ARE
4.0

# Architectural History

Mark Verwoerdt, Meg Kindelin & Lester Wertheimer

**KAPLAN** AEC EDUCATION

President: Mehul Patel
Vice President of Product Development and Publishing: Evan M. Butterfield
Editorial Project Manager: Jason Mitchell
Director of Production: Daniel Frey
Production Editor: Caitlin Ostrow
Production Artist: Virginia Byrne
Creative Director: Lucy Jenkins
Senior Product Manager: Brian O'Connor

© 2008 by Dearborn Financial Publishing, Inc.®

Published by Kaplan AEC Education
30 South Wacker Drive, Suite 2500
Chicago, IL 60606-7481
(312) 836-4400
*www.kaplanaecarchitecture.com*

Printed in the United States of America.

08  09  10  10  9  8  7  6  5  4  3  2  1

ISBN-13: 978-1-4277-7824-6
ISBN-10:     1-4277-7824-8

# CONTENTS

## WELCOME

Thank you for choosing Kaplan AEC Education for your ARE study needs. We offer updates every January to keep abreast of code and exam changes and to address any errors discovered since the previous update was published. We wish you the best of luck in your pursuit of licensure.

## THE ARE

Kaplan AEC Architecture provides the only complete, centralized source for all seven divisions of the ARE. All 50 states, five territories, and participating Canadian provinces offer the uniform NCARB Architect Registration Examination (ARE). This exam consists of seven divisions:

- Programming, Planning & Practice
- Structural Systems
- Building Systems
- Building Design & Construction Systems
- Construction Documents & Services
- Site Planning & Design
- Schematic Design

All divisions require graphic solutions to vignette graphic problems and multiple-choice questions. The exams are all administered by computer. Candidates must pass all divisions of the ARE in order to become a registered architect. Those who do not pass a division of the exam may retake it after six months. For further details on the ARE, please visit the NCARB Web site at *www.ncarb.org*.

Kaplan AEC Architecture provides a variety of study material to help you prepare for the exam: study guides, mock exams, question-and-answer handbooks, video workshops, and flash cards. All of our products can be ordered online at *www.kaplanAECarchitecture.com*, or by calling (800) 420-1429.

*The ARE is not an easy exam!* Although we cannot guarantee a passing grade, we can guarantee our material will better prepare you for the ARE.

Good luck on your examination, and in your professional career.

# COURSE PURPOSE AND PROCEDURE

This study guide is a condensed and simplified review of Architectural History, which, although not a separate division of the ARE, is covered in the multiple-choice portions of the exams. Courses covering all the divisions of the ARE are also available, and each has been prepared by the professional staff of ALS.

We advise that you set aside a definite amount of study time each week, just as if you were taking a lecture course, and carefully read all of the material. At the end of each lesson you will find a short review quiz. The quiz questions are intended to be straightforward and objective, and the answers and explanations are included to permit self-checking.

Following the last lesson, there is a Final Examination, which has been designed to simulate the style of the actual exam. Complete answers and explanations will be found on the pages following the examination, to permit self-grading.

## OVERVIEW

Architectural history is a true story—the wonderfully exciting account of people and the buildings they created. The Greeks invented not only the subject, but also the word *history*, which means an investigation or inquiry to discover the truth. By that definition, architectural history may be considered a science, although historical evidence has often been more circumstantial than factual.

The characters and adventures of history are often more fascinating than fiction. Architects such as Callicrates, Michelangelo, and Wright were real people; they lived and loved and faced human problems not unlike those we all face today. Indeed, they had problems with clients, budgets, deadlines, and the myriad concerns that continue to trouble architects today.

Architectural education, from the earliest times, has relied on historical models simply because the present has always shared an inescapable relationship with the past. Even today, we use the past to solve current problems, for example, designing a building based on historical precedent. History gives us perspective, a sense of what works and what doesn't. The old maxim that *those who fail to learn history's lessons are doomed to repeat their mistakes* applies quite literally to architecture.

Historians have always neatly categorized architectural developments by style, even though accuracy has occasionally suffered. In this course, we have followed a similar pattern for the sake of convenience. One should be aware that all historical developments bear some relationship to one another, and together they form a record of continuos evolution leading to what we are doing today. As no man is an island, neither does any structure exist apart from its society or the culture that produced it.

We are aware that exam candidates may not have been drawn to this course out of fondness for the subject. Nevertheless, we believe that developing an appreciation for architectural history will enhance one's professional practice and bring personal satisfaction as well.

This course was written by Lester Wertheimer, FAIA. Mr. Wertheimer is an architect in private practice in Los Angeles and a founding partner of ALS.

Material on the topic of sustainable design was written by Jonathan Boyer, AIA. Mr. Boyer is a principal of the firm Boyer Associates Ltd in Chicago, Illinois. He is a graduate of the University of Pennsylvania (BA) and Yale University (MArch). His firm has focused on sustainable design and environmental planning for over 30 years, with projects throughout the United States.

You are now ready to start your course in *Architectural History*. We wish you success in your examination.

# ANCIENT ARCHITECTURE

## PRIMITIVE ARCHITECTURE

Somewhere, many thousands of years ago, someone built the first structure. But who this person was or how the structure was built remains a mystery. Archeologists have never been able to determine the precise origins of construction any more than they have learned exactly how language began. The emergence of architecture followed endless centuries of primitive development.

## Paleolithic Age

As long ago as 25,000 years, during the *Paleolithic* or *Old Stone Age*, mankind's energy was concentrated on survival—the search for food. Man was a consumer, a nomad, a homeless and solitary hunter of wild game animals and a gatherer of wild plants. He took what the land offered and then moved on, as did the herds he followed. Primitive man lived and slept outside in the open air. His only shelter might have been the bough of a tree or a natural cave, but it is clear that the earliest humans created almost nothing.

## Neolithic Age

Only when man was able to free himself from this perpetual struggle for survival was civilization able to develop. During the *Neolithic* or *New Stone Age*, some 10,000 years ago, primitive men and women learned to domesticate animals and cultivate crops. This liberation was the first revolution in the story of humanity. Man now became a producer, learning to produce and store food. Thereafter, he was comparatively freed from his previous nomadic existence. With fields and herds to provide a fairly reliable source of food, and with neighbors to share the work, primitive man learned to live in a permanent village as part of a tribe. He invented many tools that made life easier—spears, fish hooks, baskets, pots, canoes—and, once settled, primitive man invented the town.

The revolutionary change from nomadic consumer to settled producer took thousands of years, as, similarly, did the development of architecture. The primitive people who plowed the soil took shelter under trees, which inspired huts that were made from branches, reeds, and mud.

PRIMITIVE HUT

**Figure 1.1**

Shepherds who lived with their flocks would lie down under the shelter of animal skins. These, when raised on branches, became the first tents. Huts, natural caves, and tents were the three primitive types of human dwellings that inspired all later architectural development.

PRIMITIVE TENT

**Figure 1.2**

*Megalithic Structures*

The Neolithic Age was also the period of *megalithic* (meaning: *great + stone*) structures that were usually erected for religious or mystical purposes. A foremost example of these impressive structures is *Stonehenge* on the Salisbury Plains in England. Here, the open ground was ringed with a series of upright stone monoliths, topped by stone lintels. Stonehenge was a highly symbolic place that was probably used for ancient worship or other mystical rites.

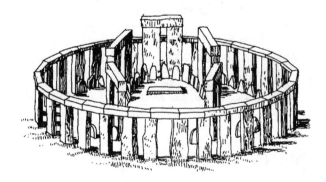

STONEHENGE RESTORED

**Figure 1.3**

Primitive architectural developments are something of a dead end. There has yet to be found a direct connection between these earliest manifestations and subsequent activities that took place in the eastern Mediterranean area many years later. In a sense, there is an architectural missing link. Therefore, we call these first tentative developments *prehistoric*.

The history of civilization—and of architecture—did not evolve at any one specific center. Rather, it emerged simultaneously at several areas of cultural development: the river valleys of the Tigris and Euphrates in Mesopotamia, the valley of the Nile in Egypt, the Indus Valley in northwest India, and the Valley of the Yangtse in China. Each of these fertile valleys provided the means by which food could be produced easily and abundantly. Which civilization came first, nobody knows for certain. We do know, however, that wherever people gathered in groups, some sort of architecture resulted. For our purposes, we shall pick up the thread of Western architectural development in the valley of the Nile.

## EGYPTIAN ARCHITECTURE

### Introduction

Egypt, mysterious land of the pharaohs, was ancient even to the ancients. It was a great nation almost 1,000 years before Moses led the Israelites out of bondage, and it was viewed by the Greeks and Romans of 2,000 years ago in much the same way as we view the ruins of Greece and Rome today.

The building forms that took shape in ancient Egypt were the forerunners of what the Western world calls its architectural heritage. The mighty Egyptian monuments are still considered to be among the most impressive structures in the history of architecture. They were

the product of a well-organized, dominant, and enduring civilization whose people lived in relative security and contentment.

To live in the Nile Valley was to be surrounded, from birth to death, by a geography and way of life of extraordinary simplicity. Under 30 dynasties of pharaohs, the political, social, and economic structure of Egypt developed into an impressive culture within a highly stable civilization. Through most of nearly 3,000 years, the way of life continued relatively unchanged. The basic architectural forms, as well, remained constant.

The ancient Egyptian culture may be viewed as one of the most successful adaptations to environment in the history of the world. Were this not so, the same expression of power and stability could not have endured for 30 centuries.

### Influences

Few countries began with a natural geography as simple and regular as that of Egypt. On each side of the Nile River was a fertile valley bordered by desert. Toward the south, the desert was flanked by mountains on each side that clearly defined the limits of human activity. The entire area resembled a great longitudinal oasis whose character was relatively uniform throughout.

#### The Nile River
The axis of this composition was the Nile River. To the ancient Egyptians, the Nile was the absolute source of all life. Each summer the Nile would swell with the torrential rains and melted snows from the south, rush north, and overflow its banks on the way to the Mediterranean. As the waters receded, a layer of fertile silt, called *black land* by the Egyptians, was deposited along the adjacent desert lands. The resulting fertility of the soil produced agri-

cultural wealth, which provided security and independence.

The Nile River additionally served as an avenue of transportation and communication. The ease and freedom of water travel to all parts of the kingdom helped to maintain a closely bound country. It was, therefore, on the banks of the Nile that the Egyptians founded their cities—for both the living and the dead. On the east bank were the temples, while on the west bank were the tombs and the royal pyramids.

The cliffs flanking the Nile Valley provided the stone that became the primary building material of the Egyptians. These quarries yielded enormous stone blocks that were ferried along the river to where they were needed. The Nile also provided mud, which the Egyptians used to produce sun-dried bricks. These were used to construct houses and other utilitarian structures that did not require the permanence of tombs and temples. Timber was scarce and therefore rarely used in permanent construction. However, wood was used sparingly in dwelling construction and more commonly for boats and mummy cases.

In all this, we can see how the Nile River exerted a profound influence on Egyptian life and the character of Egyptian buildings.

### Egyptian Religion

Another force that had a powerful influence on the development of Egyptian architecture was the religious belief of life after death. This concept of everlasting life pervaded all manners and customs. To achieve the immortality of the soul, it was essential to preserve in death all that had existed in life. Thus, we find bodies kept from decay through highly skillful methods of embalming and mummification.

It followed logically, once the corpse was preserved, that it also had to be protected by an impregnable tomb. This was more difficult, and therefore became one of the important principles of Egyptian architecture. The preservation of the soul involved several other common practices. Placed within the several chambers of the tomb were sculptured effigies and an entire household of familiar possessions—furniture, utensils, jewelry, etc. Carved or painted on the tomb walls were pictures of the family and servants of the deceased, while scenes of food and drink were included to nourish the soul.

In these various ways, the noble soul was kept alive for an eternity with everything necessary for a good life. The tomb, therefore, was not only a monument, but also a storehouse, a chapel, and a work of art. We have learned so much about the ancient Egyptian civilization because of the wealth of artifacts and information that has been discovered in excavated tombs. To know them in death is to know them as they once lived.

## Characteristics

In their desire to demonstrate the continuation of life after death, the ancient Egyptians sought to develop an eternal order in symbolic form. Thus, Egyptian architecture showed a greater adherence to established form—that is, a greater uniformity—than did the architecture of any other area. Early in their history, the Egyptians found a symbolic expression so satisfying to them that they believed that any change could only be detrimental. Originality was suppressed, deviation was discouraged, and in the course of thousands of years, very little changed.

The head of Egypt, both in politics and religion, was the pharaoh. He was considered divine, and therefore was the figurehead of the priest class. However, he was controlled by the priesthood, which became a powerful group embodying the authority, wisdom, and mystery of the age. The great temples, built to honor the numerous gods, were solely for the use of this priest class. The sacred mysteries within were never revealed to the people.

The great monuments of Egypt were built primarily by prisoners of war and vast armies of slaves. At one time, the slave class far outnumbered the free population.

### Tomb Architecture

The tombs of the ancient pharaohs took the form of the pyramid. These colossal mounds of masonry served to protect and express the perpetuity of the soul within. With the possible exception of the cone, the pyramid is the most stable of all geometric forms. Its great mass is the essence of permanence, and it is likely that this form was a conscious and logical selection.

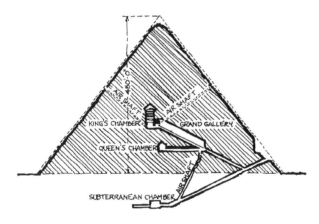

### SECTION THROUGH PYRAMID
**Figure 1.4**

The walls of Egyptian tombs were generally covered with paintings or low-carved reliefs. The *hieroglyphics*, or symbol writing, which surrounded these pictures were usually descriptions of the person and prayers that would be helpful in the afterlife. Around 1800, the key to this symbol language was discovered by Champollion. After several years of work, he broke the code of the *Rosetta Stone*, which

was a stone fragment that carried the same message in three languages, one of which was hieroglyphics.

### Temple Architecture

Egyptian temple architecture was essentially an expression in stone, and therefore, in the *trabeated* style, that is, *post-and-beam*. Columns were generously proportioned and closely spaced because the stone lintels had limited spanning capability. Continuous flat slabs of stone formed the roofs of the temples.

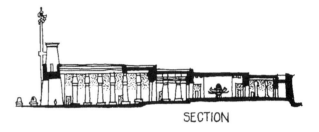

SECTION

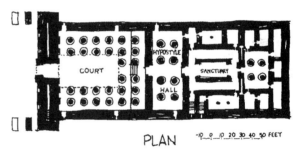

PLAN

### EGYPTIAN TEMPLE
**Figure 1.5**

Basically, the temple plan was axially organized and consisted of three parts: a colonnaded courtyard, a hypostyle hall, and a sanctuary. The entrance pylon was formed by two massive towers, with *battered*, or inclined, walls, which were united by a tall door. As one penetrated the building, the spaces became gradually smaller and darker until one reached the dark and relatively tiny sanctuary. From the open courtyard, one entered the hypostyle hall which was lit from above by clerestory openings. At the same time, the floor rose as the ceiling became lower.

## BUD & BELL CAPITALS
### Figure 1.6

Windows were virtually nonexistent for several reasons. First, the activities within the temples were mysterious and secret, not for the eyes of the average citizen. In addition, the strong light reflecting off the desert made windows unnecessary, while the desert heat and occasional sandstorms made them undesirable. Column capitals were derived from indigenous plants, such as the lotus, papyrus, and palm. The two principal capital types were the bud and the inverted bell. Incised hieroglyphics were used over all building surfaces with almost wild abandon. It had the same effect that wallpaper has today.

## Examples

The earliest historic tombs were the *mastabas*, generally constructed for the noblemen and the middle class. Small and rectangular, with battered walls and flat roofs, mastabas were faced with limestone blocks and appeared solidly permanent.

## MASTABA TOMB
### Figure 1.7

The first pyramid-shaped tomb was built around 2700 BC at Saqqara. It was the stepped **Pyramid of King Zoser** that was, strictly speaking, not a pyramid at all, but rather a series of mastabas placed one upon another. It was built by *Imhotep*, who is considered to be the first architect in history.

The most famous royal tombs are those at *Giza* from about 2600 BC. The three great pyramids of **Cheops, Chephren,** and **Mykerinus** were constructed in the conventional pyramid shape. The great pyramid of Cheops was the largest mass of stone ever erected by man. It covered 13 acres, was about 50 stories high, and its sides were oriented to the cardinal points. The essential pyramidal form was overpowering and clearly conveyed the message of authority and eternity.

## PYRAMID OF ZOSER – SAQQARA
### Figure 1.8

## THE GREAT PYRAMIDS

**Figure 1.9**

The final type of Egyptian tomb was the rock-hewn type, which was carved out of solid or "living" rock. An example of this was at Beni Hasan, where there is a fluted column believed to be the forerunner of the Greek Doric order.

## TEMPLE OF QUEEN HATSHEPSUT

**Figure 1.10**

Egypt abounded with great temples of the exclusive priest class. The largest of these was the **Great Temple of Amon** (Karnak), which was begun around 2000 BC. For several hun-

dred years, it was added to by many pharaohs until it appeared as a group of temples. The mortuary **Temple of Queen Hatshepsut** (Deir el-Bahari) was a departure in style. It consisted of three terraced courts cut into the rock and situated at the foot of dramatically vertical cliffs.

The great Pharaoh Rameses II, who was said to have fathered some 200 children, was also the most prolific of builders. Among his projects were the **Rock-Cut Temples** at Abu Simbel, before which stood enormous statues of its founder. The temple was relocated as a result of the Aswan Dam project in the 1970s.

Among the many temples constructed during the *Ptolemaic* (Greek) period, the best preserved was the **Temple of Horus** at Edfu. It was actually built about 150 years after the Parthenon, yet it adhered as rigidly to the classic Egyptian style as if it were built 1,000 years earlier.

## TEMPLE AT ABU SIMBEL

**Figure 1.11**

TEMPLE OF HORUS - EDFU
**Figure 1.12**

SPHINX

**Figure 1.13**

Standing before the temples were a great variety of *sphinxes*, which were figures with the body of a lion and the head of a man, ram, or hawk. There were also *obelisks*, or stone monoliths, which were generally placed in pairs. Many of these were removed by the Romans to Italy, where they may be seen today.

## MIDDLE EASTERN ARCHITECTURE

### Introduction

Before archeologists began to dig in what are now Iraq and Iran, almost nothing was known of the empires that flourished there 4,500 years ago. The Bible and ancient historical writings briefly mention the Babylonians and Assyrians, but the information is vague and contradictory. Of a still older people, the Sumerians, nothing at all was known until recently—not even that they had existed.

Unlike the early Egyptians, the people of these civilizations built with mud brick, not stone. Thus, the rain and shifting sands left only shapeless mounds where towers and palaces had once stood.

During the middle of the 19th century, archeologists revealed to the world that the people who settled in this area were the very first to live in cities. Other remarkable discoveries confirmed that they were the first people to use the arch in construction, study the stars, use wheeled vehicles, evolve a practical system of writing, and compile a legal code. In short, it was in this Middle Eastern area that man first became civilized: where industry, commerce, technology, and art found room to grow and expand. It is evident that, more than any other region, this area merits being called the *cradle of civilization.*

### Influences

The ancient civilizations of the Middle East, sometimes referred to as Western Asia, began to develop in the valley between the Tigris and Euphrates Rivers. This area, referred to as *Mesopotamia* (meaning: *land between the rivers*), is the one to which tradition has assigned the location of the Garden of Eden. Whether or not civilized life actually began there, this area did give birth to three of the world's great faiths: Judaism, Islam, and Christianity. We can also trace our system of chronology and astronomy to Mesopotamia, as well as the cuneiform writing that evolved into an alphabet that served as the origin of all Western written languages.

## Early Settlement

The earliest civilization of the Mesopotamian area differed in many ways from that of Egypt. The ancient Egyptian tribes came together out of mutual need and remained united for their common benefit. They lived in relative security, protected on all sides by great stretches of barren desert. This was not the case in Mesopotamia. In that arid and inhospitable region, various tribes settled on the open plains, covering as much area as they could protect. A great deal of their vitality was spent defending themselves against hostile tribes.

The area of Lower Mesopotamia, where the Babylonians, and later the Assyrians, settled, was not a land "flowing with milk and honey." It was a difficult environment that was alternately parched and flooded, depending on the season. In this alluvial district of thick mud and clay deposits, no stone was found and no trees would grow. The mode of construction that developed, therefore, was an architecture based upon the *brick*, since that was the unit of construction most easily formed from the raw materials available.

Walls were constructed of sun-dried brick and often faced with colored glazed brick. In some cases, the facing material consisted of alabaster or limestone slabs, which were generally carved with low reliefs and inscriptions. The valleys of Mesopotamia were often inundated by destructive floods. Because of this danger, and also the annoying insects that prevailed throughout the long, hot summers, towns and palaces were constructed upon enormous elevated platforms.

East of the Tigris-Euphrates Valley, on land that was higher and therefore drier, the ancient Persians settled. In this area timber was available, as was limestone and, of course, an abundance of mud and clay for brickmaking.

In general, all of the Middle Eastern civilizations were polytheistic, believing in many gods. They also believed in an afterlife, but unlike the Egyptians, there was no cult of the dead. Consequently, there was no development of monumental tombs or funerary temples as in Egypt. The temples of this area were built solely for the worship of the gods by the living.

A powerful priestly class existed whose activities included astrology. Through their study of the heavenly bodies, they interpreted the will of the gods. It was for these astrologer-priests that the monumental stepped *ziggurats* were erected.

ZIGGURAT

**Figure 1.14**

The ancient Babylonians were principally traders and merchants, in contrast to the Assyrians and Persians, who were far more warlike. The history of the Middle East comprises an endless succession of bloody battles and wars. Prisoners from these wars became the slaves who constructed the great architectural monuments.

## Characteristics

The availability of clay—and little else in the way of construction materials—led to the production of sun-dried bricks, which formed the mass of walls and palace platforms in this area. Walls were faced with colorfully glazed bricks and tiles, as well as delicately carved alabaster slabs.

The Babylonians and Assyrians both employed arches and vaulted roofs. These were developed because of the need to span wide openings with brick, a very small constructive unit. There is even evidence to suggest that the Assyrians may have developed the dome. Brick construction, therefore, is a prominent feature of Middle Eastern architecture. Columns were rarely used, since neither stone nor timber was readily available.

The architectural characteristics found in Persia are somewhat different. Persia inherited many established forms from the Assyrians, to which they added some features borrowed from Egypt. In this area, stone and some timber were available. Thus, Persian palace architecture employed a columnar expression. Wall construction, however, still utilized the conventional brick methods developed earlier. Persian roofs were probably supported by large timbers.

Even though little remains from these early periods, we can assume that Middle Eastern architecture was substantially and artfully constructed. Records have been unearthed that attest to the care, skill, and even daring that was employed by the master builders of that time. More emphatic evidence of their competence may be assumed by a law contained in Hammurabi's code that provided that *if a builder constructed a house for a man, but did not make his work strong, with the result that the house which he built collapsed and caused the death of the owner of the house, that builder shall be put to death.*

## Examples

A dramatic and characteristic structure of Babylonia was the *ziggurat.* It was a prominent tower consisting of seven layers, each of which represented a heavenly planet. Quite often, each layer was faced with glazed brick of different colors. The basic form of the ziggurat took on great meaning. Its considerable height not only made it visible for miles around, but also brought it closer to heaven.

**The Palace of Sargon** (Khorsabad) This was an enormous palace complex that covered almost 25 acres. The entire structure was built upon an elevated platform that was connected to the ground by means of broad stairways and ramps. Most of the rooms were narrow, windowless, and roofed by brick vaults. At the entrance gates were found sculpted winged bulls or lions with human heads.

**Palace Group** (Persepolis) These famous Persian structures were a strange conglomeration of ancient Eastern and Egyptian ideas. Several of the impressive structures were built by the Emperors Darius and Xerxes.

It is clear that the mighty monuments of ancient architecture can be as instructive today as they were in the past. Although the efforts of these earliest civilizations have impressed new generations for thousands of years, it may be difficult to feel a spiritual relationship with these ancient cultures that disappeared so long ago. It should be remembered, however, that valuable legacies from the Middle East and Egypt have survived for over 5,000 years, and in this respect, ancient architecture represents concepts as enduring as anything that has ever existed.

WINGED BULL

**Figure 1.15**

# LESSON 1 QUIZ

1. The earliest human tribes were nomadic because

   A. they depended on mobility to escape the ever-present danger of wild animals.

   B. they had not yet conceived of baskets, pots, and other storage receptacles.

   C. they were obliged to follow their domesticated flocks in search of grazing land.

   D. they were perpetually hunting and gathering food in new areas.

2. Among the following descriptive terms, which would NOT apply to Egyptian architecture?

   I.   Enduring
   II.  Imaginative
   III. Simple
   IV.  Symbolic
   V.   Uniform
   VI.  Delicate

   A. I, III, IV, and V      C. II and VI
   B. II, IV, and VI         D. II only

3. The temple at Abu Simbel is generally recognized for its

   A. importance as a Ptolemaic temple.

   B. unusual placement at the foot of steep stone cliffs.

   C. extraordinary stone carving and monumental statues.

   D. valuable funerary treasures of Rameses II.

4. Which of the following statements concerning the ziggurat is INCORRECT?

   A. It consisted of seven stepped layers, each representing a planet.

   B. It was erected for divine worship by the Babylonians.

   C. It was of towering height in order to be closer to heaven.

   D. It was commonly used by Middle Eastern astrologers.

5. Which of the following architectural features were applicable to the Egyptian temple?

   I.   Plan arranged about an axis
   II.  Wall generally battered
   III. Widely spaced massive columns
   IV.  Clerestory light in the hypostyle hall
   V.   Regularly spaced wall openings

   A. I, II, and IV          C. II, III, and V
   B. I, III, and IV         D. II, IV, and V

6. Which of the following statements about megalithic structures is correct?

   A. It is likely that we will never know anything factual about them.

   B. The individual parts were arranged with no semblance of geometry.

   C. It is reasonable to assume that they could only have been erected by vast armies of slaves.

   D. They were probably erected for some significant symbolic purpose.

7. The belief in an everlasting life pervaded all areas of Egyptian society. Which of the following was NOT a direct consequence of this powerful force?

   A. Bodies were kept from decay through mummification.

   B. Tombs and pyramids were located on the east bank of the Nile.

   C. Tomb walls were generally covered by paintings and hieroglyphics.

   D. The principal characteristic of all tombs was their impregnability.

8. A prominent feature of Middle Eastern architecture was

   A. the dome.

   B. trabeation.

   C. stone arches.

   D. brick construction.

9. All of the following terms refer to Egyptian architecture, EXCEPT

   A. ziggurat.          C. mastaba.

   B. obelisk.           D. pylon.

10. Egyptian temple architecture was in the trabeated style because

   A. it was the only system of construction known to the Egyptians.

   B. it was a logical expression of stone construction.

   C. an arcuated expression was not suited to the Egyptian climate.

   D. a flat-roofed expression was appropriate to the desert.

# CLASSIC ARCHITECTURE

## GREEK ARCHITECTURE

### Introduction

The story of modern man began when the Greeks, guided by intellect and the rule of law, first appeared in history. No other people exerted so profound an influence on later generations as did this ancient civilization. Greek culture and thought became the basis for the Western world, and the power of their ideas carried far beyond ancient Grecian borders. Greece was, for centuries, the source of the highest artistic and intellectual inspiration.

Even today, the Greek view of life influences our daily activities. We quote their philosophers, such as Plato, we read their epics, such as *The Iliad*, we continue to perform Greek drama, we carry on the rituals and activities of the Olympic games, and we are still guided by the Greek standards of form and beauty. A civilization whose influence has remained so powerful for almost 2,500 years certainly deserves our close attention and understanding.

### Influences

#### Philosophy

At the core of the Greek outlook was an unswerving belief in the worth of the individual. At a time when absolute monarchies ruled most of the world, the Greeks were evolving their belief that the individual must be respected for his own sake.

However, the Greek culture was full of inconsistencies, of which they were quite aware. Violence and cruelty may have been curbed, but they still existed, as did slavery, on which the Greek economy depended. There was also a certain indifference to promiscuity, infanticide, and male chauvinism, even though these practices were seen to undermine the integrity of life. And even Greek democracy was limited to a few thousand Greek-born adult males who were permitted to vote.

In the final analysis, Greek wisdom was based on respect for the human mind and body—a belief that human dignity transcended materialism. In all of Greek life, there was an aspiration to the undeviating perfection possessed by the gods on Mount Olympus.

### Theology

Greek theology was not particularly rigid or refined. The Greeks rejected the gods of Egypt and the monotheism of the Israelites; instead, they conceived a variety of Olympian gods who embodied the powers of nature. Although a priest class existed, as in Egypt, it was not at all exclusive.

### Society

The development of Greece proceeded not as a unified nation, but as a group of individual *city-states*, among which there was great rivalry and often warfare. However, all the Greek states felt a strong kinship with each other based on their common language and customs. Their homogeneity permitted them to view other nations as distinctly inferior.

During the reign of Pericles (about 450 BC), the state of Athens proposed the formation of a unified league of states in order to mount a combined defense against the warlike Persians. *The Delian League*, as it came to be called, was dominated by Athens during this productive epoch of relative peace and prosperity. This period ushered in the Golden Age of Greece, during which time the great monuments on the *Acropolis* were built. It was also a golden age of Greek philosophy, music, poetry, drama, and sculpture. In all phases of artistic, physical, and mental activity, great progress and refinements were achieved.

The Greeks were a maritime people only in the sense that they preferred to sail around the coast from city to city rather than to cross the mountains dividing them. However, in an attempt to stimulate trade, as well as provide for population expansion, the Greeks established colonies from Spain all the way to the easterly limits of the Black Sea. Had they been so inclined, they might have expanded their sphere of influence even farther. But, unlike the Romans, the Greeks had little interest in organizing an empire. Nevertheless, their journeys to other lands account for the many fine examples of Greek architecture found in southern Italy, Sicily, and elsewhere.

If ever a people made a lasting impression on the world, it was the ancient Greeks. The richness of their civilization fired the spirit and imagination of people for centuries. Other nations may have had longer histories, but none left so glorious a record of man's accomplishments.

### Geography

The geography of ancient Greece was very much as it is today: a rugged peninsula of jagged bays, with inlets extending far into the mainland and separated by mountains. Rather than vast, monotonous expanses, there were small fertile valleys bound by hard limestone ranges. The intense sunlight and clear air gave the forms an unusual clarity.

The mountains that encouraged the formation of small Greek states were also the source of great mineral wealth. Fine-grained marbles, to which the Greeks attached great importance, were found in abundance in several areas. The Pentelicus mountains near Athens provided the famous *Pentelic marble*. Good timber was also available, and was used for domestic buildings, temple roof framing, and most likely, in the early days, for the entire temple structure. With the new materials available to them, the Greeks developed a post-and-lintel style of architecture.

## The Aegean Period

According to ancient Greek literature, the classic Greeks were descended from a legendary race of heroes. Until comparatively recently, it was assumed that these heroes and their adventures were pure mythology. Now, however, we know that some of these stories were based on fact. In recent years, archeologists have uncovered evidence of a rich civilization centered at the city of Mycenae. This long-lost Mycenaean society was originally a development of an even older culture, the Minoan civilization of Crete. This period of very early Greek architecture is often referred to as the *Aegean Period*, after the Aegean Sea which surrounds the area.

The Minoans of Crete and the Mycenaeans of the southern Greek mainland represent two phases of the early Aegean Period. Both civilizations produced remarkable structures. The character of this work varied, from the refinement of *Cretan* palaces to the rough *cyclopean* masonry employed elsewhere. The latter expression resulted from the use of rough, massive stones piled one upon another. Other distinguishing features from the Aegean Period were *inverted tapered columns, corbelled arches, vaults and domes*, and *multi-storied structures*.

INVERTED   TAPERED   COLUMN
**Figure 2.1**

Examples of Aegean architecture include:

**Palace of King Minos** (Knossos, Crete) 1600 BC
The Palace of King Minos consisted of an enormous number of small, rectangular rooms grouped asymmetrically around a large central courtyard. It was multi-storied, with the first staircases in history to have regular flights and landings. Inverted tapered columns were used, which are a hallmark of Cretan architecture.

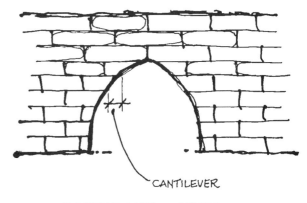

CANTILEVER
CORBELLED   ARCH
**Figure 2.2**

**Citadel** (Mycenae) 1400 BC
The Citadel was a walled city employing cyclopean masonry. At the entrance was the famous

*Lion Gate*, an ancient sculpture of two lions, carved in relief.

**Treasury of Atreus** (Mycenae) 1300 BC
The Treasury of Atreus was a *tholos* or *beehive tomb* some 50 feet in both diameter and height. A long passage led to an entrance flanked by inverted tapered columns, beyond which was the domed chamber. The stone courses of the vast dome were smoothly corbelled out, one over the other, since the principles of the arch were not yet understood.

Around 1450 BC, Crete was conquered by the Mycenaeans who passed the Cretan influence to the mainland. Two hundred and fifty years later, the tightly organized civilization of Mycenae was overwhelmed by the Dorian tribes from the north, who eventually settled in many parts of Greece, This was followed by a Dark Age of some 500 years in which the early Aegean societies disappeared and a new social order began to develop.

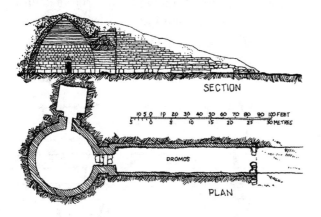

TREASURY OF ATREUS
**Figure 2.3**

## The Hellenic Period

The new social order following the Aegean Period and the Dorian conquest of the Mycenaeans gave birth to the *Hellenic Period*, which is the stage of Greek development usually associated with beauty and refinement. The archi-

tectural characteristics of this period are best illustrated by temple architecture. Since there were relatively few building types in Greece, we find that standardization, perfection, and refinement were concentrated on the predominant building type—the temple.

Originally, temple architecture was developed from the dwelling house, or *megaron*, and was probably constructed entirely of wood. It was adapted to stone when dressed stones became available as a building material. The carpentry principles that had previously applied to wood were now applied to stone, so that the new temples had all the same structural and functional members as the old. The invention of roof tiles led to the development of sloped roofs, which became the traditional roof form for stone temples. The Greeks had little interest in structural engineering. Although they knew of the arch form, they never exploited it, nor did they attempt to span large spaces with vaults or domes, as the Romans did later. Despite all its refinement, the structure of the Greek temple was little advanced beyond the structures of *Stonehenge* and *Karnak*.

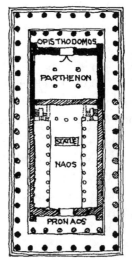

TYPICAL TEMPLE PLAN
**Figure 2.4**

The Greek temple was not used for assembly, but rather for housing a shrine. People were allowed inside to view the shrine, usually the statue of a god, but the religious rites were performed outside, in front of the temple. The exterior, therefore, was far more important architecturally than the interior space. The principal characteristic of the Greek temple was its trabeated style in stone. This post-and-beam style was expressed by way of *orders*.

HALF ELEVATION OF PARTHENON
**Figure 2.5**

An order was an entire architectural unit consisting of:

- Foundation member: base
- Supporting member: column
- Crowning member: entablature

The Greeks developed three orders:

1. *Doric*—simple, direct, perfect relation of parts, and the most widely used.
2. *Ionic*—slender, having a volute or scroll capital, and an individual base.
3. *Corinthian*—acanthus leaves on capital, used sparingly, and later the favorite of the Romans.

The most common temple features were:

- *Plan*—rectangular, occasionally irregular and rarely circular.
- *Orientation*—always faced east.
- *Dimensions*—length approximately twice the width.
- *Columns*—built in sections (drums) with fluting added later.
- *Walls*—marble blocks held together with metal clips.
- *Openings*—no windows, stone lintels over door.
- *Roofs*—timber rafters, light marble roof slabs.
- *Ornament*—carved moldings, color used freely, magnificent sculpture.

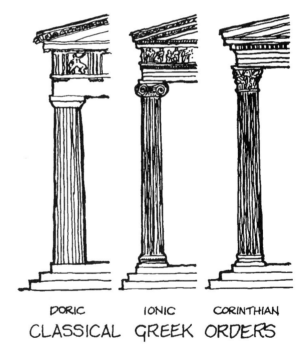

DORIC    IONIC    CORINTHIAN
CLASSICAL GREEK ORDERS
**Figure 2.6**

The Greeks employed minute adjustments of proportion in order to visually correct for optical illusions, such as:

- All columns inclined inward.
- Convex entablature and stylobate.
- *Entasis* (tapered curve) of column shafts.

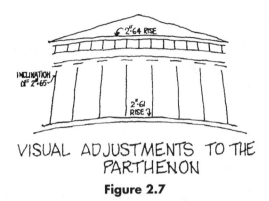

VISUAL ADJUSTMENTS TO THE
PARTHENON
**Figure 2.7**

Greek temple architecture was characterized by harmony, simplicity, and subtle refinement, the very same characteristics that pervaded all forms of art, thought, and activity during the Hellenic Period.

The Hellenic Period dates from the end of the Persian Wars to the death of Alexander (480–320 BC). The most important group of structures from this period were those built on the *Acropolis* in Athens. Under the rule of *Pericles*, an ambitious program was undertaken to make Athens the cultural and artistic center of Greece. An essential part of this program involved replacing the structures on the Acropolis that had been destroyed during the Persian Wars. The natural hill of the Acropolis was built up along the sides and flattened to form a kind of podium for the new temples. As a result, the temples were separated from the town, yet visible from a great distance. *Pheidias*, the leading sculptor of Athens, supervised the entire project, but the responsibility for the architecture of individual buildings fell to others.

The Acropolis includes the following temples:

**Parthenon** (Athens) 440 BC
Architects: Ictinus and Callicrates
Sculptor: Pheidias
The Parthenon was the most famous example of the perfected Doric style in Greek architecture. It was built to house the 40-foot-high gold and ivory statue of Athena Parthenos by Pheidias. The temple was sited on the Acropolis in such a sensitive way that it could only be seen against the sky. Built entirely of Pentelic marble, the Parthenon embodied all the typical characteristics of Hellenic temple architecture: it was simple—just a veranda of columns around a rectangular hall, it was relatively small, and it was structurally unsophisticated. However, the Parthenon was a perceptive, precise, and sensitive piece of architecture. Where earlier temples had emphasized weight and powerful proportions, the Parthenon balanced strength and grace. It was as complete and perfect a form as has ever been created.

THE PARTHENON
**Figure 2.8**

**Propylaea** (Athens) 435 BC
Architect: Mnesicles
The Propylea served as the gateway building to the sacred Acropolis. It was sited so that upon passing through it, the first glimpse of the Parthenon beyond would be from the most flattering viewpoint. The Propylaea had an ambitious plan and an appropriately monumental scale, but was abandoned after five years of construction and never completed. The front and rear colonnades were Doric, but the central passageway was lined with six slender Ionic columns, permitting a more open interior. The plan was irregular due to the *pinacotheca*, or picture gallery, at the north wing.

**Temple of Nike Apteros** (Athens) 425 BC
Architect: Callicrates
This temple of the *Wingless Victory* was a very small, almost miniature Ionic temple situated directly adjacent to the Propylaea. It had only four columns at the front and rear and a *naos* (the room that housed the sculpture) about 12 feet square. The temple was delicate in design and exquisite in every detail.

**Erectheion** (Athens) 400 BC
Architect: Mnesicles
Among Greek temples, the Erectheion, built in the Ionic style, was quite unique. It was asymmetrical in plan, irregular in its massing, and sited to avoid older centers of worship. Like the Propylaea, it too was never completed, which partly explains its unusual form. Its most unusual feature was the *Caryatid Portico*, or *Porch of the Maidens.* The roof of this small south porch was supported not by columns, but by six female figures (*caryatids*). The maidens were carved in such a graceful pose that the marble entablature they carried on their heads appeared to have no weight.

THE ERECTHEION
**Figure 2.9**

*Monuments*
The architecture of Greek monuments differed somewhat from the rigid temple design. These secondary structures were often circular or polygonal in plan, and used the Corinthian order more frequently than the others. Two such examples in Athens were the **Monument of Lysicrates** and the octagonal **Tower of the Winds**.

*Theaters*
Greek theaters were typically hollowed out of natural hills and completely open to the sky. The stage was a long, narrow platform with a permanent architectural background. The orchestra formed a complete circle in front of the stage, in which the chorus chanted or danced their comments on the action of the play. Finally, the auditorium encircled almost two-thirds of the orchestra as it rose up the hillside with tiers of marble seats. The **Theater of Dionysus** (Greek drama was originally a religious rite dedicated to the god Dionysus), in Athens, was the prototype for all Greek theaters. It was cut into the rocky foothill of the Acropolis and seated 30,000 spectators.

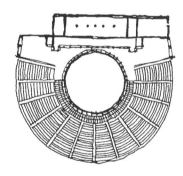

TYPICAL GREEK THEATER PLAN
**Figure 2.10**

At the center of the city, corresponding to a plaza or town square, was the *agora*, an open air meeting place for public congregation or the transaction of business. Surrounding the agora were *stoas*, which were colonnades that provided access to public law courts, gymnasiums, administrative buildings, etc.

# ROMAN ARCHITECTURE

## The Etruscans

Shortly after the Dorian tribes invaded Greece almost 3,000 years ago, another significant invasion took place in the Mediterranean. Etruscan tribes from the north landed on the Italian coast near the Tiber River. They may have come from Asia Minor, or what is now Turkey, but little else of their origin is known. The Etruscan culture was strongly influenced by Greece, and it is evident that they were a highly civilized people.

The Etruscans were skilled warriors, clever merchants, and extremely capable builders. There is little doubt that they developed the true arch form independently. In time, the Etruscans subjugated most of Italy, from the Alps in the north to the Greek colonies in the south. During this period of Etruscan domination, Rome grew from a tribal community into a city. Around the year 500 BC, the last of the Etruscan kings was deposed and Rome became a republic.

## The Romans

The *glory of Rome* was more than just a romantic notion; it was an accurate description of an extraordinary historical phenomenon. From a collection of villages near a crossing of the Tiber River, a small Latin tribe grew into a worldwide empire that stretched from England to the Persian Gulf. It was an empire to which we are all indebted—for our laws, our learning, our government, our cities, and our architecture. There remain today thousands of *Roman ruins* that serve as reminders that their impressive feats of construction were merely the outward expression of a powerful and militant people, a people who assembled the greatest empire the world has ever seen.

Rome was considered important, however, not because of its size and power, but because it embraced the intellectual and cultural achievements of the Greeks, and spread this influence across Europe. By doing so, Rome transformed a fragmented world into a single community with common respect for law, individual liberty, and public institutions. It was a respect powerful enough to endure, in some areas, for 2,000 years.

### Roman Conquest

Originally, Rome may have had little desire to rule the world. However, in an effort to protect themselves, the Romans felt that they had to control the surrounding lands. This was accomplished by neutralizing the immediate neighbors, then the new neighbors, and so on. In this way, the Romans either made allies of, or subdued through war, first the nearby cities, then the more distant villages, and ultimately all of Italy and the known world. The various peoples of the Empire were ruled by the logic of Roman law, won over by the prestige of the empire, and civilized by the Roman expressions of art and architecture. At its zenith, the Roman Empire embraced all the civilized areas of Europe, North Africa, and Western Asia, all of which constituted the known world.

The Roman Empire was built through conquest and diplomacy, but it was maintained by Rome's intelligent rule of its conquered peoples. There was no pressure to conform, no cultural traditions were destroyed, nor were social differences suppressed. Instead, the conquered peoples were absorbed into the Empire by means of a well-ordered institutional framework. It was a tribute to Roman perspicacity that insurrections were rarely attempted in any of the conquered lands. Rome may have exacted tribute from her conquered provinces, but she gave, in return, the rule of law, protection from barbarian invaders, and a commercial market for local products. Above all, Rome gave to each Roman citizen a positive belief in Rome's own glorious destiny.

### Society

It has been said that the Roman civilization was everything that the Greek civilization was not. The Athenian was inward-looking while the expansive Roman marched to the ends of the earth in pursuit of world domination. The people of Rome were sober, strong, and pragmatic. They were soldiers and statesmen, not poets or artists; they were realists concerned with practicality rather than imagination. Even the Roman religion was essentially a state policy. It was an external affair of form rather than a spiritual experience. The Roman pantheon of gods was freely borrowed from the Greeks, but in practice, the Romans preferred to glorify the Empire rather than their religion.

The Roman outlook was also dominated by obedience to authority. In Roman law, the father had absolute authority over the members of his household. It was not difficult to move from the concept of an authoritarian father to that of an authoritarian State, and finally, an all-powerful Emperor.

There was also an element of barbarism ingrained in the Romans, for even after they had acquired considerable sophistication, their popular entertainment remained, by our standards, cruel and inhuman.

What is referred to as the *decline and fall of the Roman Empire* actually occurred over a period of almost 300 years. During these last centuries, there was considerable discontent throughout Rome. Wars along the frontiers, as well as civil wars, drained the finances of the Empire. The citizens of Rome experienced inflation, taxes, dissatisfaction, and fear. By the 5th century AD, barbarian tribes had reached the city of Rome. Despite the devastation inflicted in the capital city, Rome could not be destroyed. It lived on as the seat of the new Christian church, and remains today as one of history's most fascinating monuments.

## Influences

### Materials

The mineral wealth of Italy was considerable. Among the natural materials readily available were various marbles, terra cotta, volcanic stone, Pozzolana cement, and an abundance of sand and gravel. The latter materials were used by the Romans to produce concrete. This material, together with the development of techniques for its use, enabled the Romans to overcome all previous limits of height and span.

Roman concrete was little different from the material used today; the principal difference is in the modern use of steel reinforcement. Concrete construction, as employed by the Romans, was relatively economical and easily handled by unskilled labor, whose ranks consisted primarily of slaves and idle soldiers. Concrete structures, faced with stone or brick, were popularly accepted throughout the Empire, which led to a general uniformity of style. By demonstrating their preference for concrete construction, the Romans remained independent of local materials and building styles. They did, in fact, originate the first *international style.*

Roman building types consisted of a wide variety of structures which materially expressed the authority and power of Rome. In addition, these buildings symbolized a unique social life that involved luxury and self-indulgence.

## Characteristics

The character of Roman architecture was the character of Rome itself—powerful, grand, and impressive. Its engineering accomplishments were astonishing, and rarely has its sense of planning and organization been equaled. Despite functional differences, all Roman buildings had one fundamental trait in common: they were all organized axially, frequently with crossed axes defining a center. The axis became a distinguishing attribute of Roman architecture.

A second important characteristic was found in the Roman use of interior space. Complex groups of large spaces were treated as a substance to be shaped and articulated, unlike the static way in which space had previously been handled.

Most of the basic architectural forms employed by the Romans were originally conceived by others. From Greece came the three orders in the post-and-lintel form, while from the Etruscans came the *arcuated forms*—the arch, vault, and dome. However, the way in which these forms were employed by the Romans was undeniably original. To begin with, the three Greek orders were increased to five. To the Doric, Ionic, and Corinthian orders were added the *Tuscan,* a plainer version of the Doric, and the *Composite*, which combined the Ionic and Corinthian. While the Greeks had always used these orders constructively, the Romans frequently used them for decorative, nonstructural purposes.

### Architectural Form

Roman architecture was far more varied and complicated than Greek architecture. In Greece, where life had been considerably simpler, there was only one principal building type—the temple. The Romans, however, had a multitude of building types, most of which had been unknown in prior times. Roman architects had to provide enormous uninterrupted spaces to shelter vast crowds. Had they chosen to use post-and-beam systems, there would have been a forest of columns impeding the flow of pedestrian traffic. Therefore, the Romans

became proficient in the use of arches, vaults, and domes. The arch was not only the basis of Roman architecture, but also became the basis of all subsequent European architecture.

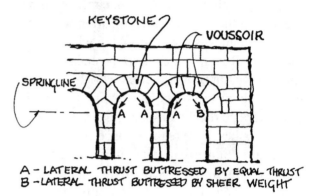

### ROMAN ARCH CONSTRUCTION
**Figure 2.11**

### Vaulting

*Semicircular vaults*, also known as *tunnel* or *barrel vaults*, were used to roof the great areas of public buildings. In the beginning, massive, continuous walls were required to support these vaults. Later, however, Roman engineers devised the means of constructing two barrel vaults that intersected at right angles. The resulting configuration, called a *cross vault* or *groined vault*, was supported at its corners by four great piers.

With the forces thus concentrated at the corners, the sides became lightweight, non-bearing walls. Windows could now be cut into these walls, thereby lighting the interior space. These ingenious vaults, together with the domed form, were employed by the Romans on a scale never even approached again until the advent of steel construction, almost 2,000 years later.

Much of this grandiose Roman work would have been impossible without their knowledge of concrete technology. They formed walls by pouring concrete between boards, and vaults and domes by casting concrete over temporary arches made of timber *centering.* Since these concrete shapes were cast in one solid mass, they had great rigidity and little lateral thrust. As employed by the Romans, concrete forms required a finished facing material, first to protect and waterproof, and second to decorate. A variety of materials was used for this purpose, including marble, stone, brick, and stucco. In later years, *mosaics* were developed to ornament walls, floors, and vaults, and their wide-ranging application became the conventional standard.

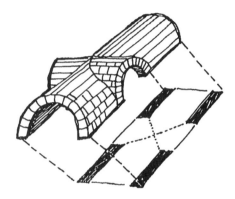

ROMAN CROSS VAULT

**Figure 2.12**

The Romans borrowed not only Greek ideas, but Greek artifacts as well. Enormous numbers of Greek statues were brought to Rome, which prompted development of the *wall niche.* This feature, originally for the display of sculpture, also appealed to the Roman sense of economy, since wall niches saved material not structurally necessary. Although the Romans actually produced more sculpture than the Greeks, in most cases it was clearly inferior.

## Examples

### Temples
Where the Greek temple had been an isolated monument on an acropolis, the Roman temple became a street feature. This made the facade most important and invariably, it was oriented to the adjacent forum, regardless of the compass point. Generally, the temple was on a raised *podium* with a great flight of steps leading to a deep *portico*, making the temple appear more like an urban monument than a place of worship. As with Greek temples, Roman temples had the same general plan and appearance wherever they were built. However, the interior space was wider than in a Greek temple because the *cella* walls were moved out at both sides to the column lines. Therefore, most of the side columns, and often those at the rear as well, were *engaged*, or attached, to the walls, rather than standing free in front of them.

Some of the more famous Roman temples include:

**Maison Carrée** (Nimes, France) 16 BC
The best-preserved Roman temple in existence, the Maison Carrée was set on a 12-foot-high podium, with broad steps leading to a deep portico of Corinthian columns. The side and rear columns were attached to the cella walls.

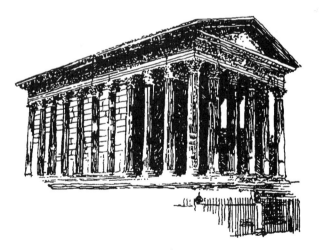

MAISON CARRÉE

**Figure 2.13**

**Temple of Vesta** (Rome) Located in the *Forum Romanum*, the Temple was the most sacred shrine in Rome. It was circular in plan and employed a Corinthian peristyle. It was maintained by the Vestal Virgins, who kept alive the sacred fire signifying the home hearth as the center of Roman life and power.

**Pantheon** (Rome) 120 AD

Architect: Hadrian

The Pantheon is the best preserved ancient building in all of Rome, mainly because of its conversion to a Christian church around the year 600 AD. The configuration of the Pantheon consisted of a vast dome resting on a circular masonry wall. Both the internal dome height and the diameter of the circular plan were 142 feet. The 20-foot-thick walls were designed to support and buttress the weight

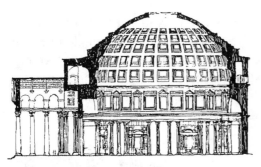

SECTION THRO' PORTICO AND ROTUNDA

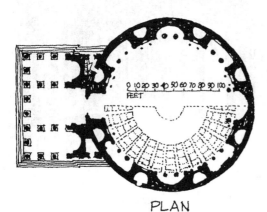

PLAN

THE PANTHEON : ROME

**Figure 2.14**

and thrust of the immense dome. On the exterior, the deep entrance portico was lined with unfluted Corinthian columns. Within the Pantheon, the hemispherical dome predominated. Its underside consisted of foreshortened *coffers* (a waffle-like pattern) which directed attention to the apex at which there was an opening called the *eye*. The light that penetrated this 30-foot-diameter eye illuminated the structure. The walls inside were relieved by niches, and a marble veneer was liberally employed inside and out. For centuries, the Pantheon has been regarded as a work of geometric perfection. It was truly one of the great structures of Roman architecture: severely simple, unified in composition, and daring in design.

### Basilicas

While the temple became an urban monument, the *basilica* served as a meeting place, site for the transaction of business, and court for the public execution of law. Basilicas represented the major link between *Classic* and *Christian architecture.* Typically, the plan was a rectangle in which the length was twice the width. The vaulted spaces were divided by supporting columns, often with galleries above the aisles. The tribunal opposite the entrance was raised and projected externally in a semicircular form. This feature evolved into the *apse* in later church architecture.

### Thermae

However, the grandest expression of Roman planning and construction were the Imperial bathing establishments, or *thermae.* Bathing was a social ritual in Rome, and the thermae served as centers of public life. They contained not only bathing rooms, but also lecture halls, game areas, libraries, theaters, shops, and gardens. Facilities for exercise, culture, business, and pleasure were combined into one vast social center. Water was conveyed to the thermae by means of aqueducts. Within the structure, water was stored and heated, while rooms were heated by means of an underground radiant warm air system. The principal bathing rooms were the *calidarium* (hot), *tepidarium* (warm), and the *frigidarium* (cool). After the collapse of the last empire, the early Christians became the authority in Rome and banned public bathing.

Two examples of thermae are:

**Baths of Caracalla** (Rome) 200 AD
The Baths of Caracalla were rigidly symmetrical in plan with a pattern of crossed axes that guided the visitor to the exact service desired. The main hall was covered by three groined vaults supported by Corinthian columns. The scale, space, and grandeur of Caracalla inspired the now demolished Pennsylvania Station in New York.

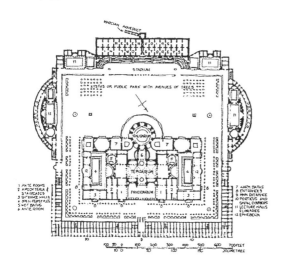

### THERMAE OF CARACALLA
**Figure 2.15**

**Baths of Diocletian** (Rome) 300 AD
Similar in plan to Caracalla, but even larger, the Baths of Diocletian could accommodate up to 3,000 bathers. The vaulted hall of the tepidarium may still be seen, since it was converted to a church in the 16th century by Michelangelo.

## Theaters
Roman *theaters* differed from Greek theaters in several respects. The Greeks required a sloping site since they knew of no other way to support the raked seating. The Romans, on the other hand, by virtue of their arched and vaulted construction, could build their theaters anywhere, even on flat ground. Other differences in Roman theaters, as compared to the Greek theaters, were: (1) the auditorium was restricted to a semicircle, (2) the chorus, as such, was eliminated, and the orchestra, where the chorus had previously performed, became a part of the Roman auditorium assigned to dignitaries, and (3) the stage was enlarged and elevated.

## Amphitheaters
The *amphitheater*, on the other hand, was a Roman invention and can be likened to two theaters set stage to stage, forming an oval auditorium around an oval arena. These facilities accommodated large crowds who gathered to view spectacles such as gladiatorial combat, battles between wild beasts, and, in later years, Christian martyrdom.

**Colosseum** (Rome) 70 AD
Architect: Vespasian
Probably the most famous Roman amphitheater is the *Colosseum* in Rome. Also known as the *Flavian Amphitheater*, the Colosseum's plan was a vast ellipse that was designed to seat 50,000 spectators. Its complex solution to circulating great crowds, using stairways, radial passages, exits, etc., attests to the brilliance of Roman planning. The facade of the outer wall was divided into four stories of superimposed orders. The composition employed a typical combination of structural arches framed by engaged columns and lintels, the effect of which tended to balance the apparent dynamic movement of the arch. The Colosseum remains the prototype for contemporary sports arenas.

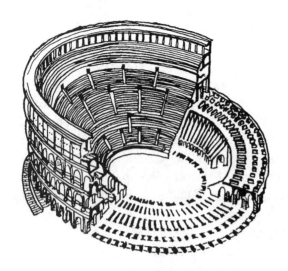

## THE COLOSSEUM
**Figure 2.16**

## ARCH OF TITUS
**Figure 2.17**

### Forums

The Roman *forum*, similar to the Greek *agora*, was a centrally-located open space surrounded by a complex of public buildings. The open space served for assemblies, market places, and social encounters. Most subsequent city planning was based on this concept of a central public square.

One of the earliest and most important forums, the **Forum Romanum**, was set between two of Rome's fabled seven hills, and was altered through the years by successive emperors. Ultimately, it became a conglomeration of public buildings having little or no connection with each other.

### Commemorative Monuments

The Romans were also the first to conceive of a freestanding arch as a monument. These *triumphal arches*, as well as *monolithic victory columns*, were erected as tangible symbols of Roman power. Triumphal arches often commemorated a victorious battle or campaign, while the victory column was erected for the glory of an individual emperor.

### Houses

When it came to individual housing, the Romans based the arrangement of the house, or *domus*, on early Etruscan dwellings, with some additional details borrowed from the Greeks. Much of our knowledge of this building type comes from the discovery of the many wealthy Roman villas in Pompeii, which were completely covered under volcanic ash from Mt. Vesuvius in 79 AD. The interior appearance of the house, not the exterior, most concerned the Romans. Consequently, the walls were high, and no windows faced the street; all the rooms looked inward. The entrance led to the *atrium*, a central court open to the sky. At the center of the atrium was an *impluvium*, or pool, used to collect rainwater. The atrium was surrounded by public rooms, while the private rooms were at the rear and built around a *peristyle*. The peristyle often contained a garden filled with fountains or sculpture. Beyond were work rooms, the kitchen, and slave quarters. Rooms in Roman houses were frequently decorated with richly colored frescoes and mosaics.

### Engineering Structures

In addition to the large number of building types developed by the Romans to shelter large crowds, they were also responsible for creating a multitude of engineering structures. For example, the Romans developed *aqueducts*, which transported water to the cities. Perhaps the finest example was the **Pont du Gard** in Nimes, France. It was 900 feet long and rose 180 feet above the river Gard on three ranges of arches. The Romans also developed bridges, city walls, entrance gates, fountains, tombs, roads, etc., many examples of which still exist today. For sheer volume of building activity, the Romans were unsurpassed, and their architectural legacy remains a matter of history.

Classic architecture laid the foundation for the developments that took place in the centuries that followed. Roman construction borrowed much from the Greeks, but it was Roman architecture, not Greek, that prevailed. The influence of Rome remained powerful and significant through the 18th century. Perhaps it is ironic that this influence extended well beyond the regions that had been ruled by the Romans.

PONT du GARD

**Figure 2.18**

# LESSON 2  QUIZ

1. Which of the following statements about the natural influences on Greek architecture is INCORRECT?

    A. The mild weather conditions in ancient Greece allowed for a great many outdoor activities.

    B. Surrounded by water as they were, the ancient Greeks developed maritime communities oriented to the sea.

    C. The rugged mountains of mainland Greece fostered individual communities physically isolated from one another.

    D. The geology of ancient Greece provided great natural wealth in the form of stone and fine-grained marbles.

2. Which of the following architectural features is usually composed of a cornice, frieze, and architrave?

    A. Entablature     C. Plinth

    B. Capital     D. Pedestal

3. The dome of the Pantheon has been called the most impressive in the world. All of the following factors contributed to its preeminence, EXCEPT

    A. it was structurally brilliant and daring in design.

    B. it was dramatically lighted above by a single opening.

    C. it was geometrically simple, being a perfect hemisphere.

    D. it was the largest dome ever created that had no lateral thrust.

4. Which of the following statements concerning the Greek temple is true?

    A. It was a totally original expression of stone construction in the trabeated style.

    B. It was developed in the post-and-beam style because the Greeks had no knowledge of the true arch form.

    C. It was created to house a shrine and, therefore, the interior space was not used for worship or assembly.

    D. It was designed for the use of the priest class, and, therefore, the greatest refinements were evident within the enclosed space.

5. Which of the following architectural features were NOT associated with the Aegean period?

    I. Surrounding peristyle

    II. Inverted tapered columns

    III. Cyclopean masonry

    IV. Corbelled arches

    V. Elevated stylobate

    A. I and V     C. II, III, and IV

    B. I, IV, and V     D. II, III, IV, and V

6. The following are several reasons why the Romans found concrete construction highly desirable. Which of these reasons is LEAST important?

A. Concrete construction was handled easily by unskilled labor, and therefore, slave labor could be fully employed.

B. The raw materials for concrete were available throughout the Empire, and therefore, concrete construction could be used almost everywhere.

C. Concrete could be formed and poured along a curved plane; therefore, arches, vaults, and domes were easily constructed.

D. Concrete technology was relatively advanced; therefore, the Romans could achieve greater spans than with any other material available to them.

7. The Parthenon has been considered one of the great masterpieces of architecture principally because it

A. exhibited the most sophisticated refinements of the perfected Doric order.

B. was a sensitive and successful merger of artistic expression and structural efficiency.

C. was a perfect solution to the problem of circulating vast groups of people.

D. was an important example of urban site planning that had considerable influence on subsequent generations.

8. Compared to Greek temples, Roman temples were

A. considered more important, because the average Roman took religion more seriously.

B. less isolated, inasmuch as they became an urban feature within the Forum.

C. far more diversified in plan and general appearance, depending on their location.

D. virtually identical, since the Romans had great admiration for Greek artistry.

9. Which of the following features could be found in the typical Roman *domus*?

I. Impluvium

II. Peristyle

III. Podium

IV. Tepidarium

V. Atrium

A. I, II, and V      C. II, III, and IV

B. I, IV, and V      D. II, III, and V

10. The use of arches, vaults, and domes by the Romans was

A. employed mainly because the Romans had knowledge of concrete technology.

B. popular because it resulted in vast, uninterrupted spaces.

C. highly valued because Romans loved power and grandeur.

D. accepted reluctantly at first because the Romans were more materially influenced by Greek trabeation.

# MEDIEVAL ARCHITECTURE

## INTRODUCTION

The Medieval period, which lasted 1,000 years, was the great age of Christian faith. From the 5th to the 15th centuries, between the grandeur of Rome and the glory of the Renaissance, was a period that has often been mischaracterized as totally bleak and barren, a dark age. Even the Renaissance term *Middle Ages* implied a prolonged hibernation before the rebirth of a classical era.

Although it was far less vigorous than the Roman era that preceded it, the Medieval period was hardly uneventful. It was, in fact, a spirited, productive, and creative time. During this period, institutions were developed that still flourish today, such as trial by jury, elected representation, banks, universities, and the capitalistic system.

Perhaps the most distinctive quality of the Middle Ages lay in its extreme paradoxes. Corruption coexisted with saintliness, ignorance with erudition, and dreadful torture with exquisite works of art. And while Medieval Europe lacked political unity, the people of this age shared a strong common bond in Christianity.

The Middle Ages consisted of four overlapping, but distinct, periods of architecture: *Early Christian, Byzantine, Romanesque*, and *Gothic*. As different as these styles were, the common belief in Christianity provided an architectural, as well as a social, unifying force. The great monuments of this period, whether in Italy, Byzantium, France, or elsewhere, were fashioned not for art's sake, as the Greeks had done, but chiefly for the greater glory of God.

## EARLY CHRISTIAN

### The Rise of Christianity

Christianity had a relatively modest birth in Judea, which was an eastern province of the Roman Empire. In the beginning, the new religion was tolerated by the Romans as merely one more among the several minority beliefs that were permitted to function without interference. This allowed the new faith to be spread more easily throughout the Empire, along Roman roads and in the common Latin language.

Although the new theology was not in actual conflict with the State, Christian scruples began to engender political disobedience. Consequently, the new religion was stigmatized and its followers were persecuted. Christians were blamed and punished by the Romans for all kinds of catastrophes: plagues, barbarian attacks, and even inflation. The first Christians executed were held responsible by the Emperor Nero for the fire that destroyed much of Rome

in 64 AD. Sporadically thereafter, the torture, execution, and martyrdom of Christians became common and acceptable.

Despite all odds, Christianity survived. Christian martyrs impressed a great many pagan Romans with their courage and devotion. In addition, this new belief caught the imagination of people who were weary of the deterioration of the Roman way of life.

The Christian church began to develop its form by assimilating existing ideas from Greek philosophy, Judaic law, and pagan rituals. Inspired converts continued to multiply, so that by the end of the 3rd century, Christianity was virtually the most powerful single force within the Empire. In the year 313 AD, the Emperor Constantine legalized the religion with the *Edict of Milan*, which granted Christians equal rights. The final triumph occurred about ten years later, when Constantine himself embraced Christianity and subsequently made it the official religion of the Roman Empire.

### Characteristics

The first church structures began to appear shortly after Christianity was legalized. Prior to that time, Christians had met clandestinely in private houses or, under pressure of Roman persecution, in the catacombs. The first church builders selected the pagan *Roman basilica* as their prototype. This spacious rectangular structure, which had served the Romans for years as a place of assembly, was essentially a nave with columned aisles. It was inexpensive to build, well lit, and had good sight lines.

#### *The Basilican Church*
The early basilican churches were designed plainly and constructed simply, since labor and materials were relatively scarce. Materials from Roman structures were frequently employed, and, consequently, many early Christian

churches contained a variety of materials and forms. Architecturally, the early Christians made no attempt to innovate; they simply provided shelter for the worshippers.

The essential functional requirement for these early churches was that worshippers had to be able to see the priest at the altar, which was located in a semicircular apse at the church's eastern end—the direction of Jerusalem and the Second Coming. The entrance was then located at the opposite end, to the west. This arrangement became so consistent that in later years, compass points could be determined by church orientation.

The importance of the altar was further emphasized by the rhythmic rows of columns on both sides of the nave. These columns carried either entablatures or semicircular arches that supported the simple timber trusses that formed the roof. The roof over the side aisles was lower than the nave roof, permitting clerestory light to penetrate the full length of the interior.

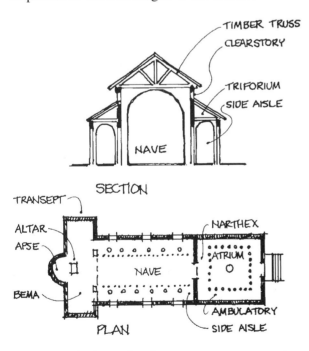

EARLY CHRISTIAN BASILICAN CHURCH
**Figure 3.1**

Architectural elaboration on the exterior was deliberately avoided. This drabness may have been dictated by economy, or perhaps it recalled earlier days, when announcing one's Christian faith meant certain persecution.

The interior of the church was another story; floors and walls were patterned in colored marbles and rich mosaics, creating an imposing and effective atmosphere.

### Baptisteries
The baptismal rite, which involved full immersion in water, was the official initiation into the church, as well as a precondition for resurrection. *Baptisteries* were usually centralized structures, either circular or octagonal in plan. Normally, each major town had only one baptistery, and since the rites were performed infrequently, a large space was required to accommodate the large number of converts.

### Tombs
Burial took place in *catacombs* outside of Rome until the end of the 4th century. Thereafter, burial in cemeteries within the city walls was permitted, and as the Roman population continued to decrease, this practice continued.

## Examples

**St. Peter's** (Rome) 330 AD
Built by: Constantine
Built near the site of St. Peter's martyrdom, this basilican church was later destroyed to make room for the present *St. Peter's Cathedral*. It had a typical colonnaded atrium leading through a narthex to a great nave with double aisles. The aisles were terminated by five arches, with the central arch referred to as the arch of triumph. Beyond the arches was a raised *bema*, or platform, and the apse.

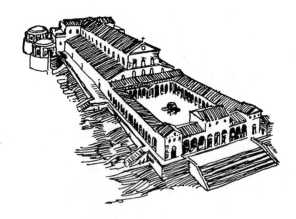

OLD ST. PETER'S - ROME

**Figure 3.2**

**S. Apollonare Nuovo** and **S. Apollonare in Classe** (Ravenna) Both of these three-aisled basilican churches were influenced by Byzantine craftsmen from Constantinople. Two new architectural features were introduced here: the *dosseret*, or impost block, which was a wide rectangular stone on a column capital used to support the arch above, and the circular *campanile,* or bell tower. Both churches were richly decorated with colored marble columns and glowing mosaics.

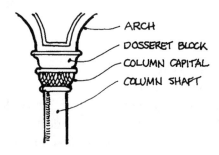

ARCH
DOSSERET BLOCK
COLUMN CAPITAL
COLUMN SHAFT

EARLY CHRISTIAN & BYZANTINE COLUMN

**Figure 3.3**

## BYZANTINE

### Division of the Empire

Some 50 years prior to the rule of Constantine, the Emperor Diocletian divided the Empire into two administrative components. Rome continued as the center of authority for the western branch of the Empire, while Byzantium served as the center for the eastern branch. After the division of the Empire, Roman life deteriorated even more rapidly than before. Rome was rife with unemployment, poor living conditions, and rebellion; the Empire was virtually bankrupt. By the year 330 AD, Constantine chose to escape the instability and dangers of Rome by moving the capital to Byzantium. Ultimately, the western branch of the Empire disappeared completely. However, the eastern branch in Byzantium—or Constantinople, as it was soon renamed—persisted and endured for another 1,000 years.

When the last years of the imperial figureheads abandoned the Roman capital, the European empire began to degenerate in disorder and confusion. Barbarian tribes assaulted every border, and ultimately they prevailed. The great light of Roman civilization faded as darkness fell over the stagnant Empire. From the 5th to the 9th centuries, cities shrank to towns, and many towns turned into desolate fields. The great Roman roads became rutted trails, villas and temples fell to ruin, and early medieval men lived in fear of hunger and disease.

The only group capable of mustering any popular support in the west was the Christian Church, to which fell the responsibilities of authority and organization. Functions previously carried out by the State were now performed by the Church. Pagans and Christians lived side by side and had essentially the same way of life. In time, the Christian faith became a common bond of strength throughout all areas of former Roman rule, and the influence of the Church became pervasive. The church unified the divided continent, and in so doing, acquired enormous power over men's minds and activities. Separation from the Church meant isolation from society and the loss of political and legal rights.

## Characteristics

Byzantium combined the artistry of Greece, the structural engineering genius of Rome, and the color and mysticism of the East. All this was skillfully exploited for the glory of Christianity, between the 4th and 15th centuries.

The predominant characteristic of Byzantine architecture was the dome, inspired by both Near Eastern and Roman examples. The great genius of Byzantine builders lay in their brilliant solution devised to cover a square or polygonal plan with a dome supported on four corner piers.

### Development of the Pendentive

Ordinarily, a dome would require some kind of circular support, such as a ring of columns or a solid round wall, in order to resist the continuous thrust around its base. The Pantheon in Rome, for example, was in effect a giant igloo, with a 20-foot-thick circular stone wall designed to resist the thrust of the dome. However, a circle is the least flexible of all plan forms, and it was incapable of meeting the functional requirements of the Christian church. The problem presented to the Byzantine architect, therefore, was to build a circular dome over a square space. The solution was eventually found in the *pendentive*.

A pendentive is a small triangular segment of a dome, or a spherical triangle, that can best be visualized if one draws a circle inscribed within a square. The four roughly triangular areas left over at the corners represent the space that had to be bridged. These four segments met to form

a circle along their upper edges while resting on four points below. Thus, the transformation from circle to square was achieved, and a dome could be constructed along the tops of the pendentives.

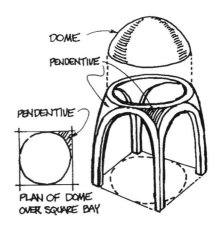

### BYZANTINE CONSTRUCTION
**Figure 3.4**

### The Domed Basilica

Since a square is only slightly more desirable than a circle as a church shape, Byzantine architects developed the *domed basilica*, which was a rectangular plan covered by a combination of domes and half domes constructed of brick, stone, or concrete.

The walls of Byzantine churches were also constructed of brick, and while the exteriors remained relatively plain, the interiors were richly decorated with colored marbles and lavish mosaics. This type of decoration, adapted from the Romans, was admirably suited to the needs of the Byzantine designers. The tiny glass or marble units were run continuously over curved surfaces and frequently placed to catch the light. The biblical figures depicted were generally highly stylized.

Dosseret blocks were set on top of the column capitals, and the capital itself gradually departed from the classic orders and evolved into a *cubiform* shape. These cubic forms were often carved in basket-weave patterns, and hence they were called *basket-type* capitals.

A major distinction between Early Christian and Byzantine architecture was in the spatial expressions conveyed. The general arrangement of the basilican church plan imparted a strong horizontal expression, with all the lines of perspective terminating at the apse. In Byzantine architecture, the emphasis was on the dome, and a vertical expression resulted, with the stress along the vertical axis, toward the apex.

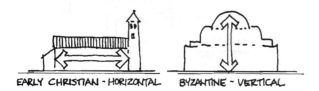

EARLY CHRISTIAN - HORIZONTAL     BYZANTINE - VERTICAL

## SPATIAL  EXPRESSION
**Figure 3.5**

## Examples

**Hagia Sophia** (Constantinople/Istanbul) 535 AD
Isidorus of Miletus and Anthemius of Tralles
Built during the reign of Emperor Justinian, this structure is considered the greatest masterpiece of Byzantine architecture and one of the finest buildings in the history of architecture. The plan of Hagia Sophia was a vast rectangle consisting of very wide aisles surrounding a huge oval nave. The nave was composed of a central square flanked by two half circles. Above the principal square were four great arches and four pendentives, all of which was supported by four massive stone piers. Above this central area was the main dome, over 100 feet in diameter and 180 feet above the floor. To the east and west of the main dome were half domes covering the circular ends of the nave, while buttressing the great dome in the east-west direction. The thrust in the north-south direction was buttressed by four huge piers which were exposed on the exterior.

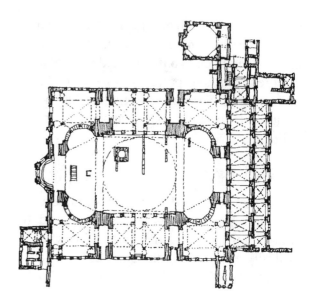

HAGIA SOPHIA - PLAN
**Figure 3.6**

The genius of Hagia Sophia was evident within the space of the church as arches, niches, and half domes combined to lead the eye upward to the climax of the great dome. The whole arrangement has been likened to a mass of soap bubbles rising out of each other. At the base of the ribbed dome were 40 windows that illuminated the interior and gave a feeling of weightlessness to the dome itself. Rich mosaics, marble, mother-of-pearl, and crisp carvings completed this superb examples of Byzantine craftsmanship.

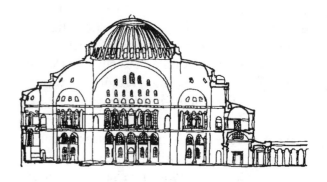

HAGIA SOPHIA - SECTION
**Figure 3.7**

**S. Vitale** (Ravenna) The plan of this church was an octagon covered by a single dome on *squinches*. The dome was built of hollow clay pots, which gave it such lightness that the problem of thrust was almost eliminated. The glory of S. Vitale was evident within the remarkable interior, including the delicately carved column capitals, dosseret blocks, and some of the finest mosaics ever created.

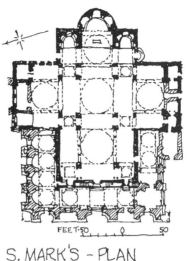

S. MARK'S - PLAN

**Figure 3.9**

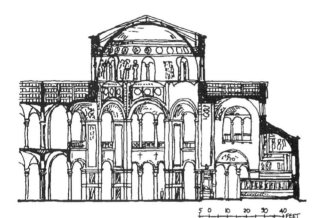

S. VITALE - SECTION

**Figure 3.8**

**S. Mark's** (Venice) 1080
The Byzantine influence extended to several remarkable structures in northern Italy, and nowhere was it more dramatic than in this great church. Once the Byzantine builders had solved the problem of setting a dome on a square, they further developed the concept by setting a series of square bays alongside one another, each with its own dome. Such was the arrangement of the nave and transepts of S. Mark's, where the Greek cross plan embodied five domes, all on pendentives. The U-shaped narthex wrapped around the front and sides. The entrance facade faced the great Piazza of San Marco and consisted of marble facing, mosaics, and sculpture that was applied intermittently up to the 15th century.

## ROMANESQUE

### The Feudal System

With the absence of the imperial system of law and order, an individual's only hope of protection rested with local chiefs powerful enough to repel hostile neighbors. A feudal system developed in which influential landowners offered their protection, and sometimes land, to neighboring countrymen in return for their agricultural labor. The peasant would work the land, pay to the feudal lord a portion of the harvest, and swear military allegiance to his lord. Because of the feudal system, early medieval communities were virtually independent, with each region relying essentially on its own resources.

### Medieval Towns

During this period, medieval towns began to develop. The construction of a church often resulted in the founding of a town, and the bishop of the church was frequently the provincial authority. Towns were designed for safety, not comfort, and a typical town was surrounded by massive stone walls, battlements, towers, and often moats. Within the city walls, streets were narrow and crooked, making them easy to defend but difficult to live with. Towns had very few open spaces and a complete absence of vegetation, since it was believed that trees and shrubs caused plagues. However, the actual cause of the epidemics was filth—stagnant water, open sewers, and garbage piled high in the narrow streets.

In contrast to the precarious physical life, there was the cloister for those spiritually inclined. The church had become a social and political power and the chief source of education, culture, and authority. The power and influence of the church pervaded all medieval life: the church provided the teachers, public officials, soldiers, and—finally—architects.

### Charlemagne

Despite the apparently absolute power of the church, an era of tension between church and state was brought about when Charlemagne attempted to reunite fragmented parts of Europe. His purpose was to restore the power and glory of Imperial Rome, and in many respects, his success was singular. In 800, Charlemagne became the Holy Roman Emperor, and the battle between church and empire was launched. Whatever political and religious difficulties it caused, Charlemagne's rule fostered the spread of knowledge and development of the arts. After Charlemagne, the Empire disintegrated and became prey to a second barbaric invasion, and, although progress was slow, gradually Europe began to assume the medieval look.

Much of the religious energy of the Romanesque period found a dramatic outlet in the Crusades. For nearly 200 years, religious enthusiasm inspired medieval crusaders to free the eastern Holy Lands from the grip of the Saracen infidels. Few holy wars have been as inhuman, protracted, or filled with such disillusionment. The crusaders recovered the holy places at an incredible cost in human suffering, but they held them for less than 100 years.

### Monastic Communities

Religious enthusiasm found material expression in the construction of churches and monastic buildings. Monastic communities had existed as early as the 6th century, but experienced an accelerated expansion in the later Middle Ages. Their influence on a disordered Europe was profound. In contrast to the medieval towns, monastic communities had gardens and fields that became proving grounds for new agricultural techniques; their libraries housed a wealth of classic manuscripts rescued from barbarian destruction; monks wove their own cloth, produced their own food and wine, and constructed their own buildings. The monks taught these useful arts to the people of the surrounding countryside, while also treating the sick in their monastic hospitals. And because of the monks' proficiency in design and construction, architecture was regarded as a sacred science for years afterwards.

## Characteristics

The early medieval years were shaped by two significant forces: the economic power of the feudal lords and the intellectual power of the monastic communities. Out of this came the Romanesque style of architecture, which was a vigorous expression of strength and faith based on classic Roman forms—principally that of the vault.

In fact, Roman structures throughout the European Empire frequently served as quarries, furnishing material for new churches. Although Romanesque buildings varied from one country to another, they had certain basic similarities. This relative uniformity resulted from several factors: (1) all the new Western European nations had formerly been parts of the Roman Empire, (2) Roman construction techniques were universally applied, and (3) the power and influence of Christianity was dominant.

### Romanesque Churches

Architectural developments concentrated almost exclusively on religious structures—churches, campaniles, baptisteries, and monasteries. The Romanesque church plan evolved from the Early Christian basilica, but it differed in several significant ways. For example, transepts were more boldly expressed, the choir was often raised on piers above a crypt, campaniles became prominent, the *triforium* was in general use, and, most important, a bay system of *ribbed vaults* was developed.

### Romanesque Vaulting

The Romanesque roof system was based on the vaulted form. In the beginning, this was simply the semicircular barrel vault or cross vault. However, these vaults were ponderous, and their construction required a forest of formwork. Thus, a new system was developed in which structural ribs—actually stone arches—were designed to replace the massive vaults. This new *rib vaulting* consisted of ribs built from small dressed stones which were bridged from arch to arch with a lightweight, nonstructural stone covering. This form of vault, with diagonal ribs dividing the bay into four parts, was known as *quadripartite vaulting*, and the six-part vaulted bay was known as *sexpartite vaulting*. Carrying these vaults were piers or columns of relatively massive proportions, which were occasionally fluted or ornamentally carved.

During this period, there was also some emphasis on the *westwork*, which was an elaboration of the west front. In addition, the tower was developed as a motif, as was the *rose*, or *wheel*, window that was located over the principal west doorway.

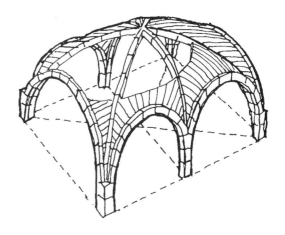

SEXPARTITE VAULT

**Figure 3.10**

## Examples

### Italian Romanesque

**Cathedral Group** (Pisa) 1000–1200

This group was one of the most representative monuments of medieval Italian architecture. Part of its extraordinary beauty resulted from the interaction of four formally related structures—the cathedral, baptistery, campanile, and *campo santo*. The **cathedral**, or *duomo*, was a *Latin cross*, five-aisle gallery basilica. Over the intersection of nave and transepts, called the *crossing*, was an elliptical dome. The exterior was composed of horizontal bands of red and white marble, and at the west were tiers of open arcades superimposed all the way up to the gable. Both within and without, delicately carved ornamentation characterized this structure. The **baptistery** was circular in plan and over 100 feet in diameter. The richness of the exterior was due principally to the Gothic additions. The **campanile** has become one of the world's most renowned structures owing to a defect in its foundation. Known as the *Leaning Tower of Pisa*, it began to tilt during construction, and now the topmost of its eight arcaded stories overhangs the base by some fourteen feet. The **campo santo** was the cemetery, and its long wall served as a background for the other structures.

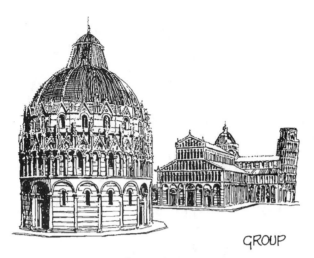

**Figure 3.11**

*French Romanesque*
**St. Etienne** (Caen, Normandy) 1070
Built by: William the Conqueror
Also known as the *Abbaye-aux-Hommes*, St. Etienne was a sexpartite-vaulted basilican church. It is historically significant because it was a direct prototype of the later, fully developed Gothic style. On the west front, for example, the entrance was flanked by two lofty, arcaded towers crowned with spires—a typical Gothic characteristic. Within the structure, the thrust of the nave vaults was resisted in a manner later emphasized during the Gothic period, by semi-barrel vaults over the triforium galleries functioning as concealed *flying buttresses*.

*English Romanesque*
The English medieval development corresponding to Romanesque is referred to as *Norman*. The Normans were an intelligent, vigorous group of Vikings who lived for over 100 years in Northern France, in an area now known as Normandy. In the noteworthy year of 1066, the Normans conquered the Saxons of England and, in that century, applied their constructive talents to many impressive church buildings.

**Cathedral** (Durham) 11th Century
Considered the greatest example of Norman architecture. The Norman nave consisted of

massive piers, set closely together, which supported ribbed vaults. Walls, supports, and all other structural elements were remarkably thick and imposing.

DURHAM  CATHEDRAL
**Figure 3.12**

## GOTHIC

## The New Style

As the medieval period advanced, the search for new ideas and new solutions continued. By the 12th century, the Romanesque style was made obsolete by dramatic architectural developments in Northern France. These developments led to a new constructive style called *Gothic*, after the barbarian tribe of Goths. This contemptuous term was devised by the 15th-century Italians who viewed the Middle Ages as a barbaric period in which classic Roman influence was finally dissipated. Nonetheless, Gothic architecture prevailed and became perhaps the most vivid architectural manifestation of the medieval years.

As it evolved, the Gothic style developed international characteristics. Bands of workmen would journey from one town to another as employment opportunities arose. Systems of communication were improving, and a new government unity began to emerge. Although the feudal system persisted, it became clear that feudalism was unable to cope with the social and economic problems created by the growth of towns, the expansion of commerce, and the birth of technology. The state became the new authority, establishing order within and repelling invasion from without. The new monarchist states administered justice, systematized legislation, and insured human rights.

## The New Cathedrals

The growth of towns was closely associated with the establishment of *cathedrals* (literally, *the bishop's seat*). Located at the very heart of town life, the cathedral often had the character of a civic building, with a variety of activities taking place both inside and out. To the medieval person, the cathedral was a school, library, art gallery, theater, hospital, and, most importantly, a house of worship.

The construction of a cathedral often took several generations, with a community devoting all of its energy to the project during this period. A cathedral site resembled a huge construction camp with its jumble of windlasses, winches, and scaffolding. Everywhere were piles of stone brought from nearby quarries in an endless procession. The construction work was contracted to groups of craftsmen, such as masons, carpenters, stone cutters, sculptors, etc. Labor was provided by uprooted peasants or serfs, with work teams frequently remaining together for years. Directing the construction was a *manager*, who procured labor and materials, and an architect, often called the *master builder*. Among all of these people, the masons and the architects were considered to be the professional elite, enjoying many special privileges.

The civic pride engendered by the construction of a cathedral served as a unifying force for the town, as well as the religious community. Through these monumental structures, people tried to prove that they were more devout and, therefore, more worthy than the people in neighboring towns. Thus, an intense rivalry began among communities to produce the grandest, tallest, and richest structures. *Siena*, after viewing the cathedral of *Florence*, decided to convert its own church into a transept for a new cathedral. *Notre Dame* in Paris raised its vaults to 114 feet. *Chartres* exceeded that with 123 feet, only to be surpassed by *Rheims* with 124 feet and *Amiens* with 138 feet. *Beauvais*, in its zeal to outstrip its rivals, overconfidently aimed towards a soaring 158 feet, and failed as parts of the structure collapsed, never to be completed.

Beyond the pride and rivalry, there was a spiritual force that dominated these great efforts. Communities chose to make their cathedrals the largest and richest monuments, focusing the entire artistic energy of the period on their construction, a testament to the powerful religious enthusiasm that existed. The soaring lines of the great cathedrals expressed a devout faith and aspiration never attained before or since.

## Characteristics

The evolution of Gothic architecture throughout Europe derived slowly from the influence of Romanesque architecture. But while Romanesque remained solid, massive, and earth-bound, Gothic architecture soared. The key features identified with the Gothic style were the *pointed arch*, the *ribbed vault*, and the *flying buttress*. However, none of these was, in fact, a totally original creation. Each of these features had been foreshadowed by adventurous Romanesque builders, here and there, who had experimented with them. One of the great Gothic accomplishments was the fusion of all these features into a totally harmonious creation.

### The Rib-and-Panel Concept

An important innovation of the Gothic style was the concentration of forces at points of support, rather than on continuous bearing walls. During the Romanesque period, it was discovered that vaults of structural ribs could replace massive vaults of solid stone, which were difficult to construct. The Gothic builders extended this *rib-and-panel* concept to the walls of churches, thereby making solid walls structurally unnecessary. What developed was a system of vertical ribs, or *piers*, at regular intervals, that were designed to support the weight of the vaults above. This novel system provided one other advantage: large windows could be used, extending from pier to pier, which permitted an abundance of light to penetrate the inner spaces of the church. With ribbed vaults and vertical piers, the structure of a Gothic church was reduced to a relatively lightweight, skeleton-like, stone framework.

### The Pointed Arch

The truly liberating feature of Gothic architecture, however, was the *pointed arch*, which was developed because of the limitations of the square bay. Since Romanesque builders invariably used Roman semicircular arches, the vaulting bay had to be square so that the ridge of the vault could be level. Obviously, two semicircles of unequal diameter, such as in a rectangular bay, would reach two different heights. The pointed arch was able to resolve this problem, since its shape could be varied as necessary, made flatter or more pointed depending on the distance to be spanned or the height to be reached. In addition, the pointed arch exerted far less lateral thrust than a round arch.

It was certainly one of the great breakthroughs of architectural history.

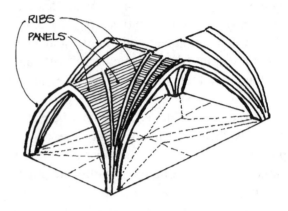

GOTHIC VAULT OVER REC-
TANGULAR COMPARTMENT

**Figure 3.13**

### The Flying Buttress

To a lesser extent, the *flying buttress* was another breakthrough. The tremendous Gothic vaults exerted enormous forces, both vertically and laterally. The downward forces were concentrated on piers, but some means had to be devised to resist the lateral thrust. At the vaulted side aisles, heavy pier buttresses perpendicular to the walls served adequately. The great lateral forces of the nave vaults, however, were another story. Pier buttresses at this point would have rendered the aisles useless. Therefore, these forces were transferred to the piers outside of the aisles by means of a connecting bridge that seemed to fly over the aisle to the outer wall of the church. The flying buttress functioned as a *prop*, or connector, transferring forces. Without it, the Gothic style could never have attained the height or openness that characterized it.

Innovative and daring though they may have been, Gothic structures were much more than mere feats of structural engineering. The aesthetic qualities of the style were made possible only because of its structural characteristics.

Gothic designers attempted to convey the emotional impact generated by the spiritual force of this period with brilliant, translucent walls of stained glass, overlaid by tracery of stone or lead, accentuating the lacy, weblike quality within the church. In the same spirit, the stone carving, which incorporated function, structure, and decoration, expressed the delicate balance of forces throughout the building. The integration of the allied arts was so complete that design, structure, and art became one.

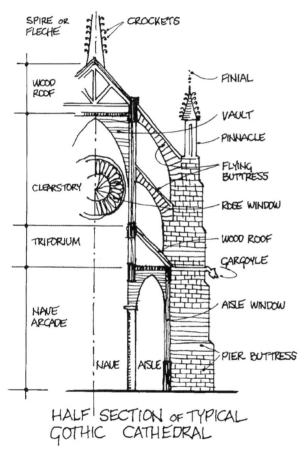

SPIRE OR FLECHE — CROCKETS

WOOD ROOF

FINIAL

VAULT

PINNACLE

FLYING BUTTRESS

ROSE WINDOW

CLEARSTORY

TRIFORIUM

WOOD ROOF

GARGOYLE

AISLE WINDOW

NAVE ARCADE

NAVE | AISLE

PIER BUTTRESS

HALF SECTION OF TYPICAL GOTHIC CATHEDRAL

**Figure 3.14**

*The Gothic Appearance*
The exterior of the Gothic church was dominated by a dramatic expression of height. Soaring buttresses crowned with pinnacles, and towers at the west surmounted by spires, all drew attention upward toward the heavens. Within the church, as well, there was a dramatic verticality, and much of the somber Romanesque feeling was replaced with an ethereal quality. Everything heavy or earthly was eliminated. Walls were brilliant with their mysterious light, and piers, ribs, and tracery glistened with gold. It was a unique and wonderfully spiritual setting.

The new cathedrals gave the people of the Middle Ages a glimpse of a world far different from anything they had ever known. Previously, they had experienced grim and heavy structures that provided shelter and protection, but little more. With the new Gothic style, they felt a dynamic and emotional spirit that expressed the intangible belief in something above and beyond themselves.

## Examples

### French Gothic
Medieval architecture was European, but after the 12th century it evolved mainly in Northern France. It is not surprising, therefore, that the Gothic style reached its most daring and brilliant heights in that country. The structural and aesthetic principles of French Gothic were carried across Europe by the great master masons, and within 400 years it had penetrated the most remote regions of the European continent. During the spirited 13th century in France, over 500 great churches were built in the Gothic style.

**Notre Dame** (Paris) Begun in 1163
Built by: Bishop Maurice de Sully
The plan consisted of continuous double aisles terminating in a *chevet*, which was a round apse surrounded by an ambulatory, off of which were chapels. Internally, Notre Dame presented a typical three-story arrangement, consisting of a nave arcade, triforium, and clerestory. The characteristic western facade had twin towers (the spires were never built), deeply recessed portals with extraordinary sculpture, and a rose

window of great beauty. Its delicate appearance was derived largely from slender flying buttresses running along both sides and around the apse.

NOTRE DAME
**Figure 3.15**

**Cathedral** (Chartres) 12th Century
An unusual feature here was the dissimilarity of the two western towers and spires, which were constructed hundreds of years apart. Chartres is perhaps most renowned for its extraordinary stained glass and admirable sculpture on the porches. Its remarkable height called for flying buttresses in three tiers, one above another.

**Cathedral** (Amiens) Begun in 1220
Regarded as the purest realization of classical high Gothic, Amiens dominated its town like a great ship, soaring to an incredible height. Nowhere was ornament integrated with structure more successfully. In addition, Amiens had unusually carved wood choir stalls and a carved wooden *flèche*.

**Cathedral** (Rheims) Rheims was the coronation church of the French kings, serving subsequently as the inspiration for Westminster Abbey. Its western facade was a product of later Gothic and remarkably ethereal in its expression. It was ornate and richly carved with over 500 exquisite statues. The three western portals of Rheims, like those at Amiens, were unusually vast and cavernous.

CHARTRES CATHEDRAL
**Figure 3.16**

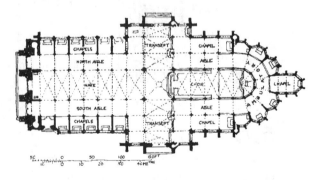

PLAN OF AMIENS CATHEDRAL
**Figure 3.17**

RHEIMS CATHEDRAL
**Figure 3.18**

MONT S. MICHEL
**Figure 3.19**

Although churches were the predominant building type during the Gothic period, the new style was employed for all structures, regardless of their purpose. This period saw the beginning of the *Loire Valley Chateaux* (country houses) such as the one at **Bloise**, as well as city halls, hospitals, castles, etc.

**Mont-St.-Michel** Begun in the 11th century
A fortified monastery, Mont-St.-Michel was restored much later by Viollet-le-Duc.

**Carcassonne** 13th Century
A fortified town that represented only one of the many secular Gothic structures. It included towers, moats, gateways, and drawbridges.

*English Gothic*
The Gothic style was adopted earlier in England than anywhere else, almost immediately developing its own individual, distinctive character. English cathedrals were longer, narrower, and lower than the French.

Transepts were more boldly projected, and the apse was generally square, in contrast to the rounded French chevet. Since nave vaults were considerably lower, flying buttresses were not nearly as common as in France. Consequently, where French cathedrals appeared complex and restless, English churches were more stately and solemn.

English medieval architecture was divided into periods roughly corresponding to the centuries. From the 11th to 16th centuries, the periods were *Anglo-Saxon, Norman, Early English, Decorated, Perpendicular*, and *Tudor*.

**Cathedral** (Salisbury) Begun in 1220
Completed in one generation, Salisbury is generally considered to be the purest example of Early English. Set on an open site, the cathedral had characteristics common to its style: double transepts, a generally horizontal emphasis, and a great central tower over the crossing crowned with the tallest spire in England—over 400 feet.

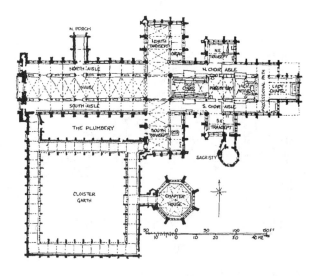

### SALISBURY CATHEDRAL-PLAN
**Figure 3.20**

**Westminster Abbey** (London) Begun in 1245
This is one of the most sacred structures in England, renowned as a coronation church, as well as a burial place for royalty and celebrated personalities. Westminster Abbey was strongly influenced by French examples, especially Rheims Cathedral, as seen in its rounded chevet, three tiers of flying buttresses, and uncharacteristic, lofty interior.

As in France, the Gothic style was not limited solely to church architecture. Other notable examples from this period include castles, such as the **Tower of London** and **Windsor Castle**, manor houses, such as **Hampton Court Palace** by Cardinal Woolsey, schools, as at **Oxford** and **Cambridge**, as well as hospitals, inns, market crosses, and bridges.

### German Gothic
German Gothic did not evolve from German Romanesque, rather, it came directly from France. Therefore, it began with designs that were essentially French. In time, owing to the availability of brick, the style became simpler. Toward the end of the 15th century, however, German builders pushed their Gothic designs to

extremes. Stones were carved in a twisted, tormented, almost fantastic way, and nonstructural ribs ran below the surface of the vaults.

**Cathedral** (Cologne) Begun in 1250
The largest Gothic church in Northern Europe, the cathedral's nave was 150 feet high, almost the height of Beauvais, and the twin towers at the west rose 500 feet. Imposing and impressive, it lacked the delicacy of French churches.

### Spanish Gothic
Several hundred years after it appeared in France, Gothic architecture arrived in Spain. Most of the traditional Gothic principles were preserved, but there were also Moorish influences, such as horseshoe arches, pierced stone tracery, and rich geometric surface decoration.

**Cathedral** (Seville) 15th Century
The largest medieval structure in Europe, the interior was ornamentally rich, but the exterior was relatively plain. The nave roof was nearly flat and the aisles had triple flying buttresses. Beside the church stood the famous campanile, the **Giralda Tower**, which had originally been the *minaret* of the Moorish mosque over which the cathedral was built.

### SEVILLE CATHEDRAL
**Figure 3.21**

### Italian Gothic

For all its beauty and grand scale, Italian Gothic architecture remained far beyond the sphere of Northern French influence. With the exception of northernmost Italy, the general character of the work was essentially Roman. Internal tie-beams were preferred to external buttresses, and surface decoration was preferred to structural articulation. The characteristically vertical expression of the North was disregarded in favor of a lower, more horizontal emphasis.

Some other unique features of Italian Gothic were flat-pitched roofs hidden by western screen walls, an absence of flying buttresses, colored marble paneling, small windows without tracery, frescoes, and mosaic decoration.

**Cathedral** (Milan) 14th–15th Century
Milan Cathedral was the second-largest church building of the Middle Ages, exceeded only by Seville. It was atypical of the late Italian Gothic because of the French and German architects who originally worked on the church. The five-aisled basilica was extremely lofty, rising 150 feet at the nave and nearly 100 feet at the side aisles. Because of the high aisles, the triforium was omitted and the small clerestory made for a dim interior. The overelaborate splendor of the exterior gave it the name *Church of a Hundred Spires*. It was a mass of white carved marble with flying buttresses, traceried windows, pinnacles, and ultimately over 6,000 individual sculptures. Its lacy appearance has been described as *petrified fireworks*.

**Cathedral** (Siena) 13th Century
This cathedral was somewhat Gothic in appearance, but not in character. Verticality and the skeletal framework were both rejected, the west facade had no towers, and the three portals employed semicircular arches. Both the interior and the exterior, as well as the square campanile, were composed of horizontal stripes of black and white marble veneer, a legacy from Italian Romanesque.

SIENA CATHEDRAL
**Figure 3.22**

**Cathedral Group** (Florence) 14th–15th Century
Arnolfo di Cambio
The group consisted of a duomo, campanile, and baptistery, all visually united by exterior colored marble panels. The duomo, **S. Maria del Fiore**, was begun around 1300 by Arnolfo di Cambio, and was intended to compete with the largest of the Gothic cathedrals. The plan was similar to a Latin cross, but the east end was really three large apses. The addition of the dome in 1420 by Brunelleschi was considered to be the beginning of the Italian Renaissance. The four-sided campanile, better known as **Giotto's Tower**, was designed by the painter Giotto. It was separate from the church and rose 275 feet. Opposite the duomo was the **Baptistery**, which was a Romanesque structure remodeled by Arnolfo di Cambio. Its octagonal

plan was 90 feet across. During the Renaissance, Ghiberti added the famous bronze doors referred to as the **Gates of Paradise**.

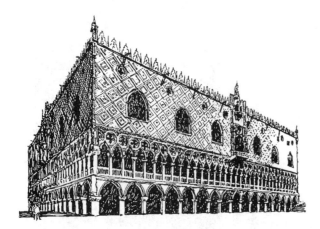

DOGE'S PALACE

**Figure 3.23**

FLORENCE CATHEDRAL

**Figure 3.24**

**Doge's Palace** (Venice) Late 14th Century Buon Brothers One of this period's finest examples of secular architecture, the Palace symbolized Venice's position as a great city of commerce and trade. The lower two stories of *ogee-arched* loggias and open arcades supported a solid third story of rose and white marble set in a geometric pattern. Set on *S. Marco Square*, the civic structure was completed during the Renaissance.

Other fine examples from the Italian period include the great church of **S. Francesco** in the hills of Assisi, resplendent with the frescoes by Giotto and Cimabue, and **S. Croce** in Florence, designed by Arnolfo di Cambio. Other famous Florentine landmarks were the town hall or **Palazzo Vecchio** and the great bridge spanning the Arno, the **Ponte Vecchio**.

By the middle of the 15th century in Italy, the Middle Ages had come to an end. The Christian faith, although still a vigorous force, was no longer the dominant concept. It slowly gave way to the secular and sovereign powers of modern Europe. The rebirth of Rome was about to take place, transforming and revolutionizing the ideas of men. The Middle Ages had run its course, but its legacy would influence future generations.

# **LESSON 3** QUIZ

1. During the Early Christian period, the Christian church was the predominant authoritative force largely because it

    **A.** owned most of the land, which was the source of all real power.

    **B.** represented the source of all education and culture of the period.

    **C.** was the only influential group capable of mustering any popular support.

    **D.** was an outgrowth of Roman rule and a logical extension of previous authority.

2. The great size and height of the Gothic vaults created enormous lateral forces. These forces were reduced, to some degree, by the development of

    **A.** pier buttresses at the external walls.

    **B.** flying buttresses over the side aisles.

    **C.** triforium spaces over the side aisles.

    **D.** pointed arches over the nave vaults.

3. Which of the following cathedrals is known for its dissimilar western towers constructed hundreds of years apart?

    **A.** Chartres        **C.** St. Mark's

    **B.** Siena           **D.** Salisbury

4. Which of the following statements regarding baptisteries is INCORRECT?

    **A.** They invariably took the form of a centralized structure, either circular or octagonal in plan.

    **B.** They had a theological association with thermae or tombs.

    **C.** They were invariably large buildings, since baptismal rites were only performed a few times each year.

    **D.** They evolved during the Early Christian period in Italy, but were obsolete by the Romanesque period.

5. In the beginning, Early Christian basilican churches were plainly designed and simply constructed, principally because

    **A.** the Christian liturgy was extremely simple and required little more than a simple rectangular space.

    **B.** the sophisticated construction techniques of the Romans disappeared with the fall of the Roman Empire.

    **C.** the materials and labor required for construction were scarce.

    **D.** the early Christians continued to feel that any elaborate expression would draw attention and lead to persecution.

6. Which of the following allied arts were important components in Gothic structures?

   I. Stone carving

   II. Wood carving

   III. Stained glass

   IV. Mosaics

   V. Portrait painting

   A. I and III

   B. I, II, and III

   C. II, IV, and V

   D. I, II, III, and IV

7. What is the principal difference between Romanesque and Gothic churches?

   A. One was horizontal in expression, whereas the other was vertical.

   B. One was solid and ponderous, while the other was lightweight and skeletal.

   C. One employed traceried stained glass, whereas the other did not.

   D. One employed rib vaulting, while the other did not.

8. One of the most significant accomplishments of the Byzantine architects was the development of the pendentive, which was used to

   A. accommodate a circular dome to an arrangement of square supports.

   B. accommodate a circular dome to a rectangular basilican church.

   C. transfer the lateral thrust of a dome to pier buttresses below.

   D. resolve the problem created by unequal vaulting arches over a rectangular bay.

9. Which of the following statements concerning medieval towns are correct?

   I. They generally followed a strict geometric pattern.

   II. They were designed principally for safety and defense.

   III. They were often planned around an open plaza or square.

   IV. They were sometimes developed around a new church.

   V. They were often ruled by the local ecclesiastical authority.

   A. I and V

   B. I, II, and IV

   C. II, IV, and V

   D. II, III, IV, and V

10. Compared with French Gothic cathedrals, English Gothic cathedrals generally

   A. appeared taller, narrower, and more complex.

   B. appeared longer, narrower, and more stately.

   C. had more sophisticated vaulting.

   D. had more sophisticated buttressing.

# RENAISSANCE ARCHITECTURE

---

**The Renaissance (1400–1700)**

**Influences**

    Humanism

    Individualism

    Invention of Printing

    Leonardo da Vinci

**Characteristics**

    Architectural Features

    Mannerism (1500–1600)

    Baroque (1600–1700)

    Proliferation of the Style

**Examples**

    Italy

        *Florence*

        *Rome*

        *Venice*

    France

    England

    Spain

## THE RENAISSANCE

The *Renaissance* movement has been defined in a number of ways: the *Age of Discovery*, the *Great Awakening*, the *Period of Enlightenment*, among others. In actuality, the Renaissance was a resurrection of the classic past, a kind of Roman Revival. The word literally means *rebirth*, and it constituted a complete resumption of the classical Roman elements and the classical system of proportion. The movement endured for some 400 years and encompassed a variety of expressions, including *Mannerism, Baroque, Rococo*, and, according to some historians, *Neo-Classicism, Greek Revival*, and *Romanticism*.

The Renaissance movement began in Italy at the end of the 14th century, as the Middle Ages were coming to a close. Giotto had just completed his campanile in Florence, Dante was writing his *Divine Comedy*, and the popes had abandoned Rome to establish the papacy in Avignon. Within less than 100 years, the Renaissance became a distinct and recognizable cultural movement, and within 200 years, the Medieval world was totally transformed.

From its focus in Italy, the Renaissance spread throughout Europe, taking a very different course in each country in which it appeared. When the movement reached its peak in Italy, around the year 1500, the rest of Europe was still completely dominated by the Late Gothic style. It was not until 1600 or so, by which time Italy was already involved with the Baroque style, that the ideas of the Renaissance were understood and assimilated elsewhere.

## INFLUENCES

The spirit of the Renaissance originated in Italy for two compelling reasons. First, Italy had not truly embraced the Gothic style and knew little of the glories of towers and vaults. In many ways, the Italians had clung to old traditions throughout the Medieval years. Secondly, the Italians remembered vividly the magnificence and splendor of the Roman Empire. The great Roman monuments surrounded them, and, in a sense, had always influenced Italian art and thought. Thus, the Italians thought of themselves as the heirs of the Romans and longed for a rebirth of their past glories.

### Humanism

The term Age of Rediscovery might more accurately describe the Renaissance. Through the study of classic works from ancient libraries, Renaissance scholars discovered the ancient humanities. These scholars, called *humanists*, were motivated, and their philosophy confirmed, by the human ideals found in the classic past.

Humanistic studies provided a more practical kind of education than did the religious studies of the Middle Ages, stressing earthly fulfillment rather than preparation for the hereafter. Although humanism accepted the existence of God, it also shared many of the intellectual attitudes of the ancient, pagan Romans. This more worldly point of view proved irresistible to those weary of the faith-oriented culture of the Middle Ages. In a short time, educated men excitedly embraced the new movement, along with Latin literature, Greek ideals, and newly excavated ruins.

### Individualism

If humanism was a goal of the Renaissance, individualism was the power behind that goal.

Medieval philosophy had stressed that life on earth was merely a transition to the eternal life. The Renaissance, on the other hand, proclaimed that life was not simply a stepping stone to heaven or hell, but something to be lived for the moment—*carpe diem*—*seize the day*. This new vision of the individual emanated from a heightened self-awareness. In this same spirit of self-interest, men began to perceive themselves as unique beings. No longer was personal identity treated with indifference; men wanted fame, to be known while alive and remembered after death. Artists began to sign their works, and the individual became as important as his or her accomplishments.

It has been said that the Renaissance was created for the merchants of Florence, who were bankers to the kings of Europe. Although this radical view ignores other influences, the fact is that the Renaissance was primarily a secular expression of royalty and commerce, just as the Gothic was primarily an expression of spirituality and faith. The great merchant families, such as the *Medici* in Florence, became the cultural leaders of their age. As merchants and patrons with great political power, the Medici were singularly responsible for palaces, paintings, literature, and the diffusion of Renaissance ideals throughout society.

### Invention of Printing

The new intellectual movement was concerned with the newly discovered classic literature. Among the great works unearthed was the *Treatise on Architecture* by *Vitruvius*, which attempted to establish the rules and standards of classical Roman architecture. With the invention of printing and the subsequent spread of knowledge, ancient authors, such as Vitruvius, had considerable influence on popular taste.

The development of printing was a giant step for civilization. After the year 1440, when

Johann Gutenburg developed his first successful press, printing grew with amazing speed—more books were printed in the 30 years that followed than had been copied by hand in the preceding 300 years. Knowledge spread swiftly and ceased to be the exclusive domain of the church. This unprecedented dissemination of knowledge generated a spirit of inquiry and free thinking that resulted in revolutionary social changes.

One important change was the Reformation, led by Martin Luther. Although the humanists did not view themselves as opponents of orthodox religion, they emphasized the importance of learning how to live, rather than how to die. The Renaissance church, therefore, became concerned with people's lives in this world, as well as the next, causing the venerable institution to be permanently split, with the new Protestant church breaking away from the old Catholic traditions.

Human knowledge was advancing everywhere during this great age of discovery. The invention of the mariner's compass led to exciting discoveries of new and foreign worlds, as Columbus, Magellan, Vasco de Gama, and other explorers opened new areas to colonization. In the world of science, as well, revolutionary ideas were advanced concerning the physical nature of mankind and the universe. In the middle of the 16th century, two radical works were published, one by Copernicus on the nature of the solar system, and the other by Vesalius on human anatomy. The effect of these two publications was cataclysmic.

## Leonardo da Vinci

Some years earlier, Leonardo da Vinci had exemplified an attitude of free thinking with his pioneering scientific inquiry. A product of this exciting age, Leonardo personified the spirit of the Renaissance. His studies encompassed anatomy, botany, mechanics, and astronomy. He conducted dissections to discover the structure of the human body; he investigated wave motion, birds in flight, and structural principles. He wrote poetry, music, and fables; he designed palaces, war machines, and churches. In his voluminous notebooks, Leonardo anticipated such inventions as the helicopter, the submarine, the machine gun, and the automobile. Finally, Leonardo was one of the greatest artists who ever lived. He exemplified the spirit of his age: he was the universal *Renaissance Man*.

With all the excitement and activity of this extraordinary period, the course of art and architecture was bound to express the changes taking place. The deeply felt interest in man, which characterized the Renaissance, found lasting expression in the arts. From the 14th century, when Giotto broke with medieval tradition to emphasize the natural, rather than the spiritual, quality of mankind, art was permanently altered. During the 200 years that separated the great Florentines— Giotto and Michelangelo—there was a revolution that changed the course of all artistic expression.

## CHARACTERISTICS

A continuous and sequential development of European architecture can be traced from the ancient civilizations of Egypt and the Middle East, through Greece and Rome, to the end of the Middle Ages. Each progressive step bore a logical relation to prior achievements. The architects of the early Renaissance, however, had little interest in this concept of evolutionary progress. They sought to express the spirit of the age, not by the use of new knowledge, but by the application of ancient history. It appeared to them that the ancients had done everything as well as it could be done, and change was desirable only if it brought one closer to the principles laid down by Rome. Renaissance architecture, therefore, was not the outcome of traditional methods, but rather the product of individual architects who looked to ancient Rome as the model, and to beauty of form as the goal.

## Architectural Features

Renaissance architecture relied heavily on familiar Roman forms. The classical Roman orders—Tuscan, Doric, Ionic, Corinthian, and Composite—were revived after nearly 1,000 years of rest. These orders were standardized by architects such as *Palladio* and *Vignola*, and were used constructively as well as decoratively. The popular Roman motif—the dome—also reappeared, and the Byzantine pendentive was adapted to fit the dome over a square compartment. The dome was frequently raised on a drum and often surmounted by a lantern—an arrangement that became a dominant architectural feature of this period.

The pointed arch, which had served the Gothic architects so well, was abandoned in favor of the semicircular Roman arch. Ribbed vaulting, too, was discarded as Renaissance architects returned to the use of ponderous semicircular vaults and cross vaults. Walls were constructed of large stone blocks, rather than the Gothic piers, and were often built of *rusticated* masonry in which each successive story became more refined. In general, Renaissance buildings took on a horizontal emphasis, as opposed to the Gothic verticality.

The intellectual spirit of the Renaissance materialized in the geometry of the compositions. In both plan and elevation, symmetry was the rule with axial lines as the guide. This followed from the Renaissance concept of design, which viewed architecture as an art of form, rather than of construction. Since architects were often painters and sculptors as well, buildings were commonly treated as two-dimensional compositions, quite independent of structural necessity.

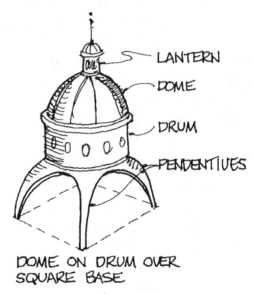

DOME ON DRUM OVER SQUARE BASE

**Figure 4.1**

## Mannerism

Within 100 years after the inception of the Renaissance, modifications of certain architectural features led to a new expression known as *Mannerism*. Mannerist design deviated from the earlier Renaissance work in several ways. First, it essentially lacked structural logic. For example, columns were *coupled* (used in pairs) or spaced unevenly. Second, classical elements were frequently used arbitrarily and capriciously. Finally, Mannerist space was often manipulated by the use of long and contrived perspectives. Vignola's **Church of the Gesu** in Rome was one of the most influential of all Mannerist buildings, and it exhibited many characteristics of this mid-Renaissance expression.

## Baroque

When members of the Medici, the great Florentine merchant family, rose to high ecclesiastical positions in Rome, the artistic center of the Renaissance also moved to Rome. It was there, at the beginning of the 17th century, that the

Mannerist style was supplanted by the *Baroque* style. Whereas Mannerism had been somewhat self-conscious and ambiguous, the Baroque was cleverly sophisticated. It was a plastic and fluent application of classical elements, used in a way that increasingly gave buildings the character of living organisms.

The Baroque had many reasons for coming into existence. For years, architects had employed the pure classic forms derived directly from ancient Rome. They were weary of the blind worship of Vitruvius, Palladio, and Vignola, who codified the rules by which architects worked. They longed for something fresh and lively. The church, too, in an effort to regain its authority, looked for a new expression with emotional, rather than intellectual, appeal. The result was Baroque—an emotional appeal manifesting itself in dramatic and original concepts. Whereas Classic and early Renaissance architecture were chiefly expressed through the limitations of the straight line, Baroque was an architecture of the curved line. Compositions from this period were asymmetrical, restless, at times violent, and frequently theatrical.

The French word *baroque* literally means bizarre or fantastic, and in many cases, that is precisely what it was. Plastic spaces were manipulated, architectural elements were deliberately distorted, and the laws of nature were often ignored. In departing from the orthodox in design, Baroque architects asserted true artistic freedom, but occasionally design freedom became confused with design anarchy. At its best, the Baroque was an expression of unusual originality. But at its worst, the results were clumsy, florid, and unmindful of true constructive principles.

## Proliferation of the Style

The social developments and cultural achievements associated with the Italian Renaissance emerged much later in the rest of Europe. The middle years of the European Renaissance stretched through the 16th and 17th centuries. In France, humanist scholars after the year 1500 paved the way for the Renaissance, but not until the reign of Francis I did the expression take hold. Unable to copy the new fashion, Francis I induced Italian artists to come to his court in order to satisfy his cultural interests. He paid lavishly, and in return, he received the services of great artists such as Cellini, Vignola, del Sarto, and Leonardo da Vinci, who died while in France.

The diffusion of the Renaissance in other countries followed a similar pattern. Italy was the fountainhead, and the Italian style was reproduced like the international style that it had become. In Spain, there was a great gap between humanist preparation and artistic achievement. After the initial groundwork was laid, some 100 years passed before the genius of Cervantes and El Greco appeared. In Germany, humanism made a strong impact, but the Renaissance did not last very long because of the swift rise of Protestantism. Although the results of the German Renaissance were often heavy handed, the Germans attained heights with the Baroque that were brilliantly original.

The proliferation of Renaissance principles in England was somewhat different from that of the other European countries. Being so far removed from the Italian source, England was unable to attract any distinguished artists from Italy. Therefore, the style arrived by means of books on architecture and through firsthand study in Rome.

One way or another, the Renaissance was ultimately assimilated throughout all of Europe. Although the development of the style, from one country to the next, was often arbitrary and illogical, the Renaissance expression remained the guiding architectural force for the next 400 years.

## EXAMPLES

### Italy

The Renaissance had its birth in Italy at the beginning of the 15th century. The Medici family in Florence became the patrons of many artists and architects, and they were responsible for several of the finest buildings of the period. From its genesis in Florence, the Renaissance spread first to Rome and then to Venice.

#### Florence
*Filippo Brunelleschi* is generally regarded as the first architect of the Renaissance. Whether or not this is true, Brunelleschi was certainly one of the earliest artists to make a pilgrimage to Rome in order to view the ruins of antiquity at their source. Having just lost a competition to *Lorenzo Ghiberti* for the design of the bronze doors on the Florence Baptistery, Brunelleschi felt the need to get away. With his friend, the sculptor Donatello, he traveled to Rome, where the two men studied and sketched the ruins of the ancient past with endless fascination.

Brunelleschi never intended to copy the Roman buildings, since they would not have suited the needs of 15th century Florence. As a matter of fact, no Renaissance architect actually copied a complete Roman model; that did not occur until the *Classic Revival* of the 18th century. Instead, Brunelleschi intended to produce a new expression using classic architectural forms to create harmony and beauty. Together with carefully measured drawings, Brunelleschi carried back to Florence a profound enthusiasm for Roman culture.

Brunelleschi's achievements were truly prodigious, and his accomplishments helped foster a change in the social status of the artist. During the medieval years, architects, painters, and sculptors had been craftsmen, much like carpenters or masons. However, during the Renaissance, there arose the modern idea of the artist as an individual who should be judged by standards different from those applied to ordinary men. In addition to elevating the position of the artist, Brunelleschi succeeded in his original intent. He helped to create a new architecture, employing classical forms, that was universally accepted and practiced for nearly 400 years.

DOME of FLORENCE CATHEDRAL
**Figure 4.2**

**Dome of Florence Cathedral** 1420
Brunelleschi
Designed as a result of a competition, this pioneer building successfully blended a Renaissance dome with a Gothic structure. The dome

was placed on a drum with windows and was constructed with a double shell. The structure was composed of Gothic ribs, in a slightly pointed shape, and crowned by a lantern, which became a typical Renaissance element.

**Foundling Hospital** Brunelleschi
Brunelleschi created here an arcade using semicircular arches supported by Corinthian columns. This early structure, like the Florence Cathedral Dome, is considered a product of the Renaissance.

FOUNDLING HOSPITAL

**Figure 4.3**

**S. Spirito** Brunelleschi
A masterpiece of geometrical planning, the design was reminiscent of the earlier *S. Lorenzo*, except that the plan was based on a square module. The nave and aisles were covered by a flat coffered ceiling, with a dome over the crossing. Classic details were employed throughout.

**Pazzi Chapel** Brunelleschi
This delightful little chapel was in the cloisters of *S. Croce*, designed earlier by di Cambio. It had a vestibule composed of six Corinthian columns and a single barrel vault. The interior was a rectangular compartment whose central space was covered by a dome on pendentives.

STO. SPIRITO - FLORENCE

**Figure 4.4**

**Pitti Palace** Brunelleschi
The largest palace in Italy after the Vatican, Pitti Palace was symmetrically composed, typically three stories in height, and geometrically disciplined. The *cortile*, or central court, faced the famous Boboli gardens.

*Michelozzo* studied architecture in Venice and was a friend and architect to *Cosimo di Medici*.

PALAZZO PITTI - FLORENCE

**Figure 4.5**

**Riccardi Palace** Michelozzo

Built for the Medici family but later occupied by the Riccardi family, it became known as the Medici-Riccardi Palace. The facades were articulated by means of graduated rusticated masonry on the three stories. The plan was essentially a square with a central, open cortile off which the principal rooms opened. The crowning cornice was typically bold, projecting some eight feet over the street.

MEDICI-RICCARDI PALAZZO - FLORENCE
**Figure 4.6**

*Il Cronaca* studied the ancient buildings of Rome as his architectural education.

**Strozzi Palace** Il Cronaca

This palace was powerful in appearance because of its massive overall rustication and the huge shadow cast by its deep overhanging cornice. All of the important rooms looked inward on the cool and quiet cortile.

*Alberti* was second only to Leonardo da Vinci as a complete Renaissance Man. He began as a theoretician and laid down the principles of design in his *Ten Books on Architecture*, which was based on the writings of Vitruvius. Alberti then set out to put his ideas into practice in a number of secular and religious buildings. He was best known for the facade of **S. Maria Novella** and for the **Rucellai Palace**, both in Florence.

*Rome*

*Bramante*, regarded as one of the leading architects of the High Renaissance, was born in Urbino just two years before Brunelleschi died. He was a master of refinement and had a great impact on subsequent Renaissance development in Italy and other European countries.

S. MARIA NOVELLA - FLORENCE
**Figure 4.7**

**Tempietto** Bramante

Perfectly exemplifying the new architecture, the Tempietto was never surpassed in its classic purity, simplicity, and repose. The small chapel followed the form of a Roman circular temple. A Roman Doric peristyle supported a straight entablature and balustrade. The dome sat on a drum which was pierced by windows.

TEMPIETTO - ROME
**Figure 4.8**

## Vatican Palace

An enormous complex of rooms, courts, and gardens, the Vatican Palace was adjacent to *St. Peter's* and used as the residence of the popes. Within the Vatican was the *Sistine Chapel*, which was later covered by the heroic paintings of Michelangelo.

*Michelangelo* was one of the geniuses of the Renaissance. Without any formal schooling, he moved from painting and sculpture to architecture. In all these arts, he was far more prolific than Leonardo da Vinci, who had been born 25 years earlier. A native of Florence, Michelangelo always considered himself principally a sculptor, and among his masterpieces were the statues of David, Moses, and the Pieta in St. Peter's, completed when he was only 23-years-old. Michelangelo's famous paintings on the vault of

the Sistine Chapel took four years to complete, and were painted as he lay on his back.

## Capitol Michelangelo

The Capitol on the hill above the Roman Forum was a planless collection of old buildings when Michelangelo began work on it. In this highly sculptural design, he remodeled the approach and stairway to the piazza, designed the great palace facades surrounding the space, and placed the equestrian statue of Marcus Aurelius at the center of the trapezoidal piazza.

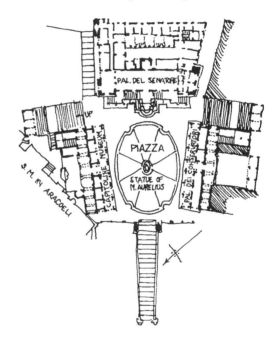

PLAN
CAPITOL at ROME
**Figure 4.9**

## St. Peter's Bramante, Michelangelo, della Porta, Maderna, Bernini, Vignola, et al.

Begun in 1506 to replace the old basilica of St. Peter's, the new St. Peter's was the ultimate centrally planned Renaissance church. One hundred and ten years later, the mother church of the Western world was completed. In the beginning, Bramante had been appointed by Pope Julius II to design the new church. Bramante's monumental plan consisted of a Greek cross within a square, with a dome about the size of the Pantheon to cover the central space. At about the time the foundations were laid, both Bramante and Pope Julius II died.

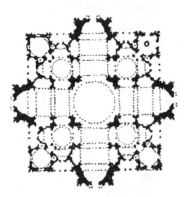

BRAMANTE'S PLAN-ST. PETER'S
**Figure 4.10**

For a number of years, no further building took place, but a number of new plans were submitted by *Raphael, Peruzzi*, and *Sangallo*. In 1546, at the age of 72, Michelangelo was appointed the new architect. His great accomplishment was to draw all the parts together to form an architectural unity. Michelangelo adhered to Bramante's Greek cross plan, but he simplified the interior and created a new and even larger dome.

Michelangelo's great dome was 137 feet in diameter and rose 335 feet above the floor. The dome sat on pendentives which were supported by piers 60 feet square. Iron chains at the base of the dome acted as a tension ring to resist the enormous thrust.

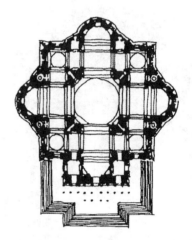

MICHELANGELO'S PLAN-ST. PETER'S
**Figure 4.12**

In succeeding years, various additions and alterations were made to St. Peter's. *della Porta* completed the dome after Michelangelo's death. *Maderna* lengthened the nave to form a Latin cross and added a new facade. *Bernini*

ST. PETER'S - PIAZZA
**Figure 4.11**

created the oval entrance piazza with imposing Tuscan colonnades, and he also designed the corkscrew spiral *baldacchino*. Finally, *Vignola* added the side *cupolas*. In all, St. Peter's was an immense and imposing church with a monumental scale that made the plan, from a practical sense, nearly unusable.

*Borromini* was one of the most innovative architects of the High Baroque. His major work was the church of **S. Carlo alle Quattro Fontane**. The plan was a subtle variation on the oval, while the exterior facade was an undulating series of convex and concave surfaces. Architecture was treated as abstract sculpture, and the result was almost perpetual fluid motion.

STA MARIA DELLA SALUTE - VENICE
**Figure 4.14**

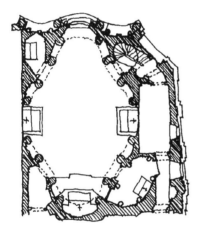

PLAN of S. CARLO ALLE QUATTRO FONTANE - ROME,
**Figure 4.13**

### Venice
*Sansovino*, a native of Florence, was trained in Rome as a sculptor and settled in Venice, where he helped spread the knowledge of the High Renaissance.

**Libreria Vecchia** Sansovino
A long, rectangular, two-story building, Libreria Vecchia was located across *S. Marco Piazzetta* from the Doge's Palace. On the ground floor was a long, arcaded loggia, and along the upper balustrade were many sculpted figures.

*Longhena* produced one of the most famous Baroque churches in Italy, **Santa Maria della Salute**. Set on the Grand Canal, it was rich in diverse elements. The octagonal plan was covered by a circular dome on a high drum. The drum was buttressed by enormous *volutes*, known as *scroll buttresses*.

*Palladio* worked chiefly in his native city of Vicenza and was regarded as the greatest architect of the Late Renaissance. His style was personal, cool, and refined, and the word *palladian* became synonymous with elegant classic architecture. Steeped in the classic traditions of ancient Rome, Palladio produced a book on architecture which gave added fame to his work. This book was later published in every country in Europe, where it became essential reading for every architect, ultimately influencing architecture more than did his actual buildings.

### Villa Rotonda (Vicenza) Palladio

The Villa Rotonda had a square plan with identical columned porticoes on each of its four sides. At the center of the plan was a circular domed hall. The main axes extended into the garden, establishing a new and formal relationship between architecture and nature. The Villa lifted residential architecture to a new level of importance, and its general scheme was the inspiration for Thomas Jefferson's **Monticello**.

VILLA ROTONDA

**Figure 4.15**

## France

France gained its first glimpse of the Renaissance when French troops invaded Italy in the late 15th century. With the expulsion of the English some years earlier, France had become a united kingdom with its capital in Paris. The earliest examples of the new style combined a curious mixture of old and new. The work was concentrated initially on *chateaux* (country houses) in the *Loire Valley*, which were strongly influenced by the presence of Italian artists.

The great power behind the later Renaissance was Louis XIV. His many projects were intended to embody his absolute authority, and they often resulted in extravagant waste and disregard for his subjects. Many years later, after the revolution and the establishment of the new republic, Napoleon III proceeded with the beautification of Paris based on the designs of *Baron Haussmann*. It was Haussmann who was responsible for the grand boulevards and charming vistas that remain today. Few churches were erected in France during the Renaissance, owing to the massive ecclesiastical building program of the Middle Ages.

CHATEAU de CHAMBORD

**Figure 4.16**

**Chateau** (Blois)
An extraordinary stylistic mixture, Blois was begun during the Gothic period, but completed by *Gaston d'Orleans*. It contained the famous spiral stairway of Francis I, which may have been designed by Leonardo da Vinci, who died in nearby Amboise.

**Chateau** (Chambord) Pierre Nepveu
Another mixture of medieval castle and Italian palace, the plan consisted of an inner and outer court, with enormous circular towers at each corner. More than 300 turrets, towers, chimneys, and pinnacles surrounded the central tower, which rose above the double spiral staircase.

**Palace** (Fontainebleau) Le Breton
This palace was designed for Francis I, and the gallery named for him served as the model for similar elongated rooms in other chateaux. On the exterior were attractive gardens, courts, terraces, lakes, and vistas.

**Louvre** (Paris) Pierre Lescot
Begun in 1546, construction continued under various architects for the next 300 years. Together with its formal gardens, the *Tuileries*, the composition of the Louvre covered over 45 acres in the heart of Paris. Today, the structure houses a valuable art collection acquired by past rulers of France, and the museum has a new pyramidal entrance designed by *I. M. Pei.*

**Palace** (Versailles) Le Vau
Built for Louis XIV towards the end of the French Baroque period, Versailles was one of the most imposing, extravagant, and ostentatious royal palaces ever built. Late 18th century additions by *Mansart* and *Gabriel* produced a megalomaniacal palace over one-third of a mile long—certainly one of the largest houses in the world. The *Petit Trianon*, on the Versailles grounds, was built by Gabriel for Madame

DuBarry, but became the favorite of Marie Antoinette. The immense and magnificent formal gardens were laid out by *Le Notre* and included several incredible fountains, avenues, lakes, canals, and vistas.

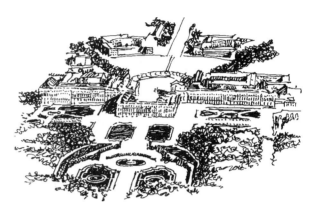

VERSAILLES
**Figure 4.17**

**Pantheon** (Paris) 1750 Soufflot
This Pantheon is not to be confused with the ancient structure in Rome. The Greek cross plan was covered by a triple-shell dome. The structure was severely Neo-Classic with a facade based on Roman temple architecture. Below the main floor were crypts in which were buried France's greatest artists, including the architect Soufflot.

**Church of the Invalides** (Paris) Bruant and Mansart
The church is considered somewhat of a transition between Baroque and *Neo-Classicism.* Bruant created a Greek cross plan within a square, over which Mansart placed his impressive dome. It was set on a high drum and constructed of three shells to reduce its weight. Beneath the center of the dome was the Emperor Napoleon's tomb.

CHURCH OF THE INVALIDES
**Figure 4.18**

**Opera House** (Paris) Charles Garnier
Designed in the classic vernacular of the mid-19th century, the Opera House was an original and sumptuous composition employing Renaissance and Baroque forms together with exaggerated eclectic decoration. It was a great influence on national opera houses built thereafter.

PARIS OPERA HOUSE
**Figure 4.19**

## England

Because of its great distance from Italy, England was the last European country to embrace Renaissance architecture, and, for some time, the English Renaissance was combined with Late Gothic. The Renaissance movement had great appeal to the English; with its emphasis on the enjoyment of life, the new spirit coincided with the end of church domination in England and the search for a rich and free life.

During the days of Elizabethan England, personalities appeared who made England one of the greatest national and colonizing powers the world had ever seen. This was the time of Sir Francis Drake and Sir Walter Raleigh, of Shakespeare, Bacon, and Spenser, as England moved towards a rich tradition in art, literature, and architecture. More than in any other country, Renaissance architecture in England was influenced by individual architects, rather than by tradition.

The original architectural revolution was, to a large degree, the work of *Inigo Jones*, an Italian-trained designer. Under the strong influence of Palladio, Jones became an ardent disciple of Italian Renaissance architecture, practicing a quiet, serene classicism, making the word *palladian* as English as it was Italian.

**Banqueting House** (Whitehall-London) 1620 Inigo Jones
Influenced by Palladio, Jones created a building of classical perfection which had enormous influence for 100 years. It was the first severely classical building in London.

BANQUETING HOUSE - LONDON

**Figure 4.20**

*Sir Christopher Wren* was the second great architectural personality of this period. Having taught science at Oxford, he approached architecture somewhat late in life. In contrast to Jones' Italian influence, Wren was a disciple of French architecture and, in fact, never visited Italy. In 1666, the *Great Fire of London* virtually destroyed the city in just nine days. Within two weeks, Wren submitted to the King his plan for a new city. Although Wren's ambitious plan was never executed, he was responsible for 53 churches in the city of London.

**St. Paul's Cathedral** (London) 1675 Sir Christopher Wren
Competing in size with St. Peter's, St. Paul's is considered to be Wren's masterpiece. It occupied the site of the medieval cathedral destroyed in the fire of 1666. Although Wren would have preferred a centralized plan, in emulation of the Italian Baroque, St. Paul's was a compromise. It had a Medieval Latin cross plan surmounted by a dominating Baroque dome on a very high drum. The facade had twin towers and a classic portico which rose in two tiers. St. Paul's was built by one architect, in 36 years, under one bishop, while St. Peter's was built by 13 architects, in 100 years, under 20 popes.

ST. PAUL'S - LONDON

**Figure 4.21**

**Royal Circus** and **Royal Crescent** (Bath)
John Wood
Early examples of urban row townhouses.

## Spain

The consolidation of the Spanish Kingdom began with the marriage of Ferdinand and Isabella. Not long afterward, in the year 1492, the Moors were ejected from Spain. In the same year, flying the Spanish flag, Columbus discovered the new world, which further added to Spain's prestige and power. The Emperor Charles V became the most powerful monarch since Charlemagne, reigning over Spain, the Netherlands, Austria, Germany, parts of Italy, as well as Mexico, Peru, and Chile in the new world. England succeeded in ousting Spain from this powerful position by defeating the Spanish Armada in 1588. From that time on, Spain's power and influence continued to decline.

Early Renaissance architecture in Spain was referred to as *Plateresque*, or the *silversmith style*, after its fine surface detail. Late Renaissance work was referred to as *Churri-guer-esque*, after the architect who introduced it to Spain. It was the equivalent of Baroque, with free and fantastic forms involving the play of light and shade.

### Escurial (near Madrid) 1580 Toledo and Juan de Herrera

Juan de Herrera, who was a pupil of Michelangelo, completed the project begun by Toledo. In the severest classical style, it housed a palace, monastery, school, and cathedral, whose dome and towers were the focal point of the vast complex.

ESCURIAL, NEAR MADRID

**Figure 4.22**

The Renaissance has left a lasting imprint on the world, not only because of the artistic and architectural masterpieces that remain, but also as a result of its creative and enlightened spirit. Centuries after the Medicis in Florence, people everywhere would look to Italy in gratitude for its exuberant culture that helped shape the quality of life throughout the world.

# LESSON 4 QUIZ

1. The Renaissance originated in Italy for which of the following reasons?

   I. Ancient Roman monuments had always influenced Italian art and thought, even throughout the Gothic period.

   II. The Italians were essentially a pleasure-seeking people, which corresponded with humanism.

   III. Religion in Italy did not exert much influence during the previous *Age of Faith*.

   IV. In many ways, the Italians had adhered to Roman traditions throughout the Medieval period.

   V. The invention of the printing press was an Italian development, and popularized ancient Roman literature.

   A. I and II
   B. I and IV
   C. II, III, and IV
   D. III, IV, and V

2. Which of the following statements concerning Renaissance architecture in England is correct?

   A. The style was originally influenced by the presence of distinguished artists from Italy.

   B. The style was accepted reluctantly at first, since the Renaissance spirit conflicted with the solemnity of the English.

   C. The style arrived late, but when it did appear, the English embraced the Baroque expression because of its unrestrained point of view.

   D. The style was initially motivated by published volumes on architecture and by individual architects, not by tradition.

3. This great church occupied the site of an earlier religious structure. Over the principal crossing was a magnificent dome set on a high drum. The original plan was in the form of a Latin cross, and at the entrance facade were twin towers and a classical Roman portico. The church described is

   A. St. Peter's.
   B. St. Paul's.
   C. Santa Maria della Salute.
   D. Church of the Invalides.

4. Palladio's fame was due to his

   A. presence at the court of Louis XIV in France.

   B. refined structures, most of which were located in Vicenza.

   C. published works, which had a greater influence than his buildings.

   D. strict adherence to classical form, with little personal modification.

5. The spirit of the Renaissance included

   I. an enthusiasm for classical culture.

   II. the search for modern methods.

   III. the concept of evolutionary progress.

   IV. a new awareness of the individual.

   V. a more worldly point of view.

   A. I, IV, and V
   B. I, II, and IV
   C. II, IV, and V
   D. II, III, and V

6. Which of the following statements regarding St. Peter's in Rome is correct?

   **A.** Although the enormous project took over 100 years to complete, the architect's original concept was finally realized.

   **B.** Michelangelo was directed by Pope Julius II to complete Bramante's plan with as few changes as possible.

   **C.** As originally designed, the great structure represented the culmination of the basilican planned Renaissance church.

   **D.** It was an impressive and imposing structure largely because of its size, as well as its scale.

7. Four famous personalities who emerged from the Renaissance period were Bramante, Borromini, Brunelleschi, and Bruant. Although their lives and work differed, they had which of the following in common?

   **A.** Their background—each was conditioned by his native country of Italy.

   **B.** Their skill and ability—each was originally trained as a painter and sculptor.

   **C.** Their architecture—each produced important domed structures that influenced later generations.

   **D.** Their epoch—they were all important artistic figures of the High Renaissance.

8. The spirit of the Early Renaissance was largely motivated by intellectual pursuits; thus the concept of design that emerged viewed architecture principally as an art of form. This was clearly demonstrated with

   **A.** curved flowing lines.

   **B.** axial symmetry.

   **C.** complete artistic freedom.

   **D.** sophisticated structural concepts.

9. Among the following architectural features, which were generally employed by the early Renaissance architects?

   **I.** Semicircular vault

   **II.** Dome on pendentives

   **III.** Ribbed vaulting

   **IV.** Pointed arch

   **V.** Classic Roman orders

   **A.** I, II, and V          **C.** II, III, and IV

   **B.** I, III, and V          **D.** II, IV, and V

10. Concerning the dome of the Florence Cathedral, which of the following statements is INCORRECT?

    **A.** Although built in the Gothic manner, it was definitely a Renaissance dome.

    **B.** It was designed by Brunelleschi, who was considered to be the first architect of the Renaissance.

    **C.** It was slightly pointed in shape, which became the Renaissance standard for subsequent domes.

    **D.** It was placed on a drum and crowned with a lantern, which deviated from Gothic practice.

# ROOTS OF MODERN ARCHITECTURE

## INTRODUCTION

The roots of *Modern Architecture* extend as far back as the 15th century, although it may be difficult for today's architects to relate Corinthian columns and classical compositions to current work. Over and above the classic details, however, the architecture of the Renais-sance developed design concepts that had significance far beyond their immediate application. For example, new ideas about space led to the discovery of *perspective*, which became the artistic standard for the next 500 years.

The invention of perspective was an outcome of *individualism*, the driving force of the Renaissance, and it emphasized the natural, rather than the spiritual, in artistic expression. In a perspective drawing, objects are seen from the unique point of view of an individual, and are depicted as they actually appear to the eye, without regard to their actual size or shape. Perspective drawing has a scientific basis and represents the beginning of the modern merger of art and science. During the later Baroque period, there was a similar scientific/artistic connection between the concept of infinity and the curvilinear compositions that appeared to have neither a beginning nor an end. The merger of art and science was to become a key principle of the modern movement in architecture.

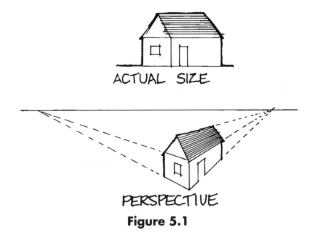

**Figure 5.1**

## The Renaissance View

The organization of large urban spaces during the 18th century developed as a result of the Renaissance wide-angle view of the world. It was an intellectual expression of formality that subordinated nature to art, best typified by the incredible gardens of *Versailles*. The influence of Versailles could later be seen as far away as **Hampton Court** in England, **Schonbrunn** in Vienna, and **Williamsburg** in Virginia.

Perhaps the most significant connection between Renaissance architecture and the work that followed was found in the spirit of discovery that blossomed during the 15th century. Intellectual curiosity led to scientific inquiry, which in turn prompted new developments in construction methods and materials that ultimately became the basis for a new architecture.

By the year 1750, the great Renaissance movement had lost its impetus. The conclusion of this epoch was confirmed by the industrial and social revolutions that subsequently took place. Years earlier, architecture had reached an impasse in which only greater elaboration of the same ideas seemed possible. Architects believed that the appropriate expression for a new building had to be based on the rules of design laid down by Palladio. Thus, architectural textbooks were followed blindly, and the results became increasingly predictable and less satisfying.

## The Role of Archeology

In time, the uninhibited and violent forms of the Baroque style gave way to a more rational expression. This gradual swing toward restraint in architecture coincided with the first serious archeological excavations. Pompeii and Herculaneum were discovered undisturbed, in the same condition in which they had been buried by volcanic activity in 79 AD. In addition, drawings of the ruins in Rome, Baalbeck, Palmyra, and Spalato were published in erudite and influential volumes.

Most significant of all, however, was the rediscovery of ancient Greece. Greek classical architecture had been completely ignored by previous ages. Even temples which were easily accessible, like those at Paestum near Naples, were newly discovered during this period. Architects began to realize that what had passed as the prototypes of classic architecture since the 15th century were really a few Roman ruins that represented a relatively narrow view of classic civilizations. These newly discovered works, particularly the temples of Periclean Athens, looked strikingly different from the designs found in Palladio's books. The publication of these examples exercised an enormous influence, helping to foster the next architectural revolution.

## Neo-Classicism

The new style which began to emerge towards the end of the 18th century was called *Neo-Classicism*, or *Romantic Classicism*. In time, it was adopted throughout Europe, in virtually the identical form. This distinct expression was based on a new kind of historical consciousness that relied more on abstract aesthetic theory than on tradition and experience. Neo-Classicism was predicated on ancient classical architecture, and its success was judged on the basis of rcheological accuracy. During the last few hundred years of the Renaissance, Roman architectural forms had been modified virtually beyond recognition. Now, a conscious effort was made to accurately portray classic compositions.

The new classical style also stressed the concept of virtue in a building, which demanded not only great size and strength, but also simplicity and nobility. Examples of this philosophy could be seen in two great monuments: the **Arc de Triomphe** in Paris, by *Chalgrin*, which was inspired by a Roman triumphal arch; and the **Brandenburg Gate** in Berlin, by *Langhans*, which was based on the *Propylaea* of the *Acropolis* in Athens.

BRANDENBURG GATE

**Figure 5.2**

### Developments in England

Several talented architects whose classically-inspired work stressed elegance, purity, and correctness appeared in England during the latter part of the 18th century. In Bath, *John Wood the Elder* and *John Wood the Younger*, father and son, developed the *English terrace house* which became the urban prototype for more than a century. In addition, they designed the **Royal Circus** and **Royal Crescent**, both of which were harmonious urban residential schemes.

BATH - AERIAL VIEW

**Figure 5.3**

Another English architect was *Robert Adam*, a true Palladian, who had a long list of great country houses to his credit. He also brought refinement into the furnishing of the house, giving rise to the elegant *Adam style.*

At the same time that Napoleon's architects were transforming Paris into a grandly-scaled metropolis. London was being modified from a provincial city to a cosmopolitan capital. The architect responsible for many of these changes was *John Nash*, an ingenious designer with a great flair for town planning. At the beginning of the 19th century, he laid out a great complex of parks, streets, terraces, and squares across the West End of London—from *Regents Park* in the north to *St. James Park* in the south.

### Soane and Schinkel

The highly imaginative and abstract projects of the Frenchmen *E. L. Boullée* and *C. N. Ledoux* had a decisive influence on the English designer *Sir John Soane*, the architect for the **Bank of England**. In his treatment of smooth surfaces, flowing interior spaces, and original detailing, Soane anticipated many 20th-century principles.

Apart from Soane, the most important and prolific architect of the Romantic phase of Neo-Classicism was *Karl Friedrich Schinkel*. In the **Schauspielhaus** and the **Alte Museum**, both in Berlin, Schinkel employed rigidly pure Grecian details in unified architectural compositions.

## Romanticism

By the beginning of the 19th century, architectural expression had become increasingly more romantic. All Neo-Classical architecture had exhibited a nostalgia for antiquity, but the new *Romantic* movement expressed more than nostalgia for the past: it expressed men's dreams and, in some cases, their fantasies. Good design was no longer enough; romantic qualities, such as charm, novelty, picturesqueness, and, above all, historical association, became necessary.

Romanticism as a style emerged for a number of reasons. First, a general discontent had developed among artists, and in an effort to free themselves of classical restraint, they adopted certain eccentricities of design. Perhaps more important, however, was the desire to escape reality, which undoubtedly represented a reaction to the *Industrial Revolution.*

SCHAUSPIELHAUS – BERLIN

**Figure 5.4**

### The Industrial Revolution

The Industrial Revolution originated in England and was, in essence, the substitution of machine power for human labor. The process had been slowly developing for many years when, late in the 18th century, the Scotsman James Watt invented a workable steam engine. By the year 1800, the steam engine had proliferated throughout mines, mills, and factories. The new machinery allowed manufacturers to produce large numbers of a product in the same amount of time and at the same cost as had formerly been required to produce one handmade product.

Suddenly it became a world of machines and engines, of iron, coal, and steam, of railroads and steamships. Speedier travel and better communications were making the world smaller, and ingenious new devices were making life easier. Science was adding daily to mankind's knowledge of the world, and the marvels of human inventiveness appeared limitless. With the Industrial Revolution came industrial progress, inexpensively manufactured goods, and the end to many backbreaking tasks. But along with the progress, there was also shoddy workmanship, vulgar industrial art, and the factory system.

The new industrial workers were mainly peasants who had formerly worked the land. In great numbers they migrated to the new industrial centers, where they provided labor for the mills and mines. In so doing, they essentially exchanged one form of bondage for another. The Industrial Revolution replaced the feudal society and released the peasants from the land. However, their survival now became dependent entirely on the owner of the factory or mine. Labor unions did not exist and workers were often treated appallingly—there was no job security and working conditions were inhuman.

Seven-year-old children frequently worked 12 to 14 hours a day for bare subsistence wages.

## Effects of the Industrial Revolution

The living conditions in the cities were equally alarming. Because of the industrial migration, manufacturing centers grew quickly and haphazardly. Families were crowded in poorly-built tenements, and, in time, conditions in the new towns and cities began to resemble those in early medieval towns. Drainage was inadequate, sewage disposal virtually nonexistent, and pure water unavailable. Because of these conditions, epidemics of cholera, typhoid, and typhus raged through cities. Whole areas were wiped out, with corpses often remaining unburied for weeks. Vice and crime became as common as hunger and disease.

Romanticism was the great escape—a rebellion against the ugliness of industrialism. Under the impulse of Romanticism, a new enthusiasm for the beauty of nature emerged, and the style which embodied this feeling was *Neo-Gothic.* Much of the credit for the establishment of this new style, especially for the English country house, went to *Horace Walpole.* His mansion, **Strawberry Hill** at Twickenham, built in 1750, became famous among connoisseurs and architects throughout Europe.

STRAWBERRY HILL

**Figure 5.5**

## Historicism

During the first half of the 19th century, the various architectural styles were collectively referred to as *Historicism.* It was, in fact, the great age of eclecticism, which was the use of styles borrowed from throughout history. The formal vernacular of architects included every style from Egypt to Late Baroque, and occasionally elements of one style were mixed with those of another. Clients began to select the style of their building out of catalogs of historical precedents, and architects were employed merely to provided a facade to an otherwise workable scheme. The accumulation of adopted forms concealed what was really happening: the entire world, including that of architecture, was changing beyond recognition.

## Alienation of the Architect

During that time, political and social power passed into the hands of the capitalist middle class, while church and state became distinctly separated. Towns grew overnight into cities, iron construction began to replace stone, and the development of paved roads, sewage disposal, and street lighting completely altered the character of cities. Throughout these developments, architects were concerned with the propriety of style, not with social or political issues. Their province was "art," and they were little concerned that most city dwellers lived in slums. It was also the beginning of a serious estrangement between architects and engineers, since architects believed that what engineers produced was not art.

The architecture of this period has been described as *a collapse of taste* because work that possessed refinement, elegance, or beauty was scarce. There were some talented designers and a few distinguished monuments from this time; however, they were all but buried under the eclectic tidal wave. The memorable structures of this period were those that were important principally for their engineering concepts. One of the benefits of the Industrial Revolution was the development of new construction materials and techniques, such as reinforced concrete, large sheets of glass, and, most importantly, the use of iron as a structural framing material.

## ENGINEERING DEVELOPMENTS

Iron was not, of course, a new material. Its use dated back to prehistoric times, but it had rarely been employed in construction. Prior to the 18th century, iron had been used mainly for fastenings or decoration, since high cost and prejudice had precluded its use for structures. But during the latter part of the century, iron began to make a tentative appearance in mills, factories, and bridges. One of the earliest examples of the latter was the **Severn Bridge** by *Abraham Darby* in 1775, in which one huge cast iron arch was used to span 100 feet. Some years later, *John Nash* used cast iron columns in the **Royal Pavilion** at Brighton, and the American engineer *James Bogardus* employed a cast iron skeleton framework for a factory in 1848.

SEVERN BRIDGE

**Figure 5.6**

Just as Victorian England was split between idealism and materialism, so too the arts continued to diverge from technology, and the chasm which separated architecture from construction widened. In Paris, the famous school of design *Ecole des Beaux-Arts* rigidly emphasized the historic styles while ignoring new methods and requirements of construction. Halfway through the 19th century,

*Henri Labrouste* used slender cast iron for the columns and vault of the **Bibliothèque Ste. Geneviève** in Paris. A few years later, Labrouste repeated this design concept in the reading room of the **Bibliothèque Nationale**, also in Paris. In both libraries, light and airy reading rooms were required, and no other material could achieve this as successfully as cast iron. These were the earliest examples of interiors that were governed by the aesthetic of metal construction, which had not yet achieved acceptance in architectural circles.

The second half of the 19th century passed with few significant architectural works. Eclecticism smothered virtually all creative energy. During this same period, however, there were three significant structural developments that were based on modern scientific technology: the enclosure of great space in the **Crystal Palace**, the spanning of great distance in the **Brooklyn Bridge**, and the reaching of great height in the **Eiffel Tower**. These eminent engineering achievements were difficult to ignore, since they mastered the three classic problems in structure.

BIBLIOTHÈQUE STE. GENEVIÈVE

**Figure 5.7**

## Crystal Palace

The Crystal Palace in Hyde Park was constructed to house the Great Exhibition of 1851 in London. This first large-scale international exhibition was organized to display mankind's progress in the 19th century. A competition for the exhibition building had drawn nearly 250 designs, all of which were rejected. Shortly afterward, *Joseph Paxton*, a horticulturist who had previously built large conservatories for the Duke of Devonshire, was asked to submit a design based on a concept he had.

CRYSTAL PALACE

**Figure 5.8**

In cast iron and glass, Paxton produced a light and airy structure of great beauty that omitted all references to past styles, and that exhibited many extraordinary features. To begin with, it was designed in nine days. Secondly, it was a masterpiece of standardization: cast iron members and glass panels were prefabricated in three months. Thirdly, it took only another three months to erect the immense structure which was, at that time, the largest building the world had ever seen—18 acres of space enclosed by nearly 1 million square feet of glass. Paxton's revolutionary Palace design brought him knighthood, a Parliament seat, and worldwide fame.

The building immediately received great acclaim and was universally judged to be an absolute tour de force. With the introduction of the structural concept of strength through precision instead of mass, the Crystal Palace foreshadowed the new age of building. And with its Regency elegance combined with advanced engineering, the Palace proved that iron and architecture were not incompatible.

## Brooklyn Bridge

The Brooklyn Bridge was designed by *John Roebling*, a young German engineer who had immigrated to Pennsylvania several years before the construction of the Crystal Palace. Working on the *Pennsylvania Canal*, Roebling developed the technology for weaving wire cable. With his new woven cable, the young engineer built many suspension structures, each with increasing sophistication and daring.

BROOKLYN BRIDGE

**Figure 5.9**

Although Roebling did not invent the suspension bridge, he did perfect both the cable and the system in order to achieve greater spans. In 1867, he designed a new bridge nearly 1,600 feet long to connect Manhattan and Brooklyn. As chief engineer, Roebling manufactured the cable, perfected the machinery that wove it, trained the workmen, and supervised the construction. The result was a suspended tension structure which has never been surpassed for efficiency, style, and beauty. The Brooklyn Bridge became an American icon, as famous and familiar as the **Capitol Building** in Washington DC.

## Eiffel Tower

The Eiffel Tower differed from the Crystal Palace and the Brooklyn Bridge in that its designer, *Gustave Eiffel*, met determined opposition from the start. Eiffel was a talented engineer who had built several fine cast iron structures around Paris, not the least of which was his exciting **Bon Marché** department store. In recognition of his proficiency and reputation, the directors of the Paris Exhibition of 1889 commissioned him to build a structure that would symbolize the event for all visitors, a practice much imitated ever since.

Eiffel's 1,000-foot-high tower became the center of a controversy that involved a great many distinguished Parisians, including the artistic elite. The design was derided, ridiculed and very nearly abandoned. Once completed, however, the "world's tallest tower" became enormously popular and has remained the most famous symbol of Paris. Eiffel's Tower was a pure engineering structure whose aesthetic was a result of its technology, which was years ahead of contemporary European practice.

EIFFEL TOWER

**Figure 5.10**

This same Exhibition of 1889 witnessed another great structure, the **Galerie des Machines**, designed by the engineer *Contamin* and the architect *Dutert*. In this vast structure, three-hinged cast iron arches spanned an amazing 380 feet in a building that was over one-quarter mile long.

It is perhaps significant that none of these designers—Paxton, Roebling, and Eiffel—was an architect. Yet each created a new technological aesthetic within the existing eclectic environment. As popular and highly-regarded as these structures became, the design establishment did not consider them related in any way to architecture. Several decades would pass before engineering and architecture would become reconciled.

## TRANSITION

The latter part of the 19th century was a period of relative prosperity and complacency. It was also a time of great technical innovation: the electric light, the telephone, wireless telegraphy, and many other modern wonders appeared during this period. But widespread dissatisfaction with eclecticism pervaded the arts. Architects, critics, and even clients began to view architectural fashion as foolish and narrow. In search of a new morality, artists appeared ready for a change.

## Arts and Crafts Movement

In England, men of great influence, such as *John Ruskin* and *William Morris*, hoped for a rejuvenation of art by returning to medieval conditions. For years, Ruskin had preached against the use of iron in architecture. Even *Viollet-le-Duc* in France considered iron-roofed markets and railway stations to be "mere sheds." Morris reacted violently against mass production which created sentimental and overly-ornamented products. Instead, he proposed to recapture the romantic world of the medieval craftsman; it was to be an *Arts and Crafts* movement, which would replace industrial mass production. From Morris to *Lutyens*, over a period of 60 years, the Arts and Crafts movement provided a nostalgic postscript to picturesque country house architecture.

In 1860, Morris commissioned *Philip Webb* to build the **Red House** at Bexley Heath in Kent. The importance of this house lay in its informality, its absence of decoration, and its simple vernacular. With their emphasis on basic form, sound materials, and good craftsmanship, Morris and Webb anticipated the Modern movement by at least 50 years. The thematic characteristics of the Red House had great appeal to architects such as *Norman Shaw, C. F. A. Voysey*, and *Sir Edwin Lutyens*, all of whom contributed to a poetic phase of European architecture.

RED HOUSE

**Figure 5.11**

## Art Nouveau

Country house architecture was not only a protest against industrialism, but it was also an attempt to move away from Historicism. Another such effort to abandon the eclectic influence was the movement known as *Art Nouveau* (literally: *new art*) that appeared during the last decade of the 19th century. The movement began principally in the applied arts, and mainly comprised ornamentation inspired by nature, and thus free from historical imitation. The favorite ornamental motifs of the Art Nouveau were the sensuous curves found in the natural forms of plants, the sea, and flowing hair. Within a short time, the new expression was found everywhere: in the lamps of *Louis Tiffany*, the drawings of *Aubrey Beardsley*, the posters of *Toulouse-Lautrec*, as well as in furniture, fabrics, typefaces, and trinkets.

Motivated by the Art Nouveau, the process of stylization placed emphasis on clarity and purity of line, which became its link with architecture. In Belgium, the architects *Henri Van de Velde* and *Victor Horta* became the principal proponents of the Art Nouveau. Horta's experiments with flexible, free curving forms resulted in his famous **Maison du Peuple** in Brussels.

SAGRADA FAMILIA

**Figure 5.12**

of the type seen on the **Carson Pirie Scott** store in Chicago. Mackintosh, on the other hand, placed no great value on the flexible ornamental line. His **School of Art** in Glasgow was strongly personal and totally devoid of historical reference. The Art Nouveau details were found in playful ornaments that were abstracted to an unusual degree.

The new expressions of design that appeared almost simultaneously in several countries were merely the outward manifestations of the great dissatisfaction that existed among designers. It became clear that until all the historical dressing was rejected, architecture could have no relevance to contemporary technology. Art Nouveau, however, served only as a protest; it was not the foundation from which 20th-century architecture was to arise. It disappeared almost as quickly as it had come. By the First World War, Art Nouveau was obsolete.

At about the same time in Barcelona, Spain, *Antonio Gaudí* was exploring similar ideas in what he called a *biological style.* In examples such as the church of the **Sagrada Familia** and the **Casa Milá**, Gaudí created free-flowing, plastic shapes that appeared to have been molded out of clay to form almost pure sculpture. Gaud"s work has frequently been referred to as *fantastic architecture.*

Two other great architects associated with the Art Nouveau movement of the 1890s were *Louis Sullivan* in America and *Charles Rennie Mackintosh* in Scotland. Sullivan created not only a new kind of architecture, but also a new kind of ornament. Realizing the potential of ductile metal, Sullivan made sensual ornament

GLASGOW SCHOOL OF ART

**Figure 5.13**

# **LESSON 5** QUIZ

1. Which of the following statements concerning the Industrial Revolution is INCORRECT?

   **A.** The Industrial Revolution originated in England and was essentially the substitution of regulated craftsmanship for unregulated manual labor.

   **B.** The new factory workers generally came from the peasantry, who migrated to the new industrial centers looking for work.

   **C.** Factory conditions were often inhuman, insecure, and dominated by factory owners.

   **D.** The original aim of the Industrial Revolution was to provide inexpensive manufactured goods that would contribute to a better life.

2. Free-flowing forms were typical of the work of

   **I.** Antonio Gaudí.

   **II.** Robert Adam.

   **III.** Victor Horta.

   **IV.** John Nash.

   **A.** I and II

   **B.** I and III

   **C.** II and III

   **D.** II and IV

3. The European style of architecture known as Neo-Classicism developed for all of the following reasons, EXCEPT

   **A.** architecture had reached an impasse in which only greater elaboration of the same ideas seemed possible.

   **B.** following the rules laid down by Palladio invariably led to predictable results that became less and less satisfying.

   **C.** the new style was a natural outgrowth of over 300 years of classical experience and tradition beginning with Brunelleschi and ending with Palladio.

   **D.** the rediscovery of ancient Greek monuments seemed to indicate that the original prototypes of Renaissance architecture were somehow fallacious.

4. Among the following qualities, which were associated with Romanticism?

   **I.** Picturesqueness

   **II.** Nostalgia

   **III.** Formality

   **IV.** Charm

   **V.** Historical association

   **A.** I, II, and IV

   **B.** I, III, and V

   **C.** II, III, IV, and V

   **D.** I, II, IV, and V

5. Which of the following statements concerning Art Nouveau are correct?

I. The movement concerned itself almost exclusively with the decorative arts, such as furniture, jewelry, and graphics.

II. The style originated in Belgium and was geographically restricted to Central Europe.

III. The movement was an attempt to abandon the eclectic influence of Historicism.

IV. The expression relied heavily on free-flowing curved lines, such as those found in nature.

V. The style proved to be merely a protest against historical allusions, and therefore only lasted about 25 years.

A. I, II, and III     C. II, IV, and V

B. III, IV, and V     D. II, III, and IV

6. The widespread 19th century notion that iron used in construction was incompatible with architecture was based on

A. the fact that iron members had no precedent in historical architecture.

B. the fact that most architects had little engineering knowledge of metal structures.

C. the preaching, writing, and influence of John Ruskin, William Morris, and Viollet-le-Duc.

D. the general understanding that engineers employed iron, but architects built with masonry.

7. Which of the following statements regarding the Crystal Palace are correct?

I. It was a masterpiece of standardization.

II. It took only three months to erect.

III. It was initially met with great controversy.

IV. It combined new technology with historical references.

V. It was built to house the Great Exhibition of 1851 in London.

A. II, III, and V     C. I, IV, and V

B. I and IV     D. I, II, and V

8. The architecture of the Historicism movement has been described as

A. soaring and spiritual.

B. imaginative and creative.

C. a collapse of taste.

D. free-flowing and natural.

9. Regarding the Arts and Crafts movement, which of the following statements is INCORRECT?

A. It was an attempt to rejuvenate art by returning to medieval conditions.

B. The movement was spearheaded by men such as John Ruskin and William Morris.

C. It was believed that sound materials and good craftsmanship could be produced with the tools of industry.

D. The Arts and Crafts movement anticipated the Modern movement by at least 50 years.

**10.** What is significant about Paxton, Roebling, and Eiffel?

**A.** Although not architects, each created a new technological aesthetic during an eclectic period.

**B.** Each rigidly followed the rules of architecture as laid down by Palladio.

**C.** Their designs were not accepted until a century later.

**D.** They used a new technology to reconcile engineering and architecture.

# AMERICAN ARCHITECTURE

## EARLY DEVELOPMENTS

During the 16th century, the exploration of North America was carried out by several of the great European powers, including Spain, France, and England. Significant colonization, however, did not begin until the following century. During the 1600s, colonists from England settled in groups along the Atlantic seaboard. The indigenous architecture of the new land consisted of primitive Native American structures such as tepees, hogans, and pueblos, but very little else.

However, the colonists chose to ignore these developments from the native culture.

Colonial architecture throughout the world has always borne the stamp of the colonizing power. This was true of Roman architecture in England and of British architecture in India. Moreover, since the climate in the new colonies was similar to that of England, American colonial architecture accurately reflected that of the mother country; in this new wilderness, the colonists built the same sort of structures they had known at home.

## Colonial Style

In 1620, the year that Plymouth was settled, the traditional architecture of England was still medieval. The earliest colonial structures, therefore, were medieval English wood-framed dwellings that were imported in their entirety to the new country. These Gothic buildings were wonderfully direct, simple, and honest in their expression of structure. After the first bleak winter, the Elizabethan prototype was suitably modified, and within 50 years after their arrival, the colonists had developed a distinctive American house.

The plan and structure of the early colonial houses were systematized and simplified into strong, obvious shapes with plain surfaces. They were two stories in height, and all the rooms were oriented to the huge, central chimney. The rooms were low, and the rough-hewn timbers which made up the frame (the English *half-timber*) were largely exposed. Covering the frame were thin, horizontal overlapping clapboards, while over the mass of the house was a steep gabled roof. Small casement windows were placed wherever light was needed, in a more or less regular pattern. After some years, when brick became available, houses were built of brick as well as timber.

Seventeenth-century colonial houses, such as the **Parson Capen House** in Massachusetts, were very simple—almost austere—but they were honest, functional, and well-suited to the new land. In later years, as the settlers moved westward across America, the *New England house* accompanied them in much the same way as the Roman structures had proliferated throughout Europe. When the design became less suited to the different climates and terrains, it suffered the fate of most ill-suited designs.

PARSON CAPEN HOUSE

**Figure 6.1**

Colonial public buildings generally conformed to the predominantly domestic scale. This was apparent in Williamsburg, which was established as the capital of Virginia in 1699. The **Capitol Building, College**, and **Governor's House** all maintained the proportions of substantial houses. Williamsburg remains today perhaps the greatest single monument of the colonial era.

GOVERNOR'S HOUSE – WILLIAMSBURG

**Figure 6.2**

## American Georgian

By the 18th century, American merchants had overcome the adversities of the new land and had prospered. In seeking the amenities of life, they looked to England, where the latest building fashion was *Georgian*. They tried to emulate this style by using building manuals, carpenter's handbooks, and architectural texts. It seemed to be of little concern to them that the original Georgian style was a stone expression; American carpenters reproduced sophisticated stone details in wood, often with craftsmanship of high quality.

The Georgian style demanded symmetry, and in the typical domestic plan, there were four rooms on each of two stories. Each room had its own fireplace, which was frequently paired and placed on the outside wall. By this time, interior finishes were considered to be important: ceilings were plastered, walls were paneled with wood, and floors were covered with wood planks. In the following years, the architecture of America continued to follow the stylistic fashions which were popular in England and the Continent.

## Federal Style

By the middle of the 18th century, the influence of the *Classic Revivals* appeared and became known in America as the *Federal Style*. One of the earliest American Palladian architects was *Peter Harrison*, whose **Redwood Library** in Newport displayed a fine Roman Doric portico. Shortly afterward, he began his **Kings Chapel** in Boston, which was the first departure from the severely plain Puritan meetinghouse.

### Thomas Jefferson

During the earliest years of the new nation, one of the most famous and influential personalities was *Thomas Jefferson*, a latter-day Renaissance man from Virginia. Jefferson authored the Declaration of Independence, served as Secretary of State under George Washington, was the third President of the United States, and achieved considerable fame as an architect. Jefferson had profound faith in Roman law and, by extension, in Roman architecture. He generally was practical and rational in the design of actual buildings, but he was completely magnetized by the Roman examples he had studied in Europe. He shared Palladio's admiration for Roman architecture, and he often spent considerable time with architectural texts searching for just the right detail.

Jefferson's design for the **Virginia State Capitol** in Richmond was a modified *Maison Carrée*; he was the first to use a pure Roman temple form for something other than its original purpose. In his own house, **Monticello**, Jefferson looked to Palladio's *Villa Capra* in Vicenza for inspiration. And in his last great design for the **University of Virginia**, Jefferson created a classically formal complex of structures that was the equal of any Roman forum. The focal point of the composition was the domed library, modeled after the *Pantheon* in Rome.

## Neo-Classicism

During the post-colonial Federal period, *neo-classic* examples proliferated throughout the new country. *Benjamin Latrobe*, who assisted Jefferson with the University of Virginia project, designed the **Bank of Pennsylvania** in Philadelphia in 1800. *Charles Bulfinch* was the architect who presided over the early growth of Boston and helped establish the architectural profession in the new republic. His **Boston State House**, from around 1800, became the standard for all subsequent domed state capitols throughout the country.

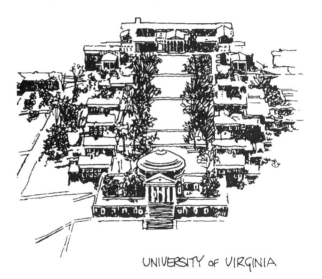

UNIVERSITY OF VIRGINIA

**Figure 6.3**

### Washington Developments

Meanwhile, in Washington DC, *Pierre Charles L'Enfant*, under the spell of *Versailles*, planned the center of the formal, grandiose city that exists today. The Baroque plan consisted of long axial avenues that radiated from the centers of power. The two major focal points were the **White House** and the **Capitol**. The White House was designed by *James Hoban*, while the Capitol was done by several designers. The original scheme of the Capitol was conceived in 1800 by *William Thornton*, and it was completed in 1827 by Bulfinch, who had become the recognized champion of the Greek revival. The great cast iron dome, which was added later, was the work of *Thomas U. Walter*, and Latrobe added his Grecian touches to the south wing, in addition to his work on the interior spaces. The grandeur of the Capitol lay mainly in its remarkable dome and great flights of steps.

BOSTON STATE HOUSE
**Figure 6.4**

By the middle of the 19th century, Neo-Classicism was the accepted architectural expression of the day—but it was the *Greek Revival*, not the Roman as Jefferson had anticipated, that became the major influence. Towns bearing Greek names like Athens, Ithaca, and Sparta were founded during this period. The earliest competition to the Classics was provided by the *Gothic Revival*. The great Gothic champion *Richard Upjohn*, through his famous **Trinity Church** in New York, generated an influence that pervaded church architecture in hundreds of small towns across the early United States.

## LATER DEVELOPMENTS

### Eclecticism

In an almost exact duplication of European developments, one historic style after another began to emerge in the greatest eclectic age America had ever seen. During the expansion following the Civil War, new fortunes were made, often by men insensitive to the arts. With little tradition to guide them, the *nouveaux riches* created projects of great size, novelty, and glitter, but generally of little substance. Rooms were ornate, overstuffed, and sentimental. An Egyptian hospital was built in Virginia, a Chinese temple in New York, and a Medieval castle in Missouri. It was a period known as the *Battle of Styles*, but according to critics, it was more like a war.

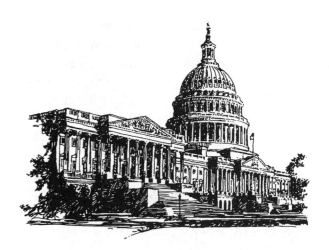

CAPITOL - WASHINGTON DC
**Figure 6.5**

Whatever originality emerged during this period was found in the way historical influences were put to use. For example, *Richard Morris Hunt*, the first American to study at the Ecole des Beaux-Arts in Paris, based his early house designs on the Gothic Revival, but the results were truly an original expression. Another influential architect was *Frank Furness* of Philadelphia, whose Gothic influence derived mainly from *Viollet-le-Duc*. His power-ful **Pennsylvania Academy of Fine Arts**, from around 1875, influenced many younger archi-tects, not the least of whom was *Louis Sullivan,* who worked for Furness for a short time.

## H. H. Richardson

Towards the end of the 19th century, two distinct trends in architecture appeared in America. One was the exploration of new techniques, led by the *Chicago School*, and the other was the *Aca-demic Style*, fostered by such firms as *McKim, Mead*, and *White.* Behind both of these trends was the giant figure of *Henry Hobson Richard-son*, one of the acknowledged geniuses of Amer-ican architecture. Richardson was trained at the Beaux-Arts in Paris, which was the main source of American academicism. In 1872, he won the competition for **Trinity Church** in Boston, which was a strong and prominent monument that made his reputation. Inspired by *French Romanesque*, Trinity Church revealed Richard-son's skillful handling of rugged masonry and his powerful sense of composition.

The church took the country by storm and gave rise to *Richardson Romanesque*, with devoted supporters in every major city. The young Rich-ardson won immediate acclaim, but while his followers became Romanesque minded, Rich-ardson himself turned away from eclecticism altogether. In his masterpiece, the **Marshall Field Warehouse** in Chicago, Richardson com-posed an honest skeleton of masonry piers and arches, relying on mass and the vertical rhythm of windows for character. The building was nor particularly progressive technologically, but it affirmed that industrial buildings could be dignified and that the aesthetic need not be bor-rowed or awkward.

MARSHALL FIELD WAREHOUSE
**Figure 6.6**

## Academicism

Richardson's genius lay in his ability to use his-torical knowledge in a modern way, and it was this quality that inspired the two most brilliant architects of the Chicago School: *Sullivan* and *Root.* In the pioneer Richardson, they found a new aesthetic for the modern movement. The New York firm of McKim, Mead, and White, on the other hand, might almost be regarded as anti-pioneers. Both *C. F. McKim* and *Stan-ford White* were trained in Richardson's office. Their early domestic buildings, such as the original **Low House** in Rhode Island, were influenced by Richardson's shingled houses, in which all historicism was abandoned. In later years, however, the McKim office turned increasingly to fashionable Roman classics for their inspiration, and with the **Boston Public Library** and **Pennsylvania Station** in New York, which was a reincarnation of the *Baths of Caracalla*, they diverted American architecture away from the Chicago School and towards Academicism.

BOSTON PUBLIC LIBRARY

**Figure 6.7**

Although the prehistory of the modern movement took place in England, the new principles were most consistently employed in the United States. Two of America's unique architectural contributions were the *balloon frame* and the *skyscraper*, both of which were connected with American industrialization.

## Balloon Framing

Balloon framing was a product of a technological revolution in the building industry. Wood was the most common natural building material in the United States. Previously, massive timbers had been held together by means of expensive handcrafted mortise-and-tenon joints. But by the mid-1880s, sawmills were able to mass produce thin, easily transported studs and joists, which could be fastened with machine-made nails. With the development of this new framing system, a formerly complicated craft, requiring highly skilled labor, became an industry. As the West was developed, balloon framing served to hasten the growth of new towns. It has been considered the most important contribution to domestic architecture.

## The Chicago School

Tall buildings utilized expensive land more economically than shorter buildings. Strangely, however, the skyscraper was born in the spacious Middle West—not in New York. This occurred for several reasons. First, Chicago had become the capital of the Midwest and the key city along the new east-west commercial axis of New York

and San Francisco. Secondly, the great Chicago Fire of 1871 had destroyed large areas of the city, providing opportunities to architects of imagination and power. Finally, Chicago had the architectural genius of Louis Sullivan.

## Early Skyscrapers

Two technological developments made tall buildings possible: the elevator and the metal frame. In 1850, *Elisha Graves Otis* developed the first practical elevator, and with each subsequent improvement in its design, building heights increased. If elevators made the skyscraper practical, the development of the steel frame, which supported its own fireproofing of masonry or terra cotta, made the skyscraper possible. *Leroy Buffington* actually designed the first tall building, but his design was never executed. Therefore, the honor of designing the first skyscraper fell to *William LeBaron Jenney* for his **Home Insurance Building** of 1883. Although this first modern building was a mere ten stories high, it must be remembered that the term skyscraper originally denoted a kind of construction, not an exceptional height.

HOME INSURANCE BLDG.

**Figure 6.8**

William Jenney is regarded as the father of the Chicago School, which included *Holabird and Roche, Burnham and Root*, and *Adler and Sullivan.* The movement laid the foundations of modern commercial architecture and the high-rise corporate centers which symbolize present-day urban development. Most importantly, the accomplishments of the Chicago School served to unite modern technology with modern architecture. Sullivan, Burnham, Holabird, and Roche had all worked in Jenney's office at one time or another, but it was Holabird and Roche who followed his principles most closely. Their **Marquette Building** of 1893 was 16 stories high, and for the first time expressed within the frame construction the large horizontal *Chicago window* with fixed center and openable sides.

RELIANCE BUILDING

**Figure 6.9**

Burnham and Root, in 1889, produced one of the great office structures of this period, the **Monadnock Building**. It was the last of the pure masonry towers, 16 stories in height with load-bearing walls six feet thick at the base.

The same firm also produced the **Reliance Building** the following year, which was amazingly modern in appearance. The aesthetics of the steel skeleton were completely expressed, with large windows extending between steel piers sheathed in terra cotta.

*Louis Sullivan*

The architect who most exemplified the Chicago School was *Louis Sullivan*. His original aesthetic inspiration was not an iron and glass building, but Richardson's Marshall Field Warehouse from 1885. Sullivan's **Auditorium Building** two years later was largely derived from Richardson's model. With his partner, *Dankmar Adler*, Sullivan produced several great structures of enormous sensitivity and lasting quality. He has been credited with the remark *form follows function.* Whether or not he actually said it, he certainly believed it. In 1890, Sullivan built the ten-story **Wainwright Building** in St. Louis, and in 1894, the **Guarantee Building** in Buffalo, which has often

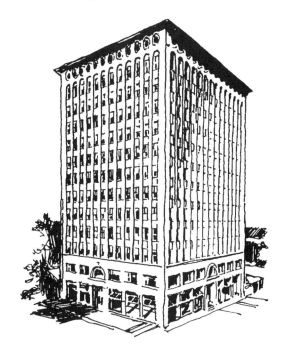

GUARANTEE BUILDING

**Figure 6.10**

been considered his masterpiece. In both examples, Sullivan stressed the vertical with expressive, uninterrupted piers. After his break with Adler in 1895, Sullivan built the **Carson Pirie Scott** store in Chicago. With its light, regular metal frame, broad fenestration, and original decoration, it was the most modern building of the Chicago School.

When Sullivan designed the Carson Pirie Scott store, his chief draftsman was the young and eager *Frank Lloyd Wright*. It was Wright who was most responsible for sustaining the principles of the Chicago School, because in a short time, a new wave of eclecticism would soon bury architecture.

CARSON PIRIE SCOTT STORE
**Figure 6.11**

## The Chicago World's Fair of 1893

The *Chicago World's Fair of 1893*, also known as the *World's Columbian Exposition*, had an extraordinary effect on American architecture: it virtually put an end to Richardson Romanesque, the developments of the Chi-

cago School, and nearly all other architectural progress that had been made up to that time. The highly respected Chicago architect Daniel Burnham was appointed chief architect, but the Fair Committee brought in *Charles McKim* as consultant. The New York firm of McKim, Mead, and White was famous, successful, and, by that time, completely under the spell of the Beaux-Arts.

In matters of design, Burnham was docile in the presence of the classicists, and the unified style dictated by McKim became *Modernized Classic*. The composition of the Fair was *neobaroque*, with crossed axes, rigid formality, and building facades derived directly from the Beaux-Arts, which in turn had come indirectly from Imperial Rome. The results of the Fair were truly incredible: people believed that in the *White City*, they were witnessing a remarkable rebirth of the greatest traditions of past ages. The Fair's classic architecture so impressed America that for years its influence was felt in almost all public buildings.

WORLD'S COLUMBIAN EXPO.
**Figure 6.12**

Only one building avoided the popular eclecticism: the **Transportation Building** by Louis Sullivan. But this marked the beginning of his unpopularity as an architect. This direct and honest structure, with its great Richardson arch, was purely original. However, its significance was lost on the America of 1893.

Travel to the Fair was almost a religious pilgrimage. Architects, artists, literary people, and almost everyone else believed that "one should mortgage one's soul to go there." Not everyone, however, was taken in by the 1893 Fair. A few individuals agreed with Sullivan that "the damage wrought to this country by the Chicago World's Fair will last half a century." Prominent among the dissenters was Frank Lloyd Wright, who in later years described these events in his autobiography. In his typically melodramatic style, Wright declared, "They killed Sullivan in 1893...and they almost killed me."

Sullivan's outburst might have seemed at the time to be the exaggerated expression of an outraged artist. As it turned out, however, he accurately prophesied what was to follow, as architectural developments moved into the 20th century.

# LESSON 6 QUIZ

1. Which of the following features were generally found in the early Colonial houses from the 17th century?

   I.   Central chimney
   II.  Gabled roofs
   III. High ceilings
   IV.  Small windows
   V.   Balloon framing

   A. I, II, and III     C. I, IV, and V
   B. I, II, and IV     D. II, III, and IV

2. During the Federal period, neo-classic buildings proliferated throughout the United States. Which of the following was NOT neo-classic?

   A. Bank of Pennsylvania in Philadelphia
   B. Boston State House
   C. The White House
   D. Trinity Church in New York

3. Which of the following statements regarding the World's Columbian Exposition of 1893 is correct?

   A. The uniform style of the buildings was Modernized Classic, which was actually a Neo-Baroque expression emanating from the Beaux-Arts.
   B. The supervising architect was Daniel Burnham, who had turned to the fashionable Roman classics for inspiration late in his career.
   C. It was an unqualified success, and its pervasive influence made possible the great projects that were later produced by the Chicago School.
   D. The one building that differed from all the others was the Transportation Building by Sullivan, who found his inspiration in ancient Rome, rather than in the Renaissance.

4. The skyscraper was first developed in the Midwest by the Chicago School because

   A. it utilized expensive land economically, and nowhere was land more expensive than in Chicago's Loop.
   B. it was made possible by the new steel framing members, which were first manufactured in the Chicago area.
   C. Chicago not only had the architectural talent, but also the opportunity to build because of the Great Fire of 1871.
   D. Chicago in the 1880s had become the commercial center of the United States and a need existed for new corporate headquarters.

**5.** From what we know of Thomas Jefferson's architectural taste, he most likely would have been attracted to which of the following?

    **A.** Pantheon by Soufflot

    **B.** Boston State House by Bulfinch

    **C.** Erectheion

    **D.** Temple of Vesta

**6.** The Richardson Romanesque style is represented best in which of the following?

    **A.** Boston Public Library

    **B.** Trinity Church in Boston

    **C.** Trinity Church in New York

    **D.** Marshall Field Warehouse

**7.** Balloon framing was made possible by the

    **A.** invention of the elevator.

    **B.** development of the steel frame.

    **C.** progressive work of Louis Sullivan.

    **D.** technological developments in the building industry.

**8.** The first American colonists

    **A.** built structures that were a precise reflection of the ones they had known in England.

    **B.** adapted elements of Native American structures to their own needs.

    **C.** used indigenous materials to build entirely new structures better adapted to their new home.

    **D.** built in the Georgian style.

**9.** Which of the following firms was NOT directly associated with the Chicago School?

    **A.** Burnham and Root

    **B.** Holabird and Roche

    **C.** McKim, Mead, and White

    **D.** Adler and Sullivan

**10.** The plan of Washington DC was created by Pierre Charles L'Enfant, who was influenced by

    **A.** Georges-Eugene Haussmann.

    **B.** the plan of Versailles.

    **C.** the work of Palladio.

    **D.** the Royal Circus.

# 20TH-CENTURY ARCHITECTURE: 1900–1980

## INTRODUCTION

For about the first 60 years of the 20th century, architecture was synonymous with *modern* architecture. It was a tangible expression, like those before it, which attempted to create a special environment for human life, while reflecting the character of its time. As the character of the age shifted towards science or space or sociology, so too did the architectural expression of the 20th century change.

Modern architecture in this multifarious period came to mean all things to all people. To some, it was the image of a steel and glass skyscraper; to others, it involved new concepts of spatial manipulation. Still others saw *modern* as anything that departed so significantly from the past that it was virtually unrecognizable. Ultimately, modern architecture simply became anything that was happening *now*.

Technological developments in transportation and communication in the 20th century made the world seem smaller and more compact, as ideas flowed swiftly and more or less freely around it. Whereas the Renaissance movement took nearly two centuries to become established in England after its birth in Florence, modern ideas of this century were transmitted around the world instantaneously. Thus, the 20th century fostered a truly international style which was part of a worldwide culture.

The appearance and substance of modern architecture differed dramatically from architecture of the past, but fundamentally, both were rooted in tradition. At first, modern structures abandoned tradition so that historical models would not become solutions for current problems. This had largely been accomplished by the time of the Second World War. In fact, the conscious effort to liberate architecture from historical precedent led architects to produce an abundance of barren forms, monotonous surfaces, sterile spaces, and, perhaps most serious of all, projects with very little human association. This *Machine Age* architecture was commonly criticized as being better suited for machinery than for people.

Tradition, however, remained very much alive, and by 1960, a reaction began against much of what modern architecture had come to represent less than a quarter century earlier. Suddenly, people, and the human environment in which they lived and worked, became the primary focus of architecture.

## NEW ECLECTICISM

The beginnings of 20th-century architecture in America were rather inauspicious. For better or worse, eclectic design dominated the practice of architecture. The World's Columbian Exposition was a tremendous public success, and its architectural concepts were embraced by the public, patrons, and architects alike, all of whom genuinely believed they were witnessing the splendid rebirth of a great cultural tradition. Among those in the architectural com-

munity, only *Louis Sullivan* protested against this regressive turn of events. Nevertheless, his **Transportation Building** for the Fair marked the beginning of the end of his architectural career.

The rebirth of *Classicism* in the 20th century (variously referred to as *Neo-, New York-,* or *Beaux-Arts Classicism*) differed from that of previous years in that it encouraged creative adaptations of style, rather than outright mimicry. A wealth of information on historic styles was now made possible by photography, which supplemented information that previously had been provided exclusively by engravings and measured drawings. This new information offered a better understanding of the historic styles. The resulting architecture, consisting of refined adaptations in a diversity of styles, replaced much of the dullness of 19th century buildings. An example was the **Lincoln Memorial** in Washington DC, designed in 1923 by *Henry Bacon.* A student of Greek architecture, Bacon chose to modify classic Greek temple proportions, emphasizing the shorter axis of the building and substituting a flat-roofed attic story for the traditional pediment and sloping roof.

LINCOLN MEMORIAL
**Figure 7.1**

Another architect whose understanding of the past was so profound that he was able to modify and simplify historic suggestions was *Bertram Goodhue.* The forms of his **Nebraska State Capitol** at Lincoln, built in 1920, were so simplified that a new style, free of eclecticism, began to emerge. This new expression was only transitional, but it indicated a firm commitment to honesty of form, thereby freeing architects, to some degree, from classical design preconceptions.

## FRANK LLOYD WRIGHT

### Career

The incredible career of *Frank Lloyd Wright* began a few years before the World's Columbian Exposition of 1893. By the time his practice was well established, eclectic design was the dominant force in the world of architecture. It was a particularly difficult time for the few who chose to pursue personal ideals, but always the individualist, Wright persevered with the skill, tenacity, and flamboyance of a true artist. His career was unmatched in the history of American architecture, spanning nearly 70 years across two centuries.

Wright's individualism was a product of his powerfully romantic nature, as well as his sensitivity to the beauty of natural forms and materials. He was considered the heir of the *Chicago School*, since he was essentially Louis Sullivan's star pupil. As an employee of the Chicago office of *Adler and Sullivan* around 1890, Wright was exposed to the organic unity found in Sullivan's work, which had been derived from *Richardson* years earlier. During those formative years, Wright displayed a keen interest in the firm's residential work, while showing little interest in its more ambitious skeleton structures.

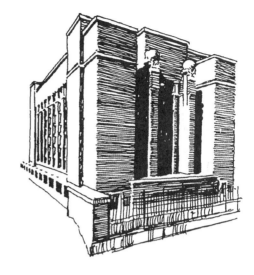

LARKIN BUILDING

**Figure 7.2**

Wright was a humanist, completely involved with the individuality and dignity of man. As with Sullivan, who rebelled against the eclectic influence of the Beaux-Arts, Wright had little use for classic forms, quoting the French author Victor Hugo approvingly when he claimed that "the Renaissance was the setting sun all Europe mistook for the dawn." Wright was a master of planning, an imaginative engineer, and a genius in the manipulation of space. Moreover, his legacy of significant works, in sheer numbers alone, is unparalleled in the history of architecture.

His earliest buildings showed the Sullivan influence in round-arched doorways and geometric ornament. But within a few years, the pure Wright expression emerged in a series of *Prairie Houses*: open, crossed axis plans, flattened hipped roofs with widely projecting eaves, long horizontal rows of windows, and a perfect marriage of building to landscape. Outstanding were the **Martin House** in Buffalo and the **Robie House** in Chicago in 1909, considered by many to be his finest dwelling.

The more enclosed and solidly monumental work of Wright appeared in the **Larkin Building** in 1904, with its soaring central office space, and **Unity Temple** in 1906, the first true monolithic reinforced concrete structure in the world. Thirty years later, Wright employed the same material to create two great tours de force: the **Johnson Wax Company** building and **Fallingwater** (the *Kaufmann House*). Both were considered daring and brilliant masterpieces.

FALLINGWATER

**Figure 7.3**

The prolific work of Frank Lloyd Wright extended over so many years and embraced such a diversity of expressions that entire periods stand out with distinction. For example, the *Japan Years* produced the **Imperial Hotel**, and the *California Years* resulted in a multitude of Mayan-influenced structures, such as the **Millard** and **Barnsdall Houses**. One of Wright's last projects, the **Guggenheim Museum**, demonstrated the creative endurance of this rare designer. It was completed in 1959, the same year in which Wright died at the venerable age of 90.

## Influence

Frank Lloyd Wright was not only a remarkable architect, he was also a furniture designer, a town planner (**Broadacre City**), a writer, and a radical preacher. Throughout his life, Wright protested, revolted, and courageously proclaimed his often unpopular or misunderstood ideas. Strangely, his influence in America was slight. In Europe, however, the significance of Wright's work had a profound effect on early 20th-century developments. Of those directly influenced by Wright were the Dutch architects *J. J. P. Oud* and *Willem Dudok.* Dudok's **Town Hall** in Hiversum freely acknowledged the influence of Wright, yet related to its urban context in a way that few of Wright's buildings did.

Wright's two rural dwellings, **Taliesin East** and **West**, in Wisconsin and Arizona, became breeding grounds for several notable architects who later developed their own individual styles. Among these were *Harwell Harris, Paolo Soleri* (of **Arcosanti** fame), as well as *Rudolph Schindler* and *Richard Neutra*, both of whom had also worked with *Adolf Loos* in their native Austria.

Rudolph Schindler came to California in 1920 to superintend the construction of Wright's Barnsdall House. Two years later, he established his own practice with his **King's Road House**. In the following 30 years, Schindler produced scores of imaginative houses, among which was the celebrated **Lovell Beach House**. In 1925, Schindler facilitated the immigration of Richard Neutra, who came to live with the Schindler family in California. Neutra's **Lovell House** (*Health House*) in 1929 gave him the opportunity to establish his own office. Two of the finest works in Neutra's long career were the **Kaufmann Desert House** in 1947 and the **Tremaine House** built the following year in Santa Barbara.

LOVELL 'HEALTH HOUSE'
**Figure 7.4**

GAMBLE HOUSE
**Figure 7.5**

## CALIFORNIA PIONEERS

At the beginning of the 20th century in California, several individualists, contemporaries of Wright, developed distinct architectural expressions. In the San Francisco Bay Area, *Bernard Maybeck*, a Beaux-Arts trained designer, developed a rich, expressionist architecture. Perhaps his finest work was the **Christian Science Church** in Berkeley from 1910. A true eclectic, Maybeck combined a Renaissance plan, Gothic tracery, Romanesque columns, and Byzantine decoration with modern industrial materials to create a sensitive and enduring work of art.

In Southern California, the pioneering *Greene Brothers* produced a fresh residential architecture that later spread throughout the country as the *California Bungalow Style.* The character of their suburban houses evolved from a love of wood and other natural materials, as well as an appreciation of Japanese design. Typical of Greene and Greene's work was the **Gamble House** in Pasadena from 1908, which exhibited their customary use of heavy, smooth timbers, projecting rafters, broad sloping roofs, and neatly shingled walls.

*Irving Gill*, who settled in San Diego a few years before 1900, produced one of the few wholly original styles of architecture in this country. His best buildings employed reinforced concrete construction that was expressed in pure and unadorned geometric compositions. The 1916 **Dodge House** in Los Angeles was a large, sprawling residence in which all of Gill's finest architectural characteristics came together in a well-balanced composition. It portended the uncompromising austerity that was to emerge during the later *international style.*

## EUROPEAN DEVELOPMENTS

At the turn of the century, Beaux-Arts Eclecticism dominated architecture throughout Europe. The general dissatisfaction among architects of the late 19th century led to transitional expressions such as *Art Nouveau.* This was the prelude or, as some have said, the false start of the modern movement. The rejection of Eclecticism was inevitable, but these reactions, which were little more than loud protests, were short-lived styles, rather than advancements.

Many Europeans were anxious to shed the motifs of historicism; this was clear in 1908 when Adolf Loos wrote his famous diatribe, *Ornament and Crime*, which demanded a formal purge of all eclectic details from new buildings. In his ascetic **Steiner House** in Vienna, Loos created unusually stark rectangular forms in reinforced concrete. In 1910, it was considered both radical and revolutionary.

STEINER HOUSE
**Figure 7.6**

In addition to the concept of structural purity, a new conviction appeared: truth in materials. An early example by *Auguste Perret* was his **25 rue Franklin Apartments** in Paris, completed in 1903. For the first time, *ferroconcrete* was used without disguise: the structural skeleton stood out plainly as an element of the exterior composition. In this and later projects, such as the church of **Notre Dame du Raincy** in 1922, Perret did for ferroconcrete what Labrouste (*Bibliothèque Ste. Geneviève* and *Bibliothèque Nationale*) had done for iron.

At about the same time, the Swiss engineer *Robert Maillart* was also experimenting with concrete. Consistently building on a single line of thought throughout his career, Maillart developed the *beamless reinforced concrete slab.* Previously, slabs had merely rested on beams and girders. Maillart later applied this and other developments to some of the most expressive and sensitive bridges and buildings of the 20th century.

In Holland, the modern movement was inaugurated with *Hendrik Berlage's* **Amsterdam Stock Exchange**, completed around 1900. The structure exhibited the power of simple masonry walls in much the same way Richardson had done some 20 years earlier. The interior of the main hall, however, was a light and airy composition of iron arches and glass.

Another iron and glass interior was created five years later by *Otto Wagner* in his **Postal Savings Bank** in Vienna. Engineering technique and architecture were totally integrated and the Bank was astonishingly pure in design. The glass vault was completely devoid of all eclectic suggestion, and it revealed the new look of *functionalism* and *rationalism*, two qualities which were soon to become architectural movements.

Simultaneously in Berlin, *Peter Behrens* embraced the new utilitarian purity in design with his industrial buildings. The **AEG Turbine Factory**, completed in 1909, was the first purely industrial building in the history of architecture. Inside, the steel frame was left exposed. Outside, broad expanses of iron and glass transformed the inner space into a dignified place of work. During the early days of the 20th century, Behrens' studio was the most stimulating in Germany. At one time or another, *Mies van der Rohe, Le Corbusier*, and *Walter Gropius* all worked in the exciting office of this great builder and teacher.

## Walter Gropius

Just prior to the First World War, a few significant buildings were produced, but these were generally isolated examples that had little immediate influence in Europe. Among those who pursued the new architecture was *Walter Gropius*, who emerged almost at once as a distinguished leader. Together with *Adolf Meyer*, Gropius demonstrated in the **Fagus Factory** of 1911 that his skill surpassed not only that of his teacher, Behrens, but also of the great Chicago engineers. In this pioneering project, the wall finally disappeared, and was replaced by a tight facade of continuous glass.

AEG TURBINE FACTORY

**Figure 7.7**

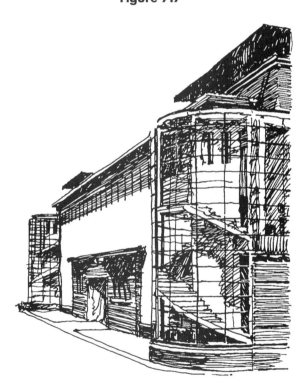

MODEL FACTORY – WERKBUND EXHIBITION

**Figure 7.8**

Gropius was also one of the original leaders of the *Deutsche Werkbund*, whose aim was to effect a collaboration between artist and crafts-

man and, on a larger scale, industry and trade. For the *Werkbund Exhibition* of 1914, Gropius created a **Model Factory** in masonry and glass. This building became a further extension of Gropius' design philosophy and influence.

## The Bauhaus

In 1919, Walter Gropius was invited to establish the first *Bauhaus* at Weimar, and the result was one of the most significant movements of modern design. With a unique staff that included *Paul Klee, Herbert Bayer, Marcel Breuer, L‡slo Moholy-Nagy, Wassily Kandinsky*, and *Josef Albers*, Gropius attempted to unite art with technology and thereby find a sound basis for modern design. Thus, the Bauhaus was not so much a movement as an idea. It became a gathering place, bringing together the accumulation of 20th-century design concepts and disseminating these through a revolutionary educational system.

In 1925, the Bauhaus was forced to leave Weimar. It was reestablished at Dessau, in a new building designed by Gropius himself. It became one of the most important structures of modern architecture. Throughout his career, two essential principles dominated the work of Walter Gropius: design through collaboration and respect for industrialization. The new **Bauhaus Building** demonstrated these convictions with great scientific rationalism. Workshops were cantilevered over the lower floor, and the entire public area was wrapped with glass curtain walls. The concrete frame was set back from the glass to give the appearance of floating interior floors, and the concept that developed was that of enclosed volume, rather than mass.

The Bauhaus fulfilled new space conceptions by organizing volumes into a unified composition. Furthermore, Gropius demonstrated that mechanization and individual freedom were not incompatible. But beyond the physical plant, the Bauhaus exerted a tremendous influence on the world of architecture: *Bauhaus* became synonymous with *modern design*.

The Bauhaus was brought to a close by Nazism; the International Style was incompatible with the repressive political climate that existed in Germany during the 1930s. Gropius arrived in the United States just prior to the outbreak of World War II and became associated with Harvard's Graduate School of Design. It was there that American architectural education began its liberation from the bondage of the Beaux-Arts system.

## Mies van der Rohe

*Mies van der Rohe* was a contemporary of Walter Gropius; both grew up in Germany, both served an apprenticeship with Peter Behrens, and both were strongly influenced by the 1910 Berlin exhibition of Frank Lloyd Wright's work. From Behrens, Mies gained practical knowledge in the use of steel, glass, and the products of industrial design. From Wright, on the other hand, Mies acquired sensitivity to the flow of space and a deep admiration of the open plan. Throughout his career, Mies' early training was reflected in a concern for disciplined details, the expert use of materials, and an almost religious passion for order.

The first building to thrust Mies into architectural prominence was the German Pavilion for the *1929 Barcelona Exhibition*, more commonly known as the **Barcelona Pavilion**. In this design, Mies was given complete freedom, since there were no exhibits and virtually no functional requirements—the Pavilion itself was the exhibit. The design consisted of an open plan, a dramatic interplay of wall and roof planes, and an opulent combination of marble, chrome, and gray glass. For the interior, Mies designed a chair, a stool, and a glass-topped

table, all of the utmost purity and refinement. Each piece of furniture, as well as the Pavilion itself, became a timeless classic. In fact, few other buildings in the world have had such an enormous influence on modern architecture.

BARCELONA PAVILION
**Figure 7.9**

Another noteworthy example of Mies' work from this period was the **Tugendhat House** at Brno, Czechoslovakia, built in 1930. Here again, spaces were defined by freestanding partitions of rich materials that were perfectly placed within the simple enclosure of glass and light metal supports. The result was a free flow of space that was defined precisely and rationally.

Mies emigrated to the United States in 1938 to escape the increasingly oppressive atmosphere of Nazi Germany. He became director of the Illinois Institute of Technology in Chicago, and, from his position as both teacher and practitioner, had a tremendous impact on Chicago and the entire country.

Mies van der Rohe's productivity increased enormously after World War II with a whole series of buildings that exploited the austerity, restraint, and sophistication of the steel frame. Among his more significant works were the **Farnsworth House** in 1950, the **Lakeshore Drive Apartments** in 1952, the **Seagram**

**Building** in 1958, with *Philip Johnson*, and his final masterpiece, the **National Gallery** in Berlin in 1968.

## Le Corbusier

Le Corbusier was the fourth major architect of the early 20th century (together with Wright, Gropius, and Mies) who had a remarkable and significant impact on the course of world architecture. Born *Charles Eduard Jenneret* in Switzerland, most of Le Corbusier's early practice centered in France. Three major influences during Le Corbusier's formative years established the direction of his future work. The first was Cubist painting, that powerful geometric approach with which Le Corbusier, as a painter, was so deeply involved. Second was the influence of the new technology which he encountered, first in Austria with *Josef Hoffman*, and later in Germany with *Peter Behrens*. The third was the influence of *Auguste Perret* from whom Le Corbusier learned the fundamentals of reinforced concrete design.

Very early in his career, Le Corbusier selected concrete as the vehicle for the architectural expression of his ideas. With his background as a painter, his earliest projects reflected a great sensitivity for composition.

Several elements of Le Corbusier's early work proved to be original and dramatic contributions to modern architecture. For example, his use of *pilotis*, or *stilts*, made a building independent of the ground below and allowed the landscape to flow freely beneath the structure. Also, the separation of the wall from the structural skeleton permitted freely composed facades. Finally, his roof gardens served to connect interior and exterior spaces, while offering outdoor terraces with elevated views. All of these elements were skillfully brought together in the **Villa Savoye** at Poissy in 1929, one of Le Corbusier's first tours de force.

Like Wright, Le Corbusier's reputation relied not only on his revolutionary architecture, but also to a large degree on his radical manifestoes. *Vers une Architecture* and *La Ville Radieuse* were powerful pieces of propaganda on the subjects of design and town planning. When he finally realized his vision of urban architecture, as in the monumental **Unité d'Habitation** in Marseilles in 1952, Le Corbusier was accused by critics of producing a cold, elitist design that ignored his own human-scale figure, the *Modulor*. It also confirmed his misunderstood statement that a house was a "machine for living." Only in later years was the Unité understood and appreciated.

The latter part of Le Corbusier's career involved the sculptural quality of concrete which he composed sensitively, almost romantically. This appeared most clearly in the brilliant pilgrimage chapel

NOTRE DAME DU HAUT – RONCHAMP
**Figure 7.10**

**Notre Dame du Haut** at Ronchamp of 1955, and the **Monastery of La Tourette** completed five years later. Both projects were magnificently sculpted works of art. In one of his final designs, the new town of **Chandigarh** in India, Le Corbusier finally put his city planning theories into practice. Each urban element was given its own identity and character, each responding brilliantly to the harsh Indian sun with rich patterns of texture and form.

SUPREME COURT - CHANDIGARH

**Figure 7.11**

Le Corbusier is considered by many to have had the most worldwide influence of any architect of the mid-20th century. Among those who were influenced by his work was the Brazilian architect *Oscar Niemeyer*, who collaborated with Le Corbusier on the **Ministry of Health Building** in Rio de Janeiro in 1936. It was this building which introduced to the architectural world the *brise soleil*, the permanent sun shield that was much copied in later years. Niemeyer, together with *Lœcio Costa*, later created **Brasilia**, the new and fresh capital of Brazil, whose forms and plan owe much to Le Corbusier's urban theories.

## EUROPEAN MODERNISM

Le Corbusier may have represented the most important influence on world architecture during the middle years of the 20th century, but there were several other Europeans whose mastery of design carried significant authority. Among these was *Erich Mendelsohn* of Germany who created several expressive concrete structures and established *Expressionism* as a genuine, though short-lived, style. His most famous structure, the **Einstein Tower**, completed in 1921, was originally designed as cast-in-place concrete. However, it ultimately was built of brick and plastered over to look like concrete. The form was totally plastic: curved surfaces, rounded corners, and a general appearance later known as *streamlined*. Mendelsohn, like so many others, left Germany prior to World War II and settled in the San Francisco Bay area where he continued to practice and teach architecture.

Another *Functionalist* of the International Style, *Marcel Breuer*, also emigrated to the United States from his native Germany. Breuer's career was long and varied, extending from the **Doldertal Flats** of 1935 in Zurich to the **Whitney Museum** of 1967 in New York. While a teacher at the Bauhaus in Dessau, Breuer designed several bent-tube pieces of furniture which have become durable classics.

*Alvar Aalto* of Finland began as an Internationalist, but soon developed a more regional humanistic approach to design. His M.I.T. dormitory, **Baker House**, was completed in 1948. Its undulating form was designed to give each room a view across the Charles River. His later **Civic Center** at Saynatsalo, from 1951, was a romantic and expressive composition of brick masses, sensitively arranged around an open court.

DOLDERTAL APARTMENTS

**Figure 7.12**

Other Europeans worthy of mention are *Gerrit Reitveld* and J.J.P. Oud, two Dutchmen who represented the *De Stijl* movement; *Gunnar Asplund* from Sweden, who designed the **Stockholm Crematorium** in 1935; *Hans Scharoun*, who created the extraordinary, organic **Philharmonic** in Berlin in 1963; and *Pier Luigi Nervi*, the Italian engineering genius, who designed the famous **Exhibition Hall** at Turin, as well as the **Palazzo dello Sport** in Rome for the 1960 Olympic Games.

## SKYSCRAPER EVOLUTION

There was perhaps no building type in the United States that exemplified the 20th century more than the *skyscraper*. It confirmed the industrial, political, and technological power of the new world, and became the major architectural symbol of America. Urban centers, such as New York, developed dense groups of towers that dominated city skylines, as cathedrals had done centuries earlier in other parts of the world.

As with other structures of this period, skyscrapers in the early part of the century were eclectic in style, based to a large extent on the all-encompassing influence of the Beaux-Arts. Curiously however, eclectic architecture seemed to avoid the Gothic style, the one historic style that had stressed verticality. Nevertheless, *Cass Gilbert* recognized the analogy between skyscrapers and cathedrals, and in 1913 in New York, he created the Gothic-inspired **Woolworth Building**, which inspired the name *Woolworth Gothic*. Reaching some 800 feet in height, it remained the world's tallest building for years.

The rapid proliferation of tall buildings created several environmental problems, the most serious of which was the relegation of streets to dark canyons, walled in by towering skyscrapers. One response to this problem was the *New York Zoning Law* of 1916, which regulated the relationship of building height to street width. This resulted in upper stories being stepped back progressively from the street line. The new law was accepted with little criticism and was the model for similar laws enacted in other urban areas. Such laws became a major determinant of skyscraper form.

## Tribune Tower Competition

The First World War interrupted, for several years, further development in tall building design. In 1922, however, the Chicago Tribune held an international competition for its new headquarters building. The event attracted an amazing range of designs that represented every architectural expression, from regressive eclectic forms to progressive modern features. Most entries, of course, were eclectic, as was the winning design by *Hood and Howells*. It was a sensitive and well-composed solution in the Woolworth Gothic style.

None of the domestic entries matched the high level of work that had been achieved in Chicago in the last decades of the 19th century. The European entries, however, were another story, with some anticipating the Bauhaus and International Styles that were to flourish later. For example, the second-prize entry, from the Finnish architect *Eliel Saarinen*, was a soaring building that emphasized mass and verticality, with no correspondence to any previous historic style.

The entry of Walter Gropius, with Adolf Meyer, was also significant. It was close in spirit to the work of the Chicago School and even resembled some of the Chicago architecture in its details. Aside from the immediate importance of the Tribune competition, it was the first instance in which European architects influenced the American skyscraper, as well as the first opportunity for an American audience to evaluate, first hand, *European Modernism.*

## International Style

In 1928, in Switzerland, a series of conferences was held by a group of modern European architects and others, all of whom embraced a new design philosophy which was intended to replace the Beaux-Arts. Called the *CIAM (Congress Internationaux d'Architecture Moderne)*, its participants gathered to discuss the state of international architecture and related design and political philosophies.

Though the strife-ridden CIAM soon lost momentum, its members more or less agreed on the characteristics of the new style. It was essentially an expression that differentiated between solid and void, mass and space, and involved smooth, unadorned surfaces, such as the ubiquitous white plastered cube pierced by steel-framed windows. In 1932, *Henry-Russell Hitchcock* and *Philip Johnson* memorialized this new architecture in a book called *The International Style*, which introduced the new work to most Americans, and gave to European Modernism its permanent label.

The international style exerted a strong influence on skyscraper design, as in the **Philadelphia Savings Fund Building**, completed in 1932 by *Howe and Lescaze.* In this early example of curtain wall design, the architects cantilevered the floors beyond the supporting columns, resulting in a wall plane of windows stretching uninterrupted from corner to corner and around the corners. The face of the building thus became alternating horizontal bands of light cladding and dark glass.

During the 1930s, tall buildings reached new heights, and the steel cage continued to be exploited as a structural concept. By 1931,

the **Empire State Building** in New York had exceeded 100 stories in height, but structurally, Sullivan's **Wainwright Building**, 40 years earlier, had been equally efficient. **Rockefeller Center** was a group of skyscrapers completed in 1939 that opened a new chapter on urban design, in the sensitive arrangement of its tall buildings relative to open spaces and street-level amenities.

## Modern Developments

For about 20 years after the end of World War II, skyscraper design was dominated by the rectilinear aesthetics of the curtain wall. Grid wall patterns were influenced by industrialized technology as well as the designs of the painter Mondrian, and design often became a search for the most elegant cover for the steel or concrete framework.

One of the finest examples from 1950 was the **United Nations Secretariat** in New York designed by *Wallace Harrison*, with an assist from Le Corbusier. It was the first strong statement of a sculptured urban element, and its 39 stories of green-tinted glass mirrored all Manhattan. The advertising value of those impressive slab walls was impossible for big business to ignore, and suddenly great American corporations were erecting skyscraping headquarters buildings in the new postwar style.

One of the most distinguished of these was **Lever House** in New York, completed in 1952, by *Gordon Bunshaft* of *Skidmore, Owings, and Merrill* (SOM). From a low glass container rose a sheer shaft of glass in which the emphasis was on space contained within the curtain walls, rather than on mass. For the first time since Rockefeller Center, New Yorkers found a generous open space at street level through which they might wander. Across Park Avenue from Lever House, Mies van der Rohe, assisted by Philip Johnson, created the **Seagram Build-**

**ing** in 1958. The monumentally powerful shaft of amber and bronze rose from a small portion of its generous site and was the ultimate in tall building purity and precision.

LEVER HOUSE

**Figure 7.13**

Most skyscrapers erected since the Seagram Building repeated lessons previously learned. However, among the more notable exceptions were the two **John Hancock Towers**—SOM's in Chicago and *I. M. Pei's* in Boston; the 1971 twin towers of *Yamasaki's* **World Trade Center** in New York; the **Sears Tower** in Chicago, built in 1974 by SOM; *Johnson and Burgee's* **Pennzoil Place** in Houston from 1977; and the **Citicorp Center** in New York, completed by *Hugh Stubbins* in 1978.

JOHN HANCOCK BLDG.- CHICAGO

**Figure 7.14**

**Figure 7.15**

## SECOND GENERATION

Modern architecture received its primary impetus from the first generation designers—Wright, Gropius, Mies, and Le Corbusier—all of whom were regarded as great masters. Those who were influenced by these pioneers constituted the second generation of modern architects, most of whom established their own influential practices, solid reputations, and loyal followings.

One of these was *Eero Saarinen*, the talented son of the Finnish architect Eliel Saarinen. His landmark projects included the **General Motors Technical Center**, the wing-shaped **TWA Terminal** in New York, **Dulles International Airport** in Washington DC, and the **CBS Building** in New York. Saarinen's assistant was *Kevin Roche*, who carried on after Saarinen's early death to create the **Ford Foundation Building** in New York and the **Oakland Museum**, a tiered concrete structure that integrated gracefully with the surrounding landscape.

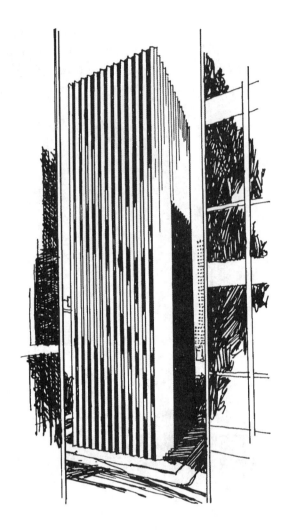

CBS BUILDING

**Figure 7.16**

JOHNSON HOUSE

**Figure 7.17**

One of Mies van der Rohe's most prolific disciples was Philip Johnson, who began by emulating the master, as in his own **Glass House** in

New Canaan, Connecticut. But in mid-career, Johnson developed a far more personal and creative approach to design. The firm of Skidmore, Owings, and Merrill was also initially inclined in a Miesian direction, but with projects such as the **U.S. Air Force Academy** in Colorado Springs, the SOM office expressed a more original point of view.

## Brutalism

A new design attitude appeared in the early 1950s that was designated *Brutalism.* The style was based, to some degree, on the crudely fabricated concrete work (*beton brut*) of Le Corbusier's later years, but it also exposed and even flaunted the structural and mechanical elements of a building. Although the new expression was received with mixed reactions, it was universally understood to represent a major assault on the international style.

*Louis Kahn* played an influential part in the formation of the Brutalist aesthetic, and he was regarded for about 20 years prior to his death in 1974 as one of America's most eminent architects. Kahn's long and quiet career suddenly burst into the limelight with his **Richards Medical Research Laboratories** in Philadelphia in 1960. This celebrated project was followed by a series of world famous commissions, which included the **Salk Institute** in La Jolla and the **Capital at Dacca** in Bangladesh.

As Kahn was influenced by Le Corbusier and Wright, so too did his own work influence many others. For example, *Paul Rudolph* recalled both Wright and Kahn in his dramatic **Art and Architecture Building** at Yale.

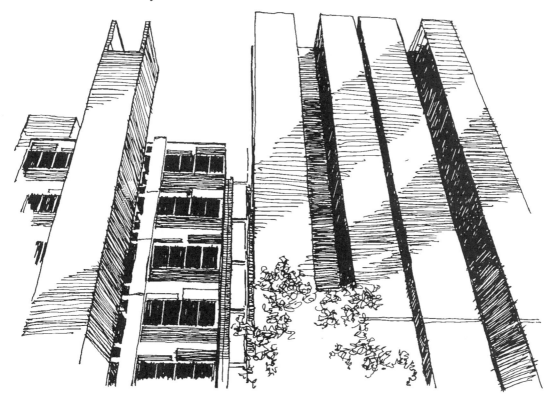

RICHARDS MEDICAL RESEARCH LABORATORIES

**Figure 7.18**

## Diverse Directions

The great diversity of architectural theory in the last half of the 20th century has been underscored by the variety of original work produced by the third generation of modern architects. *Charles Moore*, for example, who gained notoriety with his shed-roofed **Sea Ranch** project in 1966, went on to create one design after another exhibiting a variety of fantasy, illusion, and wit, as in his University of California **Faculty Center** at Santa Barbara.

YALE ART & ARCHITECTURE BLDG.

**Figure 7.19**

Another unique architectural approach involved the use of technological systems to solve the problems of shelter. The most famous proponent of this approach was *Buckminster Fuller*, neither an architect nor an engineer, whose imaginative structures stimulated loyal audiences since the early days of his **Dymaxion House**. For the Montreal Expo in 1967, Fuller created the largest geodesic dome the world had ever seen for the **United States Pavilion**. The same world's fair witnessed the tented **German Pavilion** by *Frei Otto*, and **Habitat**, the residential building-block complex designed by *Moshe Safdie*.

## HISTORY OF SUSTAINABLE DESIGN

In early human history, builders of human habitats used materials that occurred naturally in the earth, such as stone, wood, mud adobe bricks, and grasses. With nomadic tribes and early civilizations, the built environment made little impact on the balance of natural elements. When abandoned, the grass roof, adobe brick, or timber beam would slowly disintegrate and return to the natural ecosystem. Small human populations and the use of natural materials had very little impact on a balanced natural ecosystem.

But as human populations expanded and settlements moved into more demanding climates, natural materials were altered to become more durable and less natural. In fact, it is the remnants of archeology that demonstrate some of the human creations that are not easily recycled into the earth; fired clay, smelted ore for jewelry, and tools are examples of designs that will not easily reintegrate into the natural ecosystem. These materials may be reprocessed (grinding, melting, or reworking) into other human creations, but they will never be natural materials again.

As human populations expanded, there is strong evidence that some civilizations outgrew their natural ecosystem. When overused, land became less fertile and less able to support crops, timber, and domesticated animals necessary for human life. The ancient solution was to move to a more desirable location and use new natural resources in the new location, abandoning the ecologically ruined home site.

The realization that global natural resources are limited is an age-old concept. The term *conservation*, which came into existence in the late 19th century, referred to the economic management of natural resources such as fish, timber, topsoil, minerals, and game. In the United States, at the beginning of the 20th century, President Theodore Roosevelt and his chief forester, Gifford Pinchot, introduced the concept of conservation as a philosophy of natural resource management. The impetus of this movement created several pieces of natural legislation to promote conservation and increased appreciation of America's natural resources and monuments.

In the middle of the 1960s, Rachel Carson published *Silent Spring*, a literary alarm that revealed the reality of an emerging ecological disaster—the gross misunderstanding of the value and hazards of pesticides. The pesticide DDT and its impact on the entire natural ecosystem was dramatic; clearly, some human inventions were destructive and could spread harm throughout the ecosystem with alarming speed and virulence. Birds in North America died from DDT used to control malaria in Africa. Human creations were influenced by the necessities of the natural cycles of the ecosystem. Human toxic efforts could no longer be absorbed by the cycles of nature. Human activities became so pervasive and potentially intrusive that there needed to be a higher level of worldwide ecological understanding of the risk of disrupting the ecosystem.

Architects, as designers of the built environment, realize the ecological impact of their choices of architectural components, such as site selection, landscaping, infrastructure, building materials, and mechanical systems. The philosophy of sustainable design encourages a new, more environmentally sensitive, approach to architectural design and construction.

There are many credos for the approach to a new, sustainable design. Some architectural historians maintain that the best architects (Vitruvius, Ruskin, Wright, Alexander) have always discussed design in terms of empathy with nature and the natural systems. Now it is evident that all architects should include the principles of sustainable design as part of their palette of architectural best practices.

## CONCLUSION

We have seen how architects in the 20th century attempted to solve critical contemporary design problems. Next, we will look at recent developments that will lead architecture into the 21st century.

# LESSON 7 QUIZ

1. Which of the following statements regarding the Tribune Tower Competition of 1922 is most accurate?

   A. The Competition was held in Chicago because Chicago was the birthplace of the tall building and the city where the Chicago School had its greatest influence.

   B. The Competition attracted a great number of diverse designs, but they were all based on Eclecticism.

   C. The European submissions were generally more progressive than those of American architects, and in later years, they exerted a strong influence on tall building design.

   D. The winning design, by Raymond Hood, owed a considerable debt to European Modernism and bore a striking resemblance to the entry of Eliel Saarinen.

2. Breton brut, brise soleil, and pilotis were all architectural characteristics developed by

   A. Peter Behrens.     C. Oscar Niemeyer.
   B. Le Corbusier.      D. Marcel Breuer.

3. Among the following phrases, which best apply to Postmodernism?

   I.    Diversity of expression
   II.   Use of historical precedents
   III.  Austere formality
   IV.   Rigid consistency
   V.    Freedom from dogma
   A. I, II, and V      C. II, III, and IV
   B. I, III, and V     D. I, II, III, and V

4. The quintessential purpose of the Bauhaus in Dessau was to

   A. generate a revival of well-designed, handcrafted products.

   B. effect a merger between art and technology as a basis for modern design.

   C. develop a new concept of spatial organization as a basis for modern architecture.

   D. gather ideas on modern design as the basis for a new educational system.

5. Rudolph Schindler, Louis Kahn, and Paul Rudolph all had in common

   A. important architectural projects located in California.

   B. their early training in central Europe.

   C. the influence on their work, to one degree or another, of Frank Lloyd Wright.

   D. early projects that reflected Eclecticism, and later projects that reflected Rationalism.

6. Which of the following statements concerning turn-of-the-century developments is INCORRECT?

   A. The predominant architectural expression was Neo-Classic, exhibiting a widespread enthusiasm for ancient Roman forms, among others.

   B. The practice of architecture was dominated by eclectic design fostered largely by the success of the World's Columbian Exposition of 1893.

   C. The advancements in photography aided architects by supplementing historical information previously acquired exclusively through drawings.

   D. Early 20th-century eclectic designs were virtually indistinguishable from the work of the 19th century; both were inspired by ancient Roman models.

7. Around the time of the First World War, a residential expression known as the California Bungalow began to proliferate throughout much of the United States. Which of the following architects was most responsible for this development?

   A. Irving Gill

   B. Richard Neutra

   C. Frank Lloyd Wright

   D. Greene and Greene

8. Twentieth-century architecture included several pioneering projects of reinforced concrete construction. Which of the following does NOT belong in that category?

   A. Werkbund Model Factory by Walter Gropius

   B. Ronchamp Chapel by Le Corbusier

   C. Dodge House by Irving Gill

   D. Steiner House by Adolf Loos

9. The principles that dominated the work of Walter Gropius were

   I. design through collaboration.

   II. order and precision.

   III. sensitivity to natural forms and materials.

   IV. respect for industrialization.

   A. I and III        C. II and III

   B. II and IV        D. I and IV

10. Which of the following statements regarding the International Style is INCORRECT?

   A. The International Style involved austere compositions, unadorned surfaces, and a clear distinction between solid and void.

   B. The 1930s movement embraced European architectural expression, but its influence in the United States was limited to the design of tall buildings.

   C. At the CIAM conferences, architects agreed on very little, but they did concur on the general characteristics of the new architectural expression.

   D. Hitchcock and Johnson's book *The International Style* not only gave the new style its name, but contributed to the proliferation of the style in the United States.

# ARCHITECTURE IN THE LATE 20TH CENTURY AND BEYOND

By Meg Kindelin and Mark Verwoerdt

## INTRODUCTION

The one immutable truth about Modernism is that it perpetuates its own evolution. No moment in modernist history is identical to any other, and so Modernism cannot be understood as a particular style per se. It is best discussed as a method of architectural response to changing conditions in the world. Social progress, intellectual movements, technological invention, functionalism, and the drive to realize and interpret the contemporary zeitgeist have always been a part of Modernism. Yet the relative emphasis given to any one of these elements, as well as the role of history, theory, social context, and environmentalism, continue to give life to a range of possibilities that exist within the practice of "Modern Architecture."

Several styles have been popular since 1980, and some have been billed as reactions against Modernism, and in particular, against the language of the International Style. Postmodernism sought to invent its own context through a palimpsest of appropriated historical models and architectural theory. The New Urbanists and Critical Regionalists reintroduced the importance of local and regional context with a keen eye on social improvement. Deconstructivism was the most radical statement against all preconceived notions about architecture, art, or theory. Some architects, however, sought to reinvent Modernism and work within its palate to investigate themes such as transparency, texture, and surface. The super-rational high- tech style utilized architect-engineer collaborations to integrate advanced technology, daring structures, and high-performance building to reflect the zeitgeist.

In the last two decades of the 20th century, architects continued to broaden their investigations with new forms made available with the advent of three-dimensional computer modeling and advances in structural and material science. At the dawn of the Industrial Revolution, advances in industrial methods challenged architects to produce new forms using mass-produced and standardized parts. Now we see a revolution in the tools with which architects conceive their projects and often propel themselves ahead of current technological capacities.

## POSTMODERNISM

Postmodernism is a term loosely applied to works of architecture that make a break with odernism. In contrast to Modernism's austerity, Postmodernism exhibited an indulgent complexity of images and styles, quite often based on historical precedent. At its core it represented an essential shift from the formality and rigidity of the international style and the notion that there is one universally correct solution to all problems. Postmodernism had its roots in the 1950s, a time when Modernism seemed inescapably dominant, but architects such as Saarinen and Kahn were calling for richer, less sterile, solutions to architectural problems. Some Postmodern ideas came from mannerist works such as those by Lutyens and Vorsey, and others had their origins in Disneyland and the Las Vegas Strip.

Robert Venturi, one of the early Postmodernists, never denied the importance of vernacular, ordinary architecture. In *Complexity and Contradiction in Architecture*, published in 1967, he extolled the principles of compromise and accommodation. In his later work, *Learning from Las Vegas* from 1972, he argued for a mode of design that led architects to create more honest buildings. He memorably argued the difference between the "Duck" and the "Decorated Shed." He wrote

> *When Modern architects righteously abandoned ornament on buildings, they unconsciously designed buildings that were ornament. In promoting Space and Articulation over symbolism and ornament, they distorted the whole building into a duck. They substituted for the innocent and inexpensive practice of applied decoration on a conventional shed, the rather cynical and expensive distortion of program and structure to promote a duck. (Robert Venturi,* Learning from Las Vegas, *1972, p. 163.)*

Charles Moore was another of the early practitioners of Postmodernism. He looked for continuity within the history of essential forms in architecture. He identified a basic building language common to all eras, and then played with the elements' presumed definitions with ingenious wit. The juxtaposition of these building blocks, which included aedicule, path, platform, column, and threshold as well as specific elements from historic buildings, provided bold, contemporary reinterpretations for a new generation. At the *Piazza d' Italia*, 1977–78, in New Orleans, he referenced classical orders and traditional forms in a small civic plaza. Rather than build in limestone or marble with traditional methods and forms, he used low-cost materials, mismatched columns, metallic capitals, and his own face as a comic cherubim to create his plaza. An Italy-shaped platform is at the center of the circular plaza, which is surrounded by concentric rings defined by steps and colonnades. The five classic orders are represented and rendered in stainless steel and neon rather than in marble. The cheap materials began to show signs of wear shortly after construction was completed, thus allowing Moore to create a "real" ruin even as he referred to the grand classical ruins of Italy.

PIAZZA d'ITALIA

**Figure 8.1**

Michael Graves used the language of history in *The Portland Building* of 1980. The flat surfaces of this mid-rise structure are festooned with keystones, a temple front, columns, and pilasters, all rendered in soft pastels. The cornice line features a mix of numerous design ideas that are well known from a series of pastel renderings of the project. The amalgam of styles and their quasi-mannerist application is a high note of Postmodernism showing its willingness to borrow time-bound forms from the past while simultaneously freeing itself from any sort of responsibility to traditional rules of composition and organization. Anti-elitist leanings are also seen in Graves' later work, such as in his *Dolphin and Swan Hotels* of 1987. These playful, idiosyncratic, buildings have bold, colorful facades and feature whimsical creatures that act as roadside markers. The programs and forms cater to popular taste. In recent years, Graves has turned to designing low-cost home products from toasters to toilet brushes, ostensibly illustrating his belief that design is for everyone.

One of last major commissions of this movement was Philip Johnson and John Burgee's *AT&T Building* in New York City completed in 1982. The pink granite skyscraper has a clean Modernist body, yet the mutlistory base recalls Palladian windows and the gigantic pediment

has been interpreted as everything from a Chippendale highboy to an automobile hood ornament. This building also looked to New York's more decorated age of high-rises such as the Chrysler Building in reaction to prevailing minimalist forms. The project was published in newspaper headlines across the United States and was almost universally snubbed by critics. It has come to be seen as the final hurrah of the Postmodern experiment.

## NEW URBANISM

Some architects rejected the flip allusions of high Postmodernism and sought to embrace the underlying principles of classical architecture. Richard A. M. Stern called classicism "the fulcrum about which architectural discourse balances." This neo-traditionalism is evident in projects that dutifully emulate classical orders, proportions and materials and lack any sort of sardonic side glance that was common to the Postmodernists. Architects such as Leon Krier and Aldo Rossi engaged traditional forms with a real interest in the possibilities of a rigorous traditionalist approach, although expressed in a relatively abstract manner.

New Urbanism marked a neo-traditionalist return to early models of city planning and was a rebuttal to roadside strip architecture celebrated most famously in Venturi's *Learning from Las Vegas*. In the broadest sense, New Urbanist planning provided a humanist approach to landscape planning. It embraced smaller-scale development based on pedestrian use patterns rather than on the culture of the automobile. The movement also tended to embrace traditional over modern building aesthetics. Architect Leon Krier was involved with *Poundsbury Village* in Dorchester, England, a new town development founded in 1996 but modeled as an ideal village featuring the traditional buildings favored by Prince Charles. A similar project, *Celebration, Florida*, Disney's ideal planned community, was meant to evoke the simple joys of small town America and its associated values. Robert A. M. Stern and Philip Johnson were both involved with "imagineering" Celebration's houses and faux-civic buildings.

*Seaside* (1984–1991), in Seaside Florida, designed by Andres Duany and Elizabeth Plater-Zyberk, followed the principals of traditional neighborhood design and is evocative of the City Beautiful and Garden City movements. It is one of the most successful and influential New Urbanist projects. Seaside was conceived as a diminutive resort town featuring higher density living. Ample space is granted to pedestrian ways and garden paths, while cars and garages are relegated to alleys. Neighborhood interaction is encouraged by small lots and zoning restrictions that mandate generous porches on each house and prescribe each home's massing, materials, and design vocabulary. All shops and services are arranged according to the five-minute walk principle, wherein services and shops are located just a short walk from each home. While Seaside was planned as a moderately priced, 2,000 resident vacation community, it has morphed into a larger, higher-priced enclave. It has also spawned several other communities of similar design across the county.

## REGIONALISM

While Postmodernists were mining historic precedent for appropriate building vocabulary, others continued to look to local traditions to counteract the formalist, global implications of International Style Modernism. Architects looked to indigenous cultural traditions and vernacular forms to find an alternative to rampant globalization and "one-size-fits-all"

modernism. In most cases, interest in local context and tradition is paired with an interest in climate-sensitive design and sustainable building practice. However, many of these architects do not absolutely reject all modern influences.

Glenn Murcutt's (b. 1936) work combines a modernist-design vocabulary with the Australian vernacular to form a unique architecture of a time and place. In a series of buildings that began with his own house in the late 60s, he worked to find an appropriate response to the local landscape and climate and also to the vernacular building traditions around him. His signature buildings are long and narrow, generally situated on a rise to catch prevailing breezes, and shaded to manage the relentless sun. The layered building skins typically feature louvers to shade the sun and operable windows to allow natural ventilation to sweep though the spaces. He uses simple building materials that are common throughout Australia such as wood and corrugated metal in an effort to make an architecture of a particular place. The *Simpson-Fe House* of 1989–94 in New South Wales is a long, low, frame pavilion with a narrow walkway that leads the visitor through the house as if on a journey. The rooms are arranged in a row and all have easy access to natural ventilation and daylight from the adjacent veranda. The sun is managed with ample sunshades and rainwater is collected in a series of cisterns.

Other architects responding to different local climates and cultures are Will Bruder (b. 1946) and Antoine Predock (b. 1936). At the *American Heritage Center*, in Laramie, Wyoming, Predock has designed a massive truncated stone cone that is reminiscent of the nearby Medicine Bow Mountains but also recalls Native American building forms. At the *Phoenix Central Library* of 1988–95, Bruder has designed within a context older than vernacular traditions. He references the surrounding buttes and

CULTURAL CENTER OF NEW CALEDONIA

**Figure 8.2**

the geological history of the area. The library rises over the desert like a mesa or an ancient land form. Bruder also makes strong, modern sculptural moves such as using a ribbed copper cladding on the large volumes at the ends of the composition. He designs in response to climate, and the glassy southern elevation is covered with a rhythmic pattern of sunscreens. A light well, known as the crystal canyon, brings indirect light deep into the building throughout the day. His work transforms architecture into art, but does so while responding to the restrictions of building in a particular place with real climatic and programmatic concerns. Wright's influence is seen in Bruder's innovative use of newer materials and technology within in a continuum of traditional forms.

While Murcutt and Bruder have tailored their architectural response to one particular geographic area, some practitioners find appropriate responses to any number of design problems in different physical and cultural climates. The Renzo Piano Building Workshop works with local cultures and climates and uses recent technology in innovative ways to fulfill program needs. The firm's buildings do not share an overall style, but they are each a unique solution to a particular issue with a similar accommodation of local conditions paired with technological innovation.

Two small museum projects illustrate the firm's diversity. The programs call for buildings of similar size and scope, and both and have open-minded clients, but the responses in the two museums are distinct. At the *Menil Collection Museum* in Houston, the client asked that the collection be displayed in natural light, thus Piano's essential challenge was to manage the hot Texas sun and to protect the art from UV damage as it was allowed to enter the galleries. The museum is a simple modern box, but Piano covered the flat glass roof with a series of fiber-cement leaves acting as brise-soleil. The second curator also wanted the work to be displayed in natural light, but at a site in Northern Europe. The *Beyeler Foundation Museum* in Basel, Switzerland, of 1997, responds to its locality with an "intelligent roof" that, like the Menil roof, uses sunshades to manage the light in the galleries. The roof becomes a sunscreen that modulates light levels in the galleries, and consists of several layers including insulated glass panes, metal louvers, and white glass sunshades on a steel frame. His gentle interventions in the name of climatic appropriateness are known as "soft machines" and are a fusion of high-tech and low-tech responses. Piano uses natural light, sumptuous but simple stone cladding, and extends the space with outdoor water features to create a relaxed relationship between the landscape, art, and the visitor.

Another example of Piano's versatility is *The Cultural Center of New Caledonia*. Here Piano departs from a modernist vocabulary and looks to indigenous forms, but he does not merely replicate local buildings in his work. Piano's ten pavilions respond to the local climate in the same manner as the traditional buildings: by managing the humid tropical climate by acting as natural wind-driven ventilators and by shading the bright tropical sun. Over 100 feet tall, the cone-shaped volumes evoke traditional Kanak buildings that have tall roofs and are arranged in clusters. The pavilions are made from laminated wood with stainless steel rods and connections, and fuse what is locally available with what is technologically appropriate.

## DECONSTRUCTION

While the historicism of Postmodernism was playing itself out, a different way of looking at buildings was on the rise. Rather than look for complexity in pastiche and architectural one-liners, an influential group of architects chose to question the very nature of architecture as a discipline and sought to redefine the role of the architect. The last decades of the 20th century saw radical social, political, and economic changes such as the rise of a globally interconnected economy, the collapse of historical, human-scaled conceptions of time, space, and distance, and the explosive growth

of material and computer technology. As was the case at the turn of the previous century and also after World War II, a new *zeitgeist* swept art, theory, culture, and architecture into new territory. Social Theorists and philosophers, including Derrida and Foucault, engaged in discourse regarding the impact of social and political changes since the late 1960s. These literary theorists were attempting to deconstruct language in order to uncover its essential meaning or multiple meanings (in a manner that takes one beyond words into "meaning" itself). In a similar fashion, architects tried to deconstruct the formal language of buildings in order to strip building elements and spaces of their traditional associations. In this context, a new order and expression of architectural elements could emerge. These writers were championed by a new breed of architects searching for a way to understand, respond to, and ultimately shape their new world. The rise of computer technology offered these innovators new formal possibilities.

In 1988 Philip Johnson helped curate an exhibition at the MOMA in New York entitled "Deconstructivist Architecture." This exhibition identified seven major practitioners of architecture of the day, just as his 1932 MOMA show had helped to identify and codify the International Style. His list included Frank Gehry, Daniel Liebeskind, Rem Koolhaas, Peter Eisenman, Zaha Hadid, Bernard Tschumi, and the firm Coop Himmelblau. Ever involved with the most important trends in architecture, Johnson's list identified those whose work would continue to influence architectural design into the 21st century.

Among those looking to literature for an answer to the *zeitgeist*, Peter Eisenman (b. 1932) took this response to the greatest extreme. His houses of the 1960s and 1970s were harbingers of Deconstuctionism and

**Figure 8.3**

were, at best, formal and geometric experiments within the context of social theory. After years of working primarily as a theorist, he opened an office and won the commission for the *Wexner Center for the Performing Arts* at Ohio State University in Columbus. The plan is a mass of intersecting 3-D grids and sliced geometric forms meant to symbolize disunity in the arts and conflicts within Western culture. The grid is interrupted by several elements that recall previous or adjacent buildings, and thereby Eisenman questions the idea of history or art in architectural form. Other formal games include windows punched in the floors and columns that support nothing. The project is series of questions, but also manages to provide galleries, a library, and performance space.

Bernard Tschumi (b. 1944) presented a polemic at his *Parc de la Villette* of 1982–85, which was a study in fragmentation. In this public park, 42 program-free pavilions are scattered across a green lawn and painted in his signature red paint. He considered these to be follies that park-goers were meant to happen upon as they wandered the grounds. Most of the pavilions have remained empty, but a few have been commissioned for use as cafes or art spaces.

This moment of architectural questioning is answered in a more particular and subjective way by Daniel Libeskind (b. 1946). *The Jewish Museum* in Berlin was completed in 1999, only a decade after the fall of the Berlin wall. The main rectangular volume is overlaid with a jagged, irregular surface of glass and exposed structure. This ripped surface is a vivid metaphor for the sharp edges of the recent, painful memory of those whose history had been erased. The scheme is loosely based on the Star of David and is rich with textual and artistic allusions. This pulled-apart architecture reverberates more strongly than Eisenman's formalist movements of disunion and touches a disturbing cultural chord.

Working in California, Frank Gehry investigated irregular, deconstructed forms, as seen in his renovation of his own *Santa Monica House* (1978). This simple frame is made of common materials with common methods, yet in a very unexpected way, using very uncommon shapes. Chain-link fencing encloses a deck on the second floor, corrugated tin roofing clads the lower level walls, and plywood and other unfinished materials are left exposed as finished surfaces. The glass roof over the kitchen seems to have total structural and geometric independence from other elements of the house. Inside, the walls are peeled apart and cut to reveal layers beneath. Literally, the underbelly of the common house is opened to view and this changes the perception of the quiet neighborhood in which it stands.

Getty's first European commission is a clear break in many ways from his work in California. *The Vitra International Manufacturing Facility and Design Museum*, in Weil-am-Phein, Germany, was completed in 1989. Where his earlier work layered geometric forms and informal material, this project shows a more mature interest in curvature and more dynamic, sculptural forms. An assemblage of metal roofs and stucco walls express definite dynamic volumes, not just shapes. These volumes themselves are now entirely nonreferential as Gehry seeks to create a personalized style of shape-making.

At the *Guggenheim Museum Bilbao* (1991–1997) Gehry's titanium glass forms engage the working landscape and also add a sensuous new spatial experience for visitors. The project was commissioned as part of an economic plan to revitalize the area and was a collaboration between the Basque Government and Guggenheim Foundation. The success of the venture made popular the notion of the "Bilbao Effect," the sudden rise in tourism that accompanies completion of a spectacular building.

**Figure 8.5**

The building sits along a working river in a landscape of rolling hills and industrial towns. It reaches under an adjacent bridge to engage the neighborhood and provides a water feature at the river's edge. A tall form along the river is an important landmark. The building's entrance is below ground and so directs visitors to follow a rising ramp up to the interior. The atrium is an undulating internal space over 165 feet tall with galleries at the perimeter. The edges of the atrium are defined by curved volumes that are clad with various materials including glass panels on metal clips, painted wall board, and limestone panels. The galleries themselves are to be seen as art and the building appears to interact with the art displayed in its interior. The twisted overlapping forms were designed and documented for fabrication using CATIA, the 3-D modeling software used in the airplane industry, and an engineering program, BOCAD, was used to analyze the structure.

**GETTY MUSEUM**

**Figure 8.4**

This is Gehry's first use of titanium cladding, chosen because of the quality of light that it reflects. The metal is very thin and the panels seem to have a pillow-like quality due to the way they are attached to the steel frame.

## MODERNISM REINTERPRETED

Although Postmodernism and Deconstruction recommended that designers turn away from strict Modernism, this remained an important area of investigation for many architects. The Modernist language allowed investigation into themes such as transparency, surface, material, and texture. Early 20th-century modernism was mined for its clean lines, functional methods, and celebrated for its embrace of technology. I. M. Pei, at the *Grand Louvre*, Paris, (1982–94) used modern gestures and simple geometry to solve the problem posed by the expansion of the museum. The sky, a pool of water, and the very museum itself are pulled in to a formal composition at the center of the formal entry court. Pei's glass and steel pyramids are at once functional, simple, and poetic.

Richard Meier, (b. 1934) is among the most classically modern architects of this period. His work is best know for its ubiquitous white enamel panels, clearly defined grids, and simple geometries. Meier looked to the earliest ideas of Modernism for his inspiration, particularly to Le Corbusier, and his work is based on rigid geometries and proportion. As he matured he began to experiment with layered facades, transparency, and worked to enhance the quality of light in his work. Early buildings such as the *Museum fur Kunsthandwerk* of 1980–83 in Frankfort established his career. The recent *Getty Museum*, completed 1997 in Malibu, California, is his most mature work, and he uses layered facades to create depth and manage light, and he also augments his usual white

planes with panels of stone. A unique blend of classical Modernism with a completely contemporary language, the Getty Center is equal parts building and site, textured stone and painted metal panel, and solid and void. Meier claims to paint with light and uses unexpected wall penetrations and volumes to enhance the effects of daylight in this work. Known as LA's "acropolis," the billion-dollar series of buildings includes galleries, the Getty Conservation Institute, an automated tram, and extensive landscaping and site work.

Some architects have returned to a modern vocabulary and a direct application of classic modernism like Meier, but others reinterpret the tenets of the style in search of a new response appropriate to this age. Raphael Moneo's, *Museum of Roman Art* in Merida, Spain (1980–1985), is one such building that combines the old and new. The plan and overall scheme are unique blends of Modernist functional principles and Classical allusions, and the museum relates to the history of the surrounding area with the use of Roman brick and arches. The building is built around and over a Roman ruin that is displayed as part of the permanent museum collection. The program is divided into three principal masses: the galleries, the restoration labs, and the administrative areas. The plan consists of overlapping axes that are organized around a sky-lit central atrium. The plan and forms are quite modern, as is the use of the building material. Traditional Roman brick is used in a thoroughly modern way to form massive, densely-laid walls with small joints that belie the usual interpretation of the material.

Jean Nouvel augments the tenets of classic modernism with a gentle high tech aesthetic and an interest in surface details as seen in *The Arab World Institute* in Paris of the late 1980s. The building features one curved mass that contains museum spaces and that has a gently curving glass façade covered with silk-screened images of Paris. The flat curtain wall of the second rectangular library wing is covered with thousands of photosensitive lenses that open or close to manage the levels of sunlight in the adjacent spaces. The rounded, detailed lenses recall the patterns and screened panels found in Arab architecture but also provide a metaphor for the way that Arab culture is exposed or concealed in the building and in Paris. The two volumes are grouped around a square court that aligns with Notre Dame Cathedral, symbolizing a union between two cultures.

ARAB WORLD INSTITUTE

**Figure 8.6**

Nouvel's Arab Institute is part of a growing movement that looks to the building skin as a system all its own, capable of responding to environment and climate, but also a source of poetic meaning. He exploits the poetic power of the opening lens to recall the nature of a culture that is often hidden in the city, and to highlight the interplay of transparencies, the layered facades, and most critically, the daylight, which was for Nouvel the most important material in the building. In his later *Foundation Cartier* in Paris (1991–94), he again used a strict high

modern massing and geometry, but created an artful interplay between glass, reflection, and daylight. Nouvel wrote that in this project he was placing "art in the architecture, and architecture in the city" and thus blurred the distinction between the city and the building, and between the "real and virtual."

## MINIMALISM

Minimalism became a well-known and legitimate architectural style with the opening of Maya Lin's (b. 1959) *Vietnam Veterans Memorial* (1981–83) in Washington DC. Abstaining from all allusions to historical monuments or naturalistic imagery, the monument consists of two black granite slabs and 57,000 inscribed names. The two slabs comprise an angled cut into the earth, making a powerful and simple abstract statement. *The Church on Water*, in Hokkaido, Japan (1988), by Tadao Ando (b. 1941) also captures the essence of emotion and humanity with very simple gestures. The plain, poured concrete box has a large glass window that looks onto a pool of water, which holds a simple steel cross. The large glass wall of the sanctuary brings the outdoors into the worship space, and also highlights the seasonal changes in the natural landscape outside the church. The quiet, simple Modernist gestures take a second seat to the daylight, the textures, and the natural elements outside. The mood is one of rest, repose, and contemplation.

Peter Zumthor's (b. 1943) *Thermal Baths* (1997) at Vals, Switzerland, are the epitome of minimal detailing and sublime architectural composition. The baths were conceived as prehistoric stone elements emerging from the mountainside. The silent stone rooms are filled with water and look completely seamless. All the edges and spaces are detailed in an almost mute manner, and all technology related to the baths or to the building systems is hidden, allowing a somber, peaceful mood to prevail. Zumthor attempts to incorporate human experience into the built and uses architecture to evoke a sense of place, material, memory, and image. Although detailed to look utterly simple, this project required the invention of a new type of construction. The walls behave and are built solidly, without cavities, using an innovative technique dubbed "Vals composite masonry."

## HIGH TECH

Today's High-tech architecture intends to reduce structure and function to the most necessary elements. "Perfection can only be achieved if nothing can be taken away," evokes the classic Modernist maxim that "less is more." The manifestation of this High-tech philosophy ranges from a super-rational and spare aesthetic, to dazzling structural gymnastics that realize new achievements in engineering, material science, building systems, and the architect's ability to integrate them.

Architects working in this idiom collaborate closely with engineering firms to achieve new structures that challenge expected limits of roof spans, floor cantilevers, and column supports. Evanescent cable-stayed curtain walls that use special insulating and tempered glass are commonly seen in High-tech architecture as they allow maximum building performance for a (perceived) minimum use of material.

The equal marriage of technology, manufacturing, and architecture have always been a goal for some architects. Buckminster Fuller (b. 1895) was one of the iconic early pioneers and the echnologically rich *Dymaxion House* (1945) was one of his most famous works. Today's High-tech architecture is a design practice that attempts to effectively remove

the working separation between architect and engineer. Architect-engineer teams such as Helmut Jahn and Werner Sobek or Norman Foster and Ove Arup focus on utilizing the most current structural science and materials available to them in order to produce the most high-performing and structurally daring designs possible. Designer and engineer work together from the earliest sketches to create an integrated design. Invention and progress are requirements for the High-tech architects, placing them at an edge of a constantly changing and expanding architecture.

Functionalism, rationalism, and expression of industrial production are elements linking this style to early European Modernism and the international style. Advances in steel, insulating glass, cable structures, and concrete all allow for more dramatic forms than were possible in previous generations. Modernist movements have tried to free themselves from historicity and regionalism to pursue new horizons of form and so embrace this architectural style that addresses an increasingly global society.

While much early Modernism worked in a populist philosophy, high-tech is more frequently synonymous with large-scale projects such as airports, train stations, convention centers, and skyscrapers. Due to the high budgets of the projects and typically high square foot costs of the architecture, it is often governments, corporations, and high-end developers that commission High-tech projects. As a result, many of these works are major landmarks that affect the skyline, transportation patterns, and commerce at the scale of entire cities or countries.

Critics of the style see it as cold, soulless, and impersonal. High-tech architecture rejects a broad color palette and any extraneous elements that might distract from the overall composition of structure and skin. All-glass exteriors with steel and concrete structure, and stainless steel fittings and cladding are ubiquitous material combinations. Yet its ambition and the eternally evocative drive toward invention give High-tech architecture its own humanity.

## Style/Mannerism

An early example of High-tech is Norman Foster's (b. 1935) *Stansted Airport*, built 1981–1991. Foster's consistent collaboration with Ove Arup and Partners has had a great impact on architecture. High-tech style often is a good match for transportation facilities, since great efficiency is demanded for the large, open plans and building systems. The building is an efficient and simple continuous roof supported on large structural "trees." Daylight streams in from skylights in the roof as well as through the full-height glass walls at the perimeter. The transparency contributes to the successful organization of this very large building, and the visitor is able to see through the building from the roadway to the airplanes and is in no need of further orientation in the space.

Nicholas Grimshaw's (b. 1939), *Waterloo International Terminal* (1990–93) in London uses a long-span cable system as the main structural system. Grimshaw evokes the history and dynamics of the train shed with its immense volumes and diaphanous structures while making a serious statement about efficiency, cutting edge structural design, and responses to contingencies of a site. An asymmetrical, tapering, double cable-stayed truss supports the roof and is the main image of this project. The structure lends a sense of importance and lightness to an irregular and confined London rail station. The smaller western truss is placed on the outside of the building and supports glazing on the interior, achieving a continuous glazed interior with adequate clearance for the trains. This immense glass wall introduced daylight

and also became a "public showcase for the trains." Due to the irregularity of the site and truss sizes, and movement due to climate and train vibration, standardized glass panels were designed to move over one another in response to slight movements in the structural system.

Richard Rogers' (b. 1933) *Lloyd's Building* (1984) in London is remarkable for the way that it boldly expresses function and the structural and building systems. The office areas are completely open, while elevators, building systems, and other servant areas are clearly exposed at the rear of the building. These elements are clearly expressed on the exterior as individual elements that are hanging on the exposed structural system. This arrangement allows easy access for maintenance and allows easy upgrading of those elements that become obsolete through frequent use or advancing technology. Rogers' design recognizes that changing technology will require systems in the building to be significantly overhauled in the future. He designed even beyond the forefront of the technology of the era.

## Structure

Santiago Calatrava's (b. 1951) artful interpretations of natural elements into structural forms demonstrates a perfect equilibrium of architectonic and engineering principles. In his work asymmetry, dramatic cantilevers, graceful concrete forms, and operable exteriors serve to create a sense of wonder while the interiors and the site designs create a sense of architectural order. His *Lyon Satolas Railway Station* (1989–94) in Lyon, France, utilizes a series of soaring steel arches that fan from a single vertex to create the central light-filled hall that provides clear orientation for the visitor and an easily defined landmark for the surrounding city. The height and airiness of the central hall is in distinct contrast to the low, linear tube created by Calatrava's trademark wishbone piers that cover the train platforms below.

Calatrava also draws inspiration from natural movement and human or animal structures and form. The *Milwaukee Art Museum's* (2001) winglike operable sunshades draw a large crowd each time they open and close. Located just off downtown at the end of a long street, the museum complex is a magnificently sited yet unexpected Midwestern landmark. The project features a cable-stayed footbridge hung from a graceful, inclined pylon. This bridge leads to the entrance and is the main organizing axis of the project's formal composition. The sunshades qualify as public sculpture when they are open and fully extended. But the museum is more than just a mechanical curiosity: the sunshades enclose a jewel-like interior space with a stunning view of Lake Michigan.

ular to a given project and the architects design these to be easily recycled or reused.

Nicolas Grimshaw's temporary *British Pavilion* for the 1992 Seville Exposition was entirely prefabricated and assembled in Seville, Spain. It was a showcase for the articulation of structure and the ability of a small palate of materials to capture and manipulate wind, light, and water. High-tech aesthetics and structure combined to showcase local traditions and environmentally conscious passive building systems. A water wall on one side of the building served as a sculpture and also provided passive cooling. Fabric sails and roof louvers helped to shade the building and softened the harsh sunlight. Solar panels on the roof provided energy to the Pavilion. The project was designed to be taken apart at the end of the Exposition and so all elements were discrete and easily recycled.

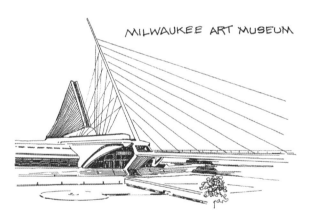

**Figure 8.7**

## Sustainability/Energy Conservation

One of the surprising tenets of the High-tech style is one of energy conservation. Although their palette of glass, steel, and concrete varies from that of other sustainable practitioners, these architects work to bring the operational costs of a building down by using less energy. Also, the components of high-tech architecture are partic-

**Figure 8.8**

Helmut Jahn's *Post Tower* (1992) in Bonn, Germany, the headquarters for the German post office, is based on simple geometries resulting in sharp edges and elegant curves. These combine to form a handsome statement of corporate identity. The distinctive shingled façade is a double skin commonly found in European high-rise buildings. It offers a highly insulated envelope that also allows fresh air to circulate. The floor-to-ceiling glass and narrow floor plate allow a maximum amount of natural light to reach the interior. These considerations give the building a low operating cost and also provide a pleasant working environment for the office staff. Helmut Jahn was educated in the pure Miesian style and he typifies the high-tech architect. He collaborates with structural and environmental engineers from the beginning of the design process in a relationship known as "Archi-neering."

PETRONAS TOWERS

**Figure 8.9**

## TALL TOWERS

Ever since the very first steel high-rises were built at the end of the 19th century, the race to construct the world's tallest buildings has been a race for civic pride and statue. The names New York or Chicago immediately call to most people's mind an image of the Empire State Building or the Sears Tower. Super-tall buildings define the visual identity of the cities that welcome them, the status of corporations who

finance them, and the careers of the architects who design them.

Caesar Pelli's (b. 1926) 1.6 billion-dollar *Petronas Towers* (1998) in Kuala Lumpur, Malaysia, emphatically demonstrates the ability of the world's tallest building to become an international cultural and commercial landmark. The tower ushered a new continent and world capital market into the global conscience. The twin 88-story towers are capped with spires that soar to 1,483 feet. The towers are linked at the 41st and 42nd floors by a double-decker skybridge. Comprising more than 8 million square feet, Petronas Towers includes a shopping mall, an interactive petroleum discovery center, an 864-seat concert hall, a mosque, and a conference center. The floor plate is based on an eight-pointed star and is said to reference Malaysian Islamic motifs. This reinforces the project's connection with national, not merely corporate, identity. The façade is reminiscent of temple spires, especially the pattern that is created by the blue glass panels that are set in aluminum frames. Other stainless steel panels help deflect the forceful Malaysian heat.

C. Y. Lee and Partners' *Taipei 101* (2004) in Taipei, Taiwan, at 508 meters, is the first building to exceed the half-kilometer mark. Holding the record with the world's tallest occupied floor and observation deck, the project is also notable for the world's fastest elevators. Based on traditional Chinese design, the rhythm of the tower is distinctive and is a departure from the orthodox, smooth Modernist line found in most high-rise buildings. The lucky number eight is found in the chamfered sections that comprise the tower.

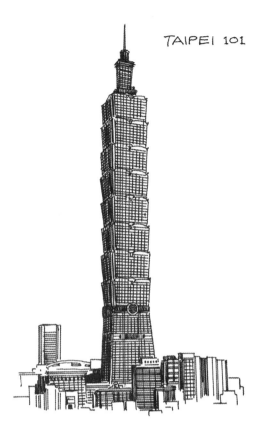

TAIPEI 101

**Figure 8.10**

## CONCLUSION

Modernism understood from the very beginning that if architecture is to remain relevant it must reflect and absorb the same influences that shape world culture. Computers and more sophisticated materials and building systems are certainly significant tools that have dramatically altered the forms that architects can produce. The vitality of discourse and theory used in architecture to develop strategies to allow architecture to emulate a changing world has proven an equally powerful tool. Change is the one constant of the discipline and those who have worked in the profession over the last 20 years have become ever more acutely aware of this premise.

Architecture at a global scale and at the local scale has been looked at extensively. What has been studied even more is the connection between the scales of inhabitation. The growing realization of how the local environment influences the city, country, and global spheres of influence, and vice-versa, has been one of the most important and difficult issues facing architecture. All of the styles we have discussed have striven for a more sophisticated, multivalent integration of physical and programmatic elements. And it is this search that will be the central challenge for the next generation as well.

The following list of structures developed since 1900 amplifies the materials of the last two lessons. The buildings have been chosen on the basis of their architectural significance or their influence on later developments. The projects have been arranged chronologically, along with their location and architect.

We have briefly described the essence of each building, and although concise, this information will be helpful in preparing for the exam. More complete descriptions and illustrations may be found in some of the books listed in the bibliography.

## Flatiron Building (New York) 1902
Daniel Burnham
Placed on a prominent, triangular site, this steel-framed structure owed much to the classical influence of the day. It had a well-defined base and shaft and a Sullivanesque capital, which were all well composed in a single, powerful volume. The 20 or so stories rose majestically from the sharp corner site and established a model for later tall buildings.

## Rue Franklin Apartments (Paris) 1903
Auguste Perret
This eight-story apartment house, where Perret himself lived, was the first example of reinforced concrete frame construction in architecture. The facade was composed of columns and beams arranged as huge timbers might have been, revealing the structure to a degree unprecedented in domestic architecture. The infilling panels were of ceramic tile decorated in relief. An interesting feature was the open roof terrace that portended the roof gardens to come.

## Larkin Building (Buffalo) 1904
Frank Lloyd Wright
The essential drama of the Larkin Building was a central, skylighted, four-story well. This soaring space was surrounded by office galleries that derived spatial unity from their outlook onto the central well. The structure and the largely unbroken exterior walls were constructed of flat bricks, and the staircase towers were strongly articulated as freestanding elements. Unfortunately, this landmark of modern design was demolished in 1950.

## Casa Milá (Barcelona) 1905
Antonio Gaudí
What has been called Gaudí's most original work was a great organic sculpture with a rhythm of undulating curves. Both in plan and elevation, the Casa, actually an apartment house, suggested a sea cliff that had been eroded and hollowed by the elements. The openings—doors and windows—were dug out of the facade and appeared as great voids. This fine example of Expressionist architecture, perhaps even late-blooming Art Nouveau, was infused with the excitement and action of nature.

POST OFFICE SAVINGS BANK

**Figure A.1**

## Unity Temple (Oak Park) 1906
Frank Lloyd Wright
This building was Wright's—and America's—first important cast-in-place concrete structure. The pebble aggregate was exposed to relieve the large plain surfaces. Most notable was the

grand interior space with its complex, interwoven relationships all softly lit from skylights set between intersecting concrete beams. The unified abstract decoration helped to make this one of Wright's best interiors.

### Robie House (Chicago) 1909
Frank Lloyd Wright
All the characteristics of the early Prairie houses were here: strong horizontal planes and masses, open interiors, bold cantilevers, and a strong attachment to the earth. Visually, this brick structure was a series of exciting planes, suggestive of a ship at sea. In its urban setting, it became one of the most celebrated residences in modern architecture.

### Gamble House (Pasadena) 1909
Greene and Greene
In the Japanese mode, Greene and Greene made wood craftsmanship the basis of architectural form. Their timber techniques were developed and fully exploited in the Gamble House, as every member went into the highly detailed skeleton structure pegged and burnished. Their work was the major inspiration for the subsequent California bungalow style, which achieved wide popularity.

### AEG Turbine Factory (Berlin) 1909
Peter Behrens
The most beautiful, the most modern, the most rational—these were some of the phrases used to describe this landmark structure of industrial architecture. The steel frame was exposed and walls of glass filled the spaces between. It was impressively monumental and, to most critics, a work of pure architecture.

### Steiner House (Vienna) 1910
Adolf Loos
Loos was extremely vociferous on the subject of decorative ornament; he felt its use should be considered a crime. It was no surprise, there-fore, that the Steiner House was designed in a style totally devoid of any decoration. The flat walls were sheer planes, punctured with carefully placed windows of large undivided panes, and the unbroken roof line was as thin as a pencil line. The Steiner House was truly ahead of its time.

### Christian Science Church (Berkeley) 1910
Bernard Maybeck
Caught between the Eclectic and the Modern, Maybeck produced a wonderfully energetic and original building. The concrete structure was enhanced with Gothic tracery carved in wood and running in provocative curves throughout. Exterior walls alternated between factory sash windows and asbestos panels. There is little doubt that this church helped foster the later Bay Area Style.

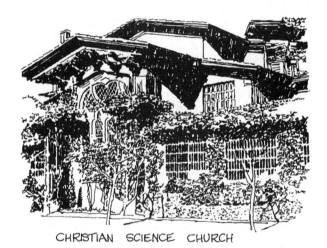

CHRISTIAN SCIENCE CHURCH
**Figure A.2**

### Fagus Factory (Alfeld, Germany) 1911
Walter Gropius
Gropius' first important commission, this shoelace factory, marked an unprecedented use of the steel frame. The cantilevered skeleton construction made possible a freestanding, three-story curtain wall of glass. With no vertical supports at the corners, the nonstructural character of the glass was emphasized. The flat roof, with no projection, helped to express the *pure cube.*

BAUHAUS

**Figure A.3**

## Model Factory, Werkbund Exhibition
(Cologne) 1914
Walter Gropius
This symmetrical building exhibited two distinct characters. On the court side, or rear, was a glass screen held by a light steel framework, which imparted the feeling of unusual lightness. On the opposite or entrance side was a facade of brick with only the narrowest slits for windows. Terminating each end were two-story, all-glass towers enclosing spiral staircases. This dramatic motif was to become an important feature in many modern buildings.

## Dodge House (Los Angeles) 1917
Irving Gill
Gill's inspiration, considered by many to be derived from Spanish mission architecture, was actually closer in spirit to the work of Adolf Loos in Vienna. The Dodge House was a brilliant composition of white cubes, unrelieved by cornices, roof overhangs, or other extraneous details. Of note was its sensitive relationship to its site through the use of terraces, arched porches, and low garden walls.

## Hallidie Building (San Francisco) 1917
Willis Polk
This relatively low building, ignored by most historians, featured a curtain wall many years before it came into common usage. For its time, there was hardly a more imaginative or daring use than in its almost totally glass facade.

## Einstein Tower (Potsdam) 1921
Erich Mendelsohn
One of Mendelsohn's first buildings, the Tower caused a mild sensation. With its curved surfaces and windows sweeping around corners, it appeared *streamlined*. Because the building's purpose was suggested by the symbolism of its form, Mendelsohn was inevitably linked to the Expressionist movement.

## Notre Dame (Le Raincy) 1922
August Perret
This church near Paris derived its character from the use of forms appropriate to reinforced concrete: slender columns, segmental vaults, and windows in the form of geometric grilles. The exposed bare bones approach conveyed a Gothic feeling rare in Modern architecture.

**Bauhaus** (Dessau) 1925
Walter Gropius
This extraordinary school of design was one of the most important buildings of the century—as noteworthy for its educational ideas as for its architectural conception. In plan, there were two large intersecting Ls that contained the separate facilities while integrating them into a coherent building complex. In the workshop wing, reinforced concrete floor slabs and supporting columns were set well back, allowing for a dramatic, uninterrupted, three-story glass curtain wall. Needless to say, the Bauhaus had an enormous influence on modern architecture.

**Lovell House** (Newport Beach) 1926
Rudolph Schindler
In this California beach house, Schindler reflected his European preference for pure form and simple surfaces while retaining, from his association with Wright, a complexity of space and structure. Five reinforced concrete frames formed the skeletal structure within which the living areas were contained. These were elevated above the beach and cantilevered beyond the frame for a dramatic ocean view.

**Weissenhof Housing Exhibition** (Stuttgart) 1927 Various Architects
This great housing exhibition was sponsored by the Deutscher Werkbund and directed by Mies van der Rohe. Among the participants were Peter Behrens, Walter Gropius, Le Corbusier, J. J. P. Oud, and Mies himself. All the architects had complete freedom, and the dramatic results represented the most progressive architectural thinking on housing and construction in Europe.

**Dymaxion House** 1927
Buckminster Fuller
"A machine for living in," Fuller's Dymaxion (*dynamic plus maximum efficiency*) House demonstrated the great technical advantages in the creation of a controlled environment. Structurally, the house was supported on a central mast containing the mechanical systems. The prototype was quite visionary, but it was rejected by most as being too mechanistic and inflexible.

**Schocken Dept. Stores** (Germany) 1927–28
Erich Mendelsohn
Among Mendelsohn's finest work were the Schocken Stores at Stuttgart in 1927 and Chemnitz in 1928. The facades of both had long bands of glass alternating with opaque bands of solid wall. The Stuttgart store was distinguished by a monumental stairway encased in a six-story, circular glass tower. The Chemnitz store was curved to follow the street on which it was sited.

**Lovell House** (Los Angeles) 1929
Richard Neutra
For the same Lovell family for whom Schindler had worked, Neutra created another tour de force with this residence, sometimes called the *Health House.* The structure was a prefabricated light steel frame that was erected in only 40 hours. The floating floor planes were pneumatically-applied concrete (gunite) suspended from cables attached to the roof. Large areas of metal sash helped to create lightness and airiness in this building, which so dramatically demonstrated the potential of modern technology.

**Villa Savoye** (Poissy) 1929
Le Corbusier
In this Villa, Le Corbusier realized his central principles of architecture: free standing pilotis, framework structurally independent of walls, open plan, free facade, and a flat roof used as a garden. The house appeared as a cube elevated on pillars, with large areas of glass facing the view on all sides. It remains one of the most influential houses in modern architecture.

**German Pavilion** (Barcelona) 1929
Mies van der Rohe
Few buildings have exerted as enormous an influence as this, the most famous of Mies' European projects. Constructed of chrome-plated steel columns, marble, and grey glass, it appeared as a precious jewel—perfect in its proportions and richly flowing in its spaciousness. The Pavilion was set on a podium that created a monumental sense of dignity. Together with the Barcelona furniture group, it has become a modern classic.

**Tugendhat House** (Brno) 1930
Mies van der Rohe
This classic house embodied Mies' preoccupation with elegant materials and flowing space. The principal living spaces were divided with freestanding walls of onyx and ebony, and the roof was supported by chromed columns. Every visible detail, down to the curtain tracks, was meticulously designed by the architect, ensuring remarkable unity and precision.

**Town Hall** (Hilversum) 1930
Willem Dudok
Although influenced by the De Stijl movement, Dudok evolved as an independent pioneer of modern architecture. The Town Hall, built entirely of bright brickwork, had a warmth characteristic of Dudok's work. Offices were arranged around an inner court with entrances along the sides and rear. It has been termed a cubistic triumph because of its well balanced composition.

**Swiss Pavilion** (Paris) 1930
Le Corbusier
In this dormitory at the Cité Universitaire, Le Corbusier elevated the four-story mass on six colossal piers. In contrast to the blank ends of the dormitory block, the long face of the building was an elegant glass curtain wall. On the opposite side was a solid curved wall, the lower part of which was constructed of natural stone. When viewed as a whole, the individualized spaces formed a distinct aesthetic unity.

**Philadelphia Savings Fund Society**
(Philadelphia) 1932
Howe and Lescaze
The PSFS Building marked a transition from the first European phase of the International Style to the second American phase. The T-shaped, 33-story tower rose without setbacks from a curved base. Cantilevered floors and ribbon windows made the principal elevation emphatically horizontal, while exposed columns on the sides emphasized verticality.

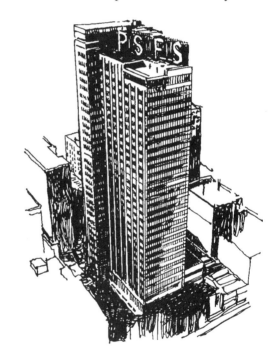

PHILADELPHIA SAVINGS FUND
**Figure A.4**

**Bellavista Housing** (Copenhagen) 1933
Arne Jacobsen
These three-story housing blocks near Copenhagen were considered to be among the finest apartments in Europe. Strongly influenced by the International Style, the smooth white-

washed apartments were staggered to give each unit an equal share of sun and view.

### Schwandbach Bridge (Berne) 1933
Robert Maillart

In a period of about 30 years, Maillart built close to 40 reinforced concrete bridges of enormous grace and efficiency. The Schwandbach Bridge, built on a curve, typically integrated the roadway into the structure. Its economy, structural efficiency, and harmonious balance made this, as well as his other projects, a work of art.

### Kaufmann House (Bear Run) 1936
Frank Lloyd Wright

Better known as *Fallingwater*, this project has become one of the most famous houses in modern architecture. Cantilevered concrete balconies, contrasted with vertical native stone walls, projected dramatically from the rock base above the water. Interior spaces opened through large glass areas to hovering terraces. It was a flawless blend of architecture and engineering, of space and structure, of poetry and technique.

### Doldertal Apartments (Zurich) 1936
Marcel Breuer

Of the three individual buildings designed, two were built, each one containing three apartments and two penthouses. In the architect's concern for the relationship between buildings and nature, garden terraces extended the interior space outward. In the lobby, a planter bed created an elegant transition from inside to out, separated only by a glass wall.

### Johnson Wax Building (Racine) 1936
Frank Lloyd Wright

Designed on a circular module, the exterior walls were built as brick screens striated with horizontal bands of glass tubing. The great workroom, surrounded by office galleries, was perhaps Wright's finest interior. It was filled with the famous mushroom columns, their flat

pads supporting a roof of translucent glass tubing. The nearby laboratory tower was added in 1950.

JOHNSON WAX

**Figure A.5**

### Ministry of Education (Rio de Janeiro) 1937
Oscar Niemeyer

This striking building was the first important work of modern architecture in Brazil. Designed by a select group of architects, including Niemeyer, Lucio Costa, Alfonso Reidy, and others, the design was strongly influenced by the chief consultant, Le Corbusier. Evidence of this can be seen in the use of reinforced concrete, rows of pilotis, and in the most dramatic feature, the brise soleil, or louvered sunscreen.

### Taliesin West (Phoenix) 1938
Frank Lloyd Wright

Wright's winter home, school, and office in the Arizona desert was planned on a triangular module, echoing the slope of the distant mountains. Battered walls of poured concrete, with large desert boulders as aggregate, formed a base for the redwood trusses and translucent canvas walls and roofs placed on them. Together with gardens and pools, the entire complex seemed to be a natural part of its colorful desert setting.

**Rockefeller Center** (New York) 1940
Reinhard, Hofmeister, Hood, and others
A landmark of urban design, the Center was conceived during the depths of the Great Depression. It was a group of office towers and multiuse spaces, designed by several architectural firms, in which each element complemented the others and together formed an extremely harmonious composition. The plazas, walks, and pedestrian amenities recognized the human element and indicated a direction for future urban design.

**Forest Crematorium** (Stockholm) 1940
Gunnar Asplund
Asplund's masterpiece was sited at the crest of a long, gently sloping hill. The approach was dominated by a large marble cross. The structure itself was utterly simple and restrained as the large portico—a timber roof supported by plain marbled columns—crowned the summit. As pure as a Greek temple, it was original and dramatic.

**Illinois Institute of Technology** (Chicago) 1940
Mies van der Rohe
As Director of Architecture at IIT, Mies was commissioned to plan the new campus. The arrangement of buildings in a series of plazas was simple but subtle. The campus was planned on a 24-foot-square grid, this modular principle exerting a strong unifying effect. All buildings were constructed of exposed, black steel frames, light brick panels, and glass. Although each of the structures was notable, Crown Hall, built in 1955 to house the architecture department, was especially brilliant.

**Kaufmann House** (Palm Springs) 1946
Richard Neutra
For the client of Wright's Fallingwater, Neutra designed what was perhaps his finest residence. Set in the hot desert, its pinwheel plan permitted light, air, and a view from several exposures. Through large areas of glass, interior spaces extended outward to terraces, patios, and gardens beyond. Flat roof planes, as well as contrasting materials and textures, were sensitively employed with elegance and precision.

**Baker House Dormitory** (Cambridge) 1947
Alvar Aalto
This dormitory at MIT was Aalto's only major work in the United States. The six-story brick structure presented a serpentine shape to one side, while the other side revealed angular and opposing masses. It served to reinforce movement that valued strong, rough shapes articulated according to their special function.

**Unité d'Habitation** (Marseilles) 1947
Le Corbusier
More like a small town than a building, this reinforced concrete structure was designed to house 100 people on each of its 16 floors. Almost all of the prefabricated apartment units were two stories high with full-length balconies and large expanses of glass. Internal shopping streets were halfway up the building, while the roof housed recreational facilities and other community services. Several of Le Corbusier's well-known elements were incorporated, including rough concrete, pilotis, and his unique modulor scale.

**Exhibition Hall** (Turin) 1948
Pier Luigi Nervi
With the goal of achieving strength through form, Nervi succeeded in developing a ferrocement that consisted of layers of fine wire mesh embedded in cement mortar. This development made possible this famous shell that remains one of his masterpieces. The enormous building consisted of a single roof structure made up of undulating prefabricated units which were sometimes only 1-1/2 inches thick.

## Equitable Savings Building (Portland) 1948
Pietro Belluschi

This pioneer building, built just after World War II, was the first sealed air-conditioned building in this country. The reinforced structural concrete frame was covered in sheet aluminum. The aluminum spandrels and tinted glass were placed in virtually the same plane as the frame, creating a smooth, reflective, and machined appearance.

## Architect's House (New Canaan) 1949
Philip Johnson

This elegant all-glass house was framed in exposed steel painted black. It was essentially one space—a transparent pavilion—in which living areas were defined by low walnut cabinets and by a brick cylinder containing a bathroom and a fireplace. The landscaped acres were an essential part of the architecture and afforded privacy as well as natural beauty. Nearby, in the years following, Johnson built a separate brick guest house, art gallery, sculpture garden, and swimming pool.

## Harvard Graduate Center (Cambridge) 1948
The Architects' Collaborative

The Architects' Collaborative (TAC), led by Walter Gropius, created seven dormitories and a commons building for the Center. They were designed around a series of quadrangles, as important to the total composition as the buildings themselves. The concrete dormitories contrasted with the steel-framed, brick-covered commons to form a variety of spaces, linked by covered walks, which were compatible with the scale of Harvard Yard.

## Architect's House (Santa Monica) 1949
Charles Eames

This house was designed of standard, mass-produced, industrial components. The walls consisted chiefly of steel windows and sliding glass doors. The metal frames were filled with transparent or translucent glass, with solid panels of red, white, or blue stucco for contrast. In the hands of an artist, the result was a light, cage-like structure of Oriental delicacy. It was an immediate success, as well as the winner of an AIA 25-year award.

## U.N. Secretariat (New York) 1950
Wallace Harrison

A thin slab of a skyscraper, this structure was strongly influenced by Le Corbusier. The short ends were solidly sheathed in white marble while the two long sides were completely covered with green-tinted glass. Since the principal axis was north-south, the 3,500 employees had a view of the East River on one side and the Manhattan skyline on the other.

U.N. BUILDING

**Figure A.6**

## Farnsworth House (Plano) 1950
Mies van der Rohe

The house consisted of three floating planes: the roof and raised floor supported between vertical columns and an adjacent exterior terrace-platform. The structure was exposed, white-painted steel into which solid glass walls were placed. At one side of the principal space, service facilities were enclosed within a wood-sheathed core, which separated living and sleeping areas. Perfect craftsmanship further enhanced the structure.

**Civic Center** (Saynatsalo) 1951
Alvar Aalto
Personal in style and closely related to the forested landscape in which it was sited, the several elements of the composition were constructed of brick and timber, all covered with copper roofing. The articulated elements of offices, council chamber, and library were sited around a raised, open courtyard—almost a miniature town square.

**Lakeshore Drive Apartments** (Chicago) 1951
Mies van der Rohe
Among the most distinctive apartments in the United States, these twin towers enjoyed a dramatic view of both the city and Lake Michigan. The steel skeletons were embellished with vertical steel mullions which not only held the all-glass walls in place, but served to emphasize the linear quality of the buildings. The towers influenced architects around the world.

**Capital City** (Chandigarh) 1951
Le Corbusier
This capital for the state of Punjab was one of the largest and most celebrated complexes of modern architecture. Le Corbusier was able to realize his theories on zoning, circulation, and traffic separation, practically without restriction. Some of the individual structures of note were the Supreme Court, the Secretariat, and the Assembly Building.

**Lever House** (New York) 1952
Skidmore, Owings, and Merrill
Gordon Bunshaft of Skidmore, Owings and Merrill (SOM) produced the first postwar commercial skyscraper in the United States that occupied less than the legal maximum area on its expensive site. The ground floor contained a lobby, walks, and gardens, while the second floor consisted of a strip of offices, raised on columns, which formed a pedestal for the thin glass-walled slab above. The green-glass tower mirrored the surrounding cityscape and became one of the most influential office towers in modern architecture.

**Connecticut General Building** (Hartford) 1954
Skidmore, Owings, and Merrill
In this building, the SOM image of contemporary urban sophistication was applied to a rural site in Connecticut. The huge three-story block was entirely glazed, offering the employees dramatic views of courtyards by Isamu Noguchi, as well as the landscape beyond. It was a modern concept that predicted corporate planning of the future.

**Notre-Dame-du-Haut** (Ronchamp) 1955
Le Corbusier
With this design, Le Corbusier shocked the world of architecture, since it was unrelated to anything that preceded it. It was as much a piece of sculpture as it was architecture—revealing another facet in the personality of the recognized master. Light penetrated the interior through a narrow space between the roof shell and walls. In addition, windows of various sizes were scattered along the curved walls. In all, the building represented a variety of subtle experiments in the use of light, form, and color.

**U.S. Air Force Academy** (Colorado Springs) 1956
Skidmore, Owings, and Merrill
At a spectacular site in Colorado, a gigantic paved platform was created to carry the seven enormous buildings. Each of the buildings was tailored with Miesian purity, leading to criticism that they were relentlessly repetitious, even inhuman. In this vast composition, the chapel, with it aluminum-clad tetrahedral frames, became the dominating element.

## General Motors Technical Center
(Warren, Michigan) 1956
Eero Saarinen
This incredible complex of 25 buildings was dispersed around a 22-acre artificial lake to form the research center for the world's largest corporation. It was the ultimate in industrial architecture, detailed with machine-like precision, and incorporating steel frames, aluminum, glass, porcelain enamel, and brilliant walls of glazed ceramic brick. Courts, gardens, and pools softened the industrial impact and affirmed the human element.

## U.S. Embassy (New Delhi) 1958
Edward Stone
Offices and reception areas were composed around a rectangular pool, open to the sky but protected from the sun by a suspended mesh of gold anodized aluminum. Exterior openings were concealed and protected by a grille of pierced tile, while broad overhangs supported by slender gold columns protected the walls.

## Seagram Building (New York) 1958
Mies van der Rohe
With the help of Philip Johnson, Mies created what has been called the last word in tall building elegance. Similar in detail to his Chicago apartments, this project used superior materials: bronze sheathing for the steel frame, amber-tinted glass, green marble, travertine, and pink granite. The slender tower was set well back from the street, creating a generous plaza with pools.

## Capital City (Brasilia) 1958
Oscar Niemeyer
The master plan of Brasilia, the new capital of Brazil, was selected by an international jury in an open competition won by Lucio Costa. The plan essentially comprised two axes that intersected at right angles, one of which curved into the residential areas. The plan provided a superb framework for Niemeyer's monumental buildings, such as the Presidential Palace, Congress Building, and the Cathedral. The whole was a rational setting for a well-organized community life in a dignified capital city.

## Guggenheim Museum (New York) 1959
Frank Lloyd Wright
The concrete spiral ramp, which was the essence of this unique structure, had fascinated Wright for at least 35 years. At the Guggenheim, he created a totally enclosed space, lighted from above, that was both a gallery and a continuous means of circulation. It was criticized as being in conflict with its environment as well as its purpose, but it offered visitors an incomparably exhilarating experience.

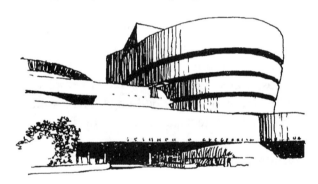

GUGGENHEIM

**Figure A.7**

## Monastery of La Tourette (Eveux) 1960
Le Corbusier
The plan was a courtyard enclosed on three sides by monks' cells and on the fourth side by the church, which was cut into the sloping site. The side was lit by huge light funnels which literally emerged from the earth. The monks' cells were lifted high in the air and supported by narrow concrete columns. The entire composition had a sculptural unity of form cast in rough concrete—a further exploration of Le Corbusier's guiding principles.

**Pirelli Building** (Milan) 1960
Gio Ponti
With Pier Luigi Nervi as structural engineer, Ponti achieved his masterpiece in this unique structure. Roughly hexagonal in plan, the sides were tapered like a ship's bow. Four giant piers supported the building and were revealed on the exterior, becoming thinner and lighter as they rose higher. Its distinctive, powerful shape and size dominated the skyline but lent an elegance to the surrounding area.

**Richards Medical Research Building** (Philadelphia) 1960
Louis Kahn
One of Kahn's finest buildings, this structure was perhaps the most influential and imitated American building of the 1960s. Individual tower groupings, containing laboratories, utilities, and stairways, were vigorously composed to produce forms symbolic of their functions. The functionalism was made monumental and grand.

**Dulles Airport** (Washington DC) 1961
Eero Saarinen
Perhaps the most important innovation at this gateway airport was the development of the mobile lounge, which separated the jet traffic and the terminal traffic. Vehicular circulation was simplified by a separation of levels. The distinctive structure consisted of a cable-suspended concrete hammock slung between two rows of leaning, tapered pylons, between which were large sheets of tinted glass.

**TWA Terminal** (New York) 1962
Eero Saarinen
One of Saarinen's most controversial structures, this terminal building borrowed its form from the inspiration of flight. Concrete was sculpted into an expressive space containing a restaurant, snack bar, and other passenger ser-

vices. Of interest were the arched tube-tunnels that led to the waiting airplanes.

**Art & Architecture Building** (New Haven) 1963
Paul Rudolph
This dramatic building on the Yale campus was a bold composition of towers, which housed service elements, and work-space slabs bridging between them, all surrounding a central core space. Both inside and out, horizontal and vertical masses intersected, creating a variety of spatial experiences. Concrete walls were heavily striated in a corduroy-textured surface pattern, emphasizing its durability. Despite its drama, this tour de force was criticized as a functional failure.

**Carpenter Center** (Cambridge) 1963
Le Corbusier
In this Center for the Visual Arts at Harvard University, Le Corbusier created pure, articulated volumes that were enclosed by flat or curved smooth concrete walls. A ramp supported on slender columns led pedestrians through the spaces and made the composition entirely accessible, while remaining respectful of the urban environment. This project was Le Corbusier's only completed architectural example in America.

**First Unitarian Church** (Rochester) 1964
Louis Kahn
Kahn's experiments with windows and other means of introducing daylight culminated in this modern but poetic church. The massing and exterior profiles of the concrete block structure were designed to shield the interior spaces from glare. Individual spaces and wall openings were highly articulated and sensitively composed.

FIRST UNITARIAN CHURCH

**Figure A.8**

**Society Hill Apartments** (Philadelphia) 1964
I. M. Pei
As part of a comprehensive urban renewal, Pei designed three 30-story towers, at the base of which were several three-story row houses. The row houses, planned around courtyards, maintained the scale and harmony of several rehabilitated houses in the area. The concrete towers were graceful and well-proportioned refinements of Pei's earlier and successful *Kips Bay Plaza* project.

**Civic Center** (Chicago) 1964
C. F. Murphy
This graceful structure was actually designed by Jacques Brownson, a disciple of Mies van der Rohe, who tried to extend the steel and glass vernacular beyond what had previously been done. The floors were framed with great steel girders permitting structural bays 48 × 87 feet, the largest in any skyscraper that existed at the time. The structure was sheathed in Corten steel, which weathered to a dark brown. It occupied only 30 percent of its site, which allowed a granite-paved plaza to be created that was later enhanced by a Picasso sculpture.

**CBS Building** (New York) 1964
Eero Saarinen
Saarinen's last major building was an image of quiet corporate strength. Rising out of a sunken plaza, the freestanding concrete shaft was emphasized vertically by the unbroken sweep of the granite-clad triangular piers. The use of black granite led to its nickname *Black Rock*. The closely spaced piers provided an ever-changing pattern of open and closed as one moved around the building.

**Marina City** (Chicago) 1964
Bertrand Goldberg
Dramatically situated on the Chicago River, in the heart of the Loop, these twin 60-story towers quickly became an identifying symbol for Chicago. Each circular concrete tower had 450 apartments in its upper two-thirds, with the lower third comprising a continuous parking ramp. The cylindrical core carried services and utilities while serving as a rigid structural element. A theater, auditorium, stores, restaurants, recreational facilities, and a marina for 700 boats completed the urban composition.

**Venturi House** (Chestnut Hill, PA) 1964
Robert Venturi
Venturi's house for his mother was one of the projects that initiated the revolution against

Modernism by substituting symbolic content for structure and formal space. The stuccoed volume had a split gable and a variety of Mannerist forms. Within the house, space was determined strictly by function, with no preconceived concept of a rational order.

### Guild House (Philadelphia) 1965
Venturi and Rauch

This apartment for the elderly was disturbing to most architects, since it broke so sharply with the conventional approach. With this building, Venturi demonstrated his belief in compromise or the *principle of accommodation.* The concrete frame was covered with brick, and various standard windows were cut in where necessary; thus, the entire design was functionally, rather than technologically, expressed. In celebrating the ordinary, Venturi used an identifying sign far too large and crowned the entire project with a gold-anodized television antenna.

### Ghirardelli Square (San Francisco) 1965
Wurster, Bernardi, and Emmons

With the help of landscape architect Laurence Halprin, the Wurster firm converted the historic bay-front chocolate factory into an urban center of fine shops, restaurants, and humanly-scaled outdoor spaces. This project, perhaps more than any other in this country, provided the inspiration to conserve and reuse fine old structures, rather than destroy them after their original usefulness was gone. As a retail concept and an environment to bring pleasure, Ghirardelli Square was an immediate success.

### Deere & Co. Building (Moline, IL) 1965
Eero Saarinen

Beautifully sited and eloquently detailed, the suburban setting and structure were in total harmony. The Cor-Ten steel frame was exposed and relieved only by tinted glass panels. It was a rational and orderly composition that set an admirable pattern for later suburban corporate headquarters.

### Salk Institute (La Jolla) 1965
Louis Kahn

On a dramatic site overlooking the Pacific Ocean, Kahn created an academic village of research laboratories. Structure and services were combined in generously proportioned structures in which Kahn's ideas about *servant* and *served* spaces were clearly revealed. The concrete was refined to a degree rarely seen before—density, color, and meticulous joinery were truly remarkable. The intellectual atmosphere was enhanced by an impressive scale complemented by the well-proportioned and boldly expressed elements of structure.

### Capital City (Dacca, Bangladesh) 1966
Louis Kahn

In his design for the "Second Capital," in what was originally East Pakistan, Kahn utilized vast masonry walls that were carefully pierced by circles, triangles, and diamonds. The richly geometric plans were composed with simplicity, clarity, and an almost Beaux-Arts formality. The forms exploited light and structure to the utmost, creating an opulent spatial order appropriate to the traditions of the area.

### Sea Ranch (Northern California) 1966
Moore, Lyndon, Turnbull, and Whitaker (MLTW) This residential resort development, north of San Francisco, demonstrated the application of Charles Moore's shack-style architecture to a larger, more complex project. Individual apartment units were assembled in a single, bold structure while preserving a diversity and individual identity for each unit. Heavy timber framing, vertical wood siding, a variety of shed roofs, and individual bay windows helped to create an exciting interplay of volumes and spaces.

SEA RANCH

**Figure A.9**

**Faculty Club** (Santa Barbara) 1967
Charles Moore (MLTW)
Evoking the Colonial vernacular that was part
of the Santa Barbara tradition, Moore created
a composition of red tile roofs, wood timbers,
and white stuccoed walls, which translated into
a completely original and contemporary architectural interpretation. The interior of the main
dining room was a virtual stage set of imagery
that featured eclectic components combined
with 20th-century details, such as hanging neon
flags.

**Ford Foundation Building** (New York) 1967
Roche and Dinkleloo
One of Kevin Roche's most celebrated buildings, this structure was located in mid-Manhat-
tan. Offices were arranged along two sides of
the site, while the remainder of the space was
devoted to a full-height, glass-enclosed interior
garden. All the offices on each level overlooked
this grand space, while each was exposed to the
casual passerby. Floor framing was of exposed
steel, though the exterior glass walls were composed in their own scale with little reference to
floor levels.

**U.S. Pavilion** (Montreal) 1967
Buckminster Fuller
Fuller once proposed covering an entire city
with one of his *geodesic domes*, and many
thought he came close to it with his great dome
at Expo '67. Fuller's dome employed lightweight standard parts to produce the maximum
enclosed volume with the minimum enclosing
surface. The gigantic enclosed space was filled
with an imaginative display by the *Cambridge
Seven*.

**Habitat** (Montreal) 1967
Moshe Safdie
For Expo '67, Safdie created a building-block
pile of prefabricated concrete residential units
that caused a mild sensation when it was built.
The boxlike units were carefully arranged to
provide roof terraces, individual views, and the
utmost privacy attainable, within the limits of
the high-density development. The entire composition resembled the architecture of Italian
hill towns or ancient pueblos.

BOSTON CITY HALL

**Figure A.10**

**City Hall** (Boston) 1968
Kallmann, McKinnell, and Knowles
Created as the result of a competition, the City Hall was strongly influenced by Le Corbusier's *Monastery of La Tourette*, as in the multitiered windowed cornice. The rugged and highly sculptured composition was set in a generous plaza, making it remarkably accessible. The design intent was to make the people of Boston feel involved in their government.

**John Hancock Building** (Chicago) 1968
Skidmore, Owings, and Merrill
This enormous 100-story steel and glass shaft, tapering as it swept skyward, forever changed the Chicago skyline. A community within itself, the bottom half contained offices, while apartments were located above. Commercial facilities, recreational features, and parking for over 1,000 cars were also provided. In addition to the pronounced batter, the tower was distinguished by the enormous diagonal bracing that was exposed on all four sides.

**Bank of America Building** (San Francisco) 1970
Wurster, Bernardi, and Emmons
This 52-story tower was the result of the collaboration between the Wurster firm and Pietro Belluschi, who was the design consultant. The form was heavily jagged—reminiscent of the San Francisco bay window—since each office was provided a commanding view of the bay. Sheathed in reddish-brown marble, the various elements of the shaft ended at different heights, creating an almost casual, crystal-like effect at the building's summit.

**Kimball Art Museum** (Fort Worth) 1972
Louis Kahn
For this project, Kahn employed a classically organized composition in which galleries were imaginatively lighted from above. The structure was sophisticated and sensitively arranged in a parklike setting. The tranquillity of the arrangement made the building appear timeless.

**Hyatt Regency Hotel** (San Francisco) 1972
John Portman
Beginning in 1967 with the first Hyatt Regency in Atlanta, Portman created some of the most exuberant spaces of the 20th century. In San Francisco, access balconies to rooms were arranged around a central skylighted atrium, and the balconies were staggered inward as they rose higher. Within the atrium was a delightful arrangement of well-scaled pools, sculpture, trees, exposed elevators, and furnishings. It became at once an active and popular urban meeting place, not unlike a city square, filled with light, color, and sound.

**World Trade Center** (New York) 1972
Minoru Yamasaki
The 9 million square feet of the World Trade Center were arranged in twin towers that were flanked by low buildings and a plaza larger than the *Piazza San Marco* in Venice. Though the 110 stories equaled those of the *Sears Building* in Chicago, the pair of filigreed towers were shorter by approximately 100 feet.

HYATT REGENCY

**Figure A.11**

**Sears Tower** (Chicago) 1973
Skidmore, Owings, and Merrill
Rising 110 stories, this giant tower was well
over a quarter mile in height and the world's
tallest building for the next 25 years. The
composition consisted of nine 75-foot-square
structural tubes, seven of which terminated at
various elevations as the building rose, until
only two tubes remained at the very top. The
entire shaft was clad with a curtain wall using
bronze-tinted glass. The building's population
of around 16,000 created circulation problems
on a massive scale that were solved by ingenious double-decked elevator shafts and 102
high-speed elevators.

**Pacific Design Center** (Los Angeles) 1976
Cesar Pelli
This vast collection of designer showrooms
was encased in a scaleless wrapping of blue
glass that emphasized volume, rather than
mass. The exterior form appeared as a giant
extrusion, with the projection of a few simple
geometric shapes and culminating in a semicircular vaulted galleria. The massive bulk of the
structure created its own scale of urban monu-
mentality—a shiny object in the landscape, too
immense to ignore.

**Bronx Development Center** (New York) 1977
Richard Meier
Considered to be Meier's crowning achievement, this treatment center for the mentally dis-
abled was a large group of four-story buildings
enclosing a spacious courtyard. The structural
steel frame was wrapped with a clear anodized
aluminum skin, which was pierced by flush
windows with rounded corners. The total effect
was a strict composition of sleek, machine-
made forms. It was sophisticated, refined, and
entirely consistent with Meier's orderly and
skillful work.

**Pennzoil Place** (Houston) 1977
Johnson and Burgee
Twin trapezoidal office towers of dark anodized
aluminum on a steel frame were mirror images
in plan separated by a ten-foot slot of space.
The tops of the towers were angled towards
each other, with the same angle repeated at the
glazed entrance atrium that rose eight stories
from the street into the slot. The geometrically
powerful composition was seen as a prototype
of monumental urban sculpture.

**Centre Pompidou** (Paris) 1977
Piano and Rogers
The six-level megastructure, called *Place
Beaubourg*, was created as the result of an
international design competition, and it consti-

tuted perhaps the most sensational example of high technology architecture. In this center for art and culture, the architects created universal spaces within a totally exposed structure. The basic grammar was glass and steel in cast components. Outside the structure, mechanical pipes, ducts, and molded-glass escalator tubes were exposed and painted in brilliant primary colors. The cultural facilities attracted an immediate audience, but the unusual building created as much agitation among Parisians as the Eiffel Tower had nearly a century before.

## National Gallery/East Building
(Washington DC) 1978
I. M. Pei
Actually three small museums in one, the East Building was trapezoidal in plan in order to fit the oddly-shaped site. It was purely geometric, classic, and innovative—all based on a consistent triangular theme. The solid walls were completely covered with marble that matched the original National Gallery, but the spaces within were remarkably open and brilliant, lighted from glass skylighted roofs above.

## Museum of Contemporary Art
(Los Angeles) 1986
Arata Isozaki
Formed of simple geometric shapes, red sandstone and green aluminum. A generous plaza unites two separate building volumes.

## Le Grand Arche de la DŽfense
(Paris) 1983–1989
Johan Otto von Spreckelsen
Revisiting the triumphal arch for the modern age and combining it with skyscraper typologies.

## Roof Top Office (Vienna) 1989
Coop Himmelblau
Mechanized skylight of a law office, resembling a lightning bolt or a huge bird. Not a part

of Deconstructionist Movement but became an important work of the era.

## Art Tower Mito (Mito Japan) 1986–90
Arata Isosaki
An art center complete with cultural center, concert halls, and exhibition spaces. A 100-meter tower of trapezoidal sections creates a strong landmark and visual memory.

## Water Temple (Awaki Island, Japan) 1989–90
Tadao Ando
Traditional shrine sits below grade and is accessed via a pathway leading under an elliptical lily pond.

## Umeda Sky Building (Osaka, Japan) 1993
Hiroshi Hara and Atelier
Essentially two 173-meter towers connected with a "floating garden observatory," this connection at the top of the building features a giant circular opening.

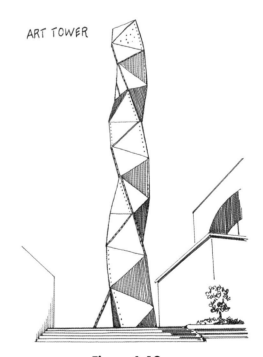

**Figure A.12**

**San Francisco Museum of Modern Art**
(San Francisco) 1995
Mario Botta
Handsomely patterned red brickwork forms
a solid, massive base above which projects a
striking black-and-white striped cylindrical
oculus.

**Kansai International Airport**
(Osaka, Japan) 1988–95
Renzo Piano
A man-made island between sky and water and
land, the whole design is a disk with only a
portion of it visible above ground. 1.7 kilome-
ter long main terminal.

**St. Ignatius** (Seattle) 1996
Stephen Holl
Conceived as "seven glass bottles in a concrete
box," each programmed area receives a differ-
ently colored filtered light. Walls of the buildings were precast on the ground and lifted into
place like jigsaw pieces. Windows and other
openings admit light in very indirect and inven-
tive directions.

**Campo Volantin Footbridge**
(Bilbao, Spain) 1997
Santiago Calatrava
Curved, steel platform resembling a spine is
stayed by cables hung from a single, arching
steel pipe.

**Dominus Winery** (Yountville, CA) 1996–1998
Herzog and DeMueron
Napa Valley Wine storage and office building conceived as a single modern rectangular
volume that is built into the vineyards. The
glass surfaces are covered by gabions filled
with local stone of various sizes and tones that
create layers of transparency and provide delicate filtered light in parts of the building. Stone
"cladding" also helps modulate temperature in
the building.

**Landesgartenschau Pavilion**
(Weil-am-Rhein, Germany) 1996–1999
Zaha Hadid
An event and exposition garden that rises out of
the landscape as a series of interlocking pathways. Rooms are stretched along these interior
pathways allowing light to enter the underground spaces.

**Reichstag Cupola** (Berlin, Germany) 1999
Norman Foster
The renovation of the German Reichstag
included a new glass dome with an observation
within. Mirrored surfaces in the dome allow
visitors to look down into the legislative areas.

**Dutch Pavilion** (Hanover Expo) 2000
MVRDV
Dutch materials and new Dutch aesthetics combine to form a distilled and artificial landscape
of Holland that recalls historic land-making
projects in the country. Also an experiment in
how far model making as an architectural process can be taken.

**Sony Center** (Berlin, Germany) 2000
Helmut Jahn
Reinvigorating the Potsdamer Platz for a new
millennium, this collection of residential, commercial, and retail buildings are topped with a
dramatic glass and fabric umbrella structure.

**Experience Music Project**
(Seattle) 1995–2000
Frank Gehry
Dedicated to Jimi Hendrix and inspired by
forms such as the Stratocaster, this interactive
music museum features a distinct undulating
metal façade.

**Seattle Central Library** (Seattle) 2004
Rem Koolhaas
Contained in a latticed, glass façade, the stacks
of this library are situated on a continuous, spi-

raling four-story ramp. The startling novel form of the library is synonymous with its role as a container for new information and media.

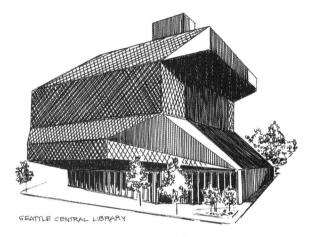

SEATTLE CENTRAL LIBRARY

**Figure A.13**

The following glossary defines a number of terms, many of which have appeared on past exams. While this list is by no means complete, it comprises much of the terminology with which candidates should be familiar. You are therefore encouraged to review these definitions as part of your preparation for the exam.

## A

**Abacus**   A plain square slab forming the topmost member of a capital.

**Acanthus**   A plant with thick, fleshy leaves used as a model for carved ornament on Corinthian capitals.

**Acropolis**   A citadel in an ancient Greek city, usually on a high plateau.

**Aesthetics**   The study of what is beautiful. In architecture, beauty as perceived by the senses and emotions.

**Agora**   An open-air market or meeting place in ancient Greece.

**Amphitheater**   An elliptical or circular space surrounded by rising tiers of seats, used by the Romans for gladiatorial contests.

**Apse**   A semicircular area at the east end of a church; originally contained an altar.

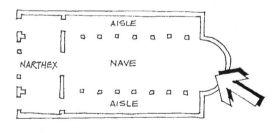

**Figure G.1**

**Apteral**   A Classical style building with columns on the end, but not on the sides.

**Aqueduct**   A structure, in the form of a channel or bridge, used by the Romans to transport water.

**Arabesque**   Surface decoration using intricate flowing lines and geometric patterns.

**Arcade**   A group of arches on columns or pillars, which are either freestanding or attached to a wall.

**Arch**   A curved structure composed of wedge-shaped elements, used to span an opening.

**Architrave**   The lowest member of the entablature, which extends from column to column.

**Arcuated**   Describing construction that uses arches.

**Astylar**   A term used to describe a facade without columns.

**Atrium**   An inner court open to the sky, but surrounded by a roof.

## B

**Baldacchino**   A freestanding canopy supported by columns symbolically sheltering an altar, throne, or tomb.

**Balloon Framing**   A method of wood framing construction that was developed in the mid-1880s.

**Baptistery**   A building used for baptismal services.

**Barrel Vault**   See **Tunnel Vault.**

**Base**   The lowest part of a structure.

**Basilica**   In Roman architecture, an oblong building used for public administration, from which early Christian churches evolved.

**Basket-Type Capital**   See **Cubiform.**

**Batter**   The inclined face of a wall.

**Bay**   The unit of space between the supporting columns of a building.

**Bema**   The raised stage used by the clergy in Early Christian churches.

**Boss**   An ornamental knob covering the intersection of ribs in a vault or ceiling.

**Bracket**   A small projecting member used to support a weight.

**Brise-Soleil**  A permanent sun shield covering the windows of a building.

**Buttress**  A mass of masonry built against a wall to provide additional strength.

# C

**Campanile**  The bell tower of a church, usually detached from the rest of the building.

**Capital**  The topmost feature of a column.

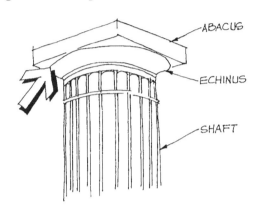

CAPITAL

**Figure G.2**

**Caryatid**  A sculptured human figure used as a column or support.

**Cella**  The main body of a Greek or Roman temple. See **Naos.**

**Centering**  The temporary scaffolding used to support an arch or vault.

**Chancel**  The eastern part of a church reserved for the choir and clergy.

**Chapel**  A separate place of worship in a church, usually in honor of a specific saint.

**Chateau**  A French country house or castle.

**Chevet**  The French term for the east end of a church containing the apse and ambulatory.

**Chicago Window**  A large horizontal window with a fixed center and openable sides.

**Ciborium**  See **Baldacchino.**

**Clerestory**  A portion of a building that rises above adjacent rooftops and has windows admitting daylight to the interior.

**Cloisters**  Roofed or vaulted passages connecting a church with the other parts of a monastery.

**Coffers**  Sunken or recessed square or octagonal panels of a ceiling.

**Colonnade**  A row of columns carrying an entablature or arches.

**Column**  A circular upright support, consisting of a base, shaft, and capital.

**Composite**  A Roman order whose capital combines Ionic and Corinthian elements.

**Corbel**  A small projecting element used for the support of horizontal members.

**Corinthian**  A Greek order having acanthus leaves on the capital.

**Cornice**  The topmost section of an entablature.

**Cortile**  A courtyard surrounded by arcades.

**Crenelation**  The notched battlement of a palace or fortification that shielded the warrior while allowing space for firing weapons.

CRENELATION

**Figure G.3**

**Crocket**  A decorative ornament projecting at regular intervals from the outer angles of spires and pinnacles.

**Cross Vault**  Two tunnel vaults that intersect at right angles. Also known as a Groined Vault.

**Cubiform**  In Byzantine architecture, a cubic form of column capital often carved in geometric patterns resembling basket weaving. Also known as a Basket-Type Capital.

**Cupola**  A small dome that crowns a structure.

**Crossing**  The space where the transept crosses the nave and chancel of a church.

**Cyclopean Masonry**  Rough, massive stones piled one upon another, used by the Greeks during the Aegean Period.

**D**

**Dentils**  Small square blocks used in Ionic and Corinthian cornices.

**Dipteros**  A building with a double row of columns on each side.

**Dome**  A vaulted structure with a circular plan.

**Doric**  The oldest and simplest of the classical orders of Greek architecture.

**Dosseret**  A block or slab set on top of a capital for additional support of the arch above.

**Figure G.4**

**Drum**  A cylindrical shell that supports a dome or cupola.

**Duomo**  An Italian cathedral.

**E**

**Echinus**  The curved moulding supporting the abacus in Doric capitals.

**Eclectic**  Describing architecture derived and assembled from various historic periods and styles.

**Engaged Column**  A column attached to, or partly built into, a wall or pier.

**Entablature**  The upper part of a Greek or Roman order, comprising architrave, frieze, and cornice.

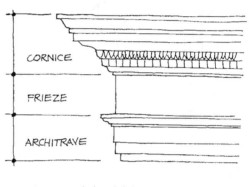

**Figure G.5**

**Entasis**  The swelling or outward curve of a column shaft, designed to counteract the optical illusion that would occur if the column were straight.

**Eye**  An opening at the apex of a dome that allows in light.

**F**

**Fan Vault**  Vaulting in which all the ribs radiate from one point, in the shape of a fan.

**Ferroconcrete**  Concrete reinforced with wire mesh.

**Finial**  The small, ornamental feature at the top of a pinnacle or gable.

**Flamboyant**  A late French Gothic term used to describe window tracery carved in the shape of flames.

**Flèche**   A slender spire rising from the ridge of a roof, often over the crossing.

**Flute**   The vertical grooving on the shaft of a column.

**Flying Buttress**   A stone arch that transmits the thrust of a vault or roof across the intervening space to a buttress.

**Forum**   In ancient Rome, a centrally located open space surrounded by a complex of public buildings.

**Frieze**   The part of the entablature between the architrave and the cornice.

**G**

**Gable**   The triangular portion of a wall at the end of a pitched roof.

**Gargoyle**   A projecting water spout, carved in the form of a grotesque figure, either human or animal.

**Greek Cross**   A cross with four arms of equal length.

**Greek Orders**   The three column types used in ancient Greek architecture. See **Doric, Ionic,** and **Corinthian.**

**Groin**   The curved edge formed by the intersection of two vaults or surfaces of a vault.

**Groined Vault**   See **Cross Vault.**

**H**

**Hypaethral**   Used to describe a building without a roof and open to the sky.

**Hypostyle**   A large space over which the roof is supported by massed rows of columns, as in the forest-like halls of Egyptian temples.

**Impluvium**   The rainwater basin in the center of an atrium in a Roman house.

**I–K**

**Ionic**   A Greek order which had a volute or scroll capital.

**Keystone**   The central stone of a rib vault or arch.

**L**

**Lantern**   A circular structure of open construction on the roof or dome of a building.

**Latin Cross**   A cross with a long nave and short crossing transepts.

**Lintel**   A structural member placed over an opening and supporting construction above.

**M**

**Machicolation**   A projecting parapet with floor openings through which boiling oil or stones were dropped on the enemy below.

MACHICOLATION
**Figure G.6**

**Mastaba**   An Egyptian tomb, built above ground, with sloping sides and a flat roof.

**Megalithic**   Describing great Neolithic stone structures, usually erected for religious or mystical purposes.

**Megaron**   The principal large hall in Mycenaean and Greek architecture.

**Modular**   Composed of standardized units or sections for easy construction or flexible arrangement.

**Modulor**   Le Corbusier's system of proportioning based on the male human body.

**Monolith**   A single block of stone, usually in the form of a column or monument.

**Mosaic**    Inlaid tile work of colored glass or marble used to ornament floors, walls, and vaults.

**Moulding**    A narrow projecting band of stone used on walls or columns.

**Mutule**    A projecting flat block above the triglyphs on the underside of a Doric cornice.

## N

**Naos**    The principal inner room of a Greek temple containing the statue of the deity.

**Narthex**    The open porch of a church or vestibule at the entrance end of a church.

**Nave**    The central portion of a church used by the congregation.

**Niche**    A recess set in a wall to hold a statue or decorative object.

## O

**Obelisk**    A tall, tapering shaft of stone, square in section and pyramidal on top.

OBELISK

**Figure G.7**

**Ogee**    A double curved shape made up of a convex and concave curve, applied to a molding or arch.

**Ogivale**    A term used to describe Gothic architecture in France.

**Order**    A classical column arrangement, including the base, shaft, and capital, which supports the entablature.

**Organic**    Describing architecture having direct form and economy of materials, as is common to natural organisms. Term used by Frank Lloyd Wright and followers.

## P

**Pediment**    The triangular gabled end of a temple roof above the entablature.

**Pendentive**    A spherical triangle by means of which a circular dome is supported over a square or polygonal compartment.

**Peripteral**    Descriptive of a building surrounded by a single row of columns.

**Peristyle**    An open space or a building surrounded by a range of columns and colonnade.

**Perspective**    A technique for drawing objects from the unique point of view of an individual, as they actually appear to the eye.

**Pier**    A solid masonry support, usually fatter than a column.

**Pilaster**    An engaged rectangular pillar projecting slightly from a wall.

**Pillar**    An upright structure of any shape used as a building support.

**Piloti**    The French term for a column that raises a building off the ground, as used by Le Corbusier.

**Pinnacle**    A spherical upright structure crowning a spire or buttress.

**Plinth**    A flat slab member beneath the base of a column, or the projecting base of a building.

**Podium**    A continuous low wall that forms a base for the construction above.

**Pointed Arch**    An arch with a pointed crown used to span a rectangular or square bay.

**Portico**   A structure covered by a roof and supported by columns on at least one side, usually attached to a building as an entrance porch.

**Pronaos**   An open vestibule at the front of a temple, enclosed by side walls, with columns in front.

**Pylon**   A masonry tower with a central opening, forming the entrance to an ancient Egyptian temple.

# Q

**Quadripartite Vault**   A rib vault divided into four compartments.

**Quoins**   Corner stones used at the exterior angles of buildings to visually indicate strength.

QUOINS

**Figure G.8**

# R

**Rib**   A projecting structural member used to carry the infilled panels of a vault.

**Rococo**   A style that evolved from the Baroque, using various materials to achieve a lavish, ornamental effect.

**Roman Orders**   The column types developed in Rome, based on the Greek orders. See **Tuscan and Composite.**

**Rose Window**   A round window in a Gothic church, usually of stained glass, whose mullions converge like wheel spokes. Also known as a Wheel Window.

**Rustication**   A form of masonry in which roughened blocks are separated from each other by recessed joints giving a rich and contrasting texture to an exterior wall.

# S

**Semicircular Vault**   See **Tunnel Vault.**

**Sexpartite Vault**   A vault containing six compartments.

**Shaft**   The part of a column between the base and the capital.

**Skyscraper**   A tall building with many stories, generally supported by a steel or concrete framework.

**Soffit**   The underside of a building element.

**Spandrel**   The triangular space between the curves of adjacent arches.

SPANDREL

**Figure G.9**

**Sphinx**   A figure with the body of a lion and the head of a man, ram, or hawk.

**Spire**   A tall tapering structure rising from a tower or roof and ending in a point.

**Squinch**   The corner filler of masonry placed diagonally at the interior angle of a square structure to make the upper space an octagon.

**Stoa**   A detached portico used as a meeting place.

**Stylobate**   The masonry base on which a colonnade is placed.

## T

**Tessera** The small pieces of glass, stone, or marble use in mosaics.

**Thermae** Roman public baths; the principal bathing rooms were the calidarium (hot), tepidarium (warm), and frigidarium (cool).

**Tholos** A circular domed building.

**Trabeated** Describing construction employing the post-and-beam form.

**Tracery** The delicate ornamental work forming the upper part of a Gothic window.

**Transept** The transverse part of a cruciform church at right angles to the main axis of the church.

**Triforium** The space in a church that is open to the nave and falls between the sloping roof over the aisle and the aisle vaulting.

**Triglyphs** Vertically grooved blocks, separated by metopes, which form a distinguishing feature in a Doric frieze.

**Triumphal Arch** A monument designed as an arch.

**Tunnel Vault** The simplest form of vault, having the form of a very deep arch. Also known as a Barrel, Wagon, or Semicircular Vault.

**Tuscan** One of the Roman orders, which was a simplified version of the Greek Doric order.

**Tympanum** The triangular surface bounded by the sloping and horizontal cornices of a pediment. Also, the area between the lintel of a doorway and the arch above it.

## V

**Vault** An arched structure, usually made of stone or brick, forming a ceiling over a building.

**Vestibule** A passage or anteroom between the outer door and the interior parts of a building.

**Viaduct** A bridge for carrying a road over a valley, usually consisting of several arched spans.

**Volute** The spiral scroll of an Ionic or Corinthian capital.

**Figure G.10**

**Voussoirs** Wedge-shaped blocks used to form an arch or vault.

## W

**Wagon Vault** See **Tunnel Vault.**

**Westwork** The monumental western front of a Romanesque church.

**Wheel Window** See **Rose Window.**

## Z

**Ziggurat** A mud-brick stepped pyramid in Mesopotamian sacred architecture.

# BIBLIOGRAPHY

The following list of books is provided for candidates who may wish to do further research or study in architectural history. Most of the books listed below are available in college or technical bookstores, and all would make welcome additions to any architectural bookshelf. In addition to the course material and the volumes listed below, we advise candidates to review regularly the many professional journals, which are available at most architectural offices.

*A History of Architectural Styles*
Baumgart
Praeger

*The Architecture of America*
Burchard & Bush-Brown
Atlantic-Little, Brown

*A Concise History of Western Architecture*
Jordan
Harcourt, Brace, Jovanovich

*A History of Architecture on the Comparative Method*
Fletcher
Batsford

*American Architecture & Urbanism*
Scully
Praeger

*Architects on Architecture*
Heyer
Walker & Co.

*Encyclopedia of Modern Architecture*
Hatje (Editor)
Abrams

*Macmillan Encyclopedia of Architects*
Placzek (Editor)
The Free Press

*Modern Architecture*
Scully
Braziller

*Pioneers of Modern Design*
Pevsner
Penguin Books

*Space, Time, and Architecture*
Giedion
Harvard Press

*The Architecture Book*
White
Knopf

## Lesson One

**1. D**  During the *Paleolithic Age*, approximately 25,000 years ago, man did not know how to domesticate animals or cultivate crops. In order to survive, he followed the wild herds and searched for edible plants (D is correct; A, B, and C are incorrect). Once man learned to produce and store food during the *Neolithic Age*, he was able to settle, and civilization began to develop.

**2. C**  Egyptian religion focused on the afterlife and affected every aspect of Egyptian life, including architecture. Early in their history, the Egyptians found a symbolic architectural expression of an eternal order that so satisfied them that they believed any change to it would be harmful. Consequently, originality and imagination were suppressed (II). Also, because of the emphasis on eternity in religion and the use of stone, Egyptian temples and tombs were large, permanent buildings. The pyramidal form, for example, was overpowering, conveying the idea of authority and eternity, certainly not delicacy (VI). Remember, this question asks for the terms which do NOT apply to Egyptian architecture. The terms enduring (I), simple (III), symbolic (IV), and uniform (V) accurately describe the style, while imaginative (II) and delicate (VI) do not. Therefore, the correct answer is C.

**3. C**  The *Rock-Cut Temples* at Abu Simbel include enormous statues of Rameses II at the entrance (correct answer C). It was not one of the temples built during the Ptolemaic (Greek) period (A is incorrect), and it was not at the foot of steep, stone cliffs, as was the Temple of Queen Hatshepsut (B is incorrect). Tombs, not temples, contained funerary treasures (D is incorrect).

**4. B**  The *ziggurat* was a prominent tower consisting of seven layers, each representing a heavenly planet (A). It was high in order to be closer to heaven (C), so that the astrologer-priests could better use it (D). However, the ziggurat was built for astrological purposes, and not for divine worship (B is the incorrect answer we are seeking).

**5. A**  Egyptian temples were arranged about an axis (I), generally had battered walls (II), and had clerestory light in the hypostyle hall (IV). Because the stone lintels could not span a great distance, columns were closely spaced and generously proportioned (III is incorrect). Also, because of the desert heat and glare, as well as sandstorms, windows were virtually nonexistent (V is incorrect). Therefore, A is the correct answer.

**6. D**  *Megalithic* (stone) structures were usually erected for religious or mystical purposes (correct answer D). Some, such as *Stonehenge*, were designed geometrically with an inner and outer circle, with the upright stone monoliths evenly spaced (B is incorrect). Although we do not know much about these structures, we do have some basic facts, such as the type and origin of the stone used (A is incorrect). In addition, there is no evidence that armies of slaves erected these structures (C is incorrect).

**7. B**  Because Egyptian religion emphasized eternity, it was important to preserve the bodies of the dead for the afterlife. Therefore, mummification was developed (A), and tomb walls were covered with paintings and hieroglyphics describing the person, prayers, and scenes of food and drink (C). In addition, the tombs were impregnable (D). However, tombs and pyramids were located on the west bank of the Nile, not the east (B is the incorrect statement, and therefore the correct answer).

8. **D**  The availability of clay in the Middle East led to the development of the sun-dried brick and the widespread use of brick construction (D is correct). The area had no stone, so these civilizations did not have stone arches (C is incorrect), nor was the trabeated style used (B is incorrect). Although there is evidence to suggest that the Assyrians may have developed the dome, it was not a prominent architectural feature (A is incorrect).

9. **A**  All of the terms refer to Egyptian architecture, except ziggurat (A), which was Middle Eastern. An obelisk (B) was a stone monolith, a mastaba (C) was a tomb, and a pylon (D) was an element used in temple design.

10. **B**  Because stone was the primary material used in Egyptian temples, the trabeated style (post-and-beam) was the appropriate expression (correct answer B). The Egyptians knew other systems of construction (A is incorrect), as seen by the brick construction used in dwellings. And, although a flat-roofed expression may have been appropriate to the desert, it was more a consequence of the trabeated style than the cause of it (D is incorrect), nor was an arcuated expression unsuitable to the Egyptian climate (C is incorrect).

## Lesson Two

1. **B**  The geography of ancient Greece very much influenced the development of the Greek culture. The rugged peninsula, with its jagged bays and deep inlets, separated by mountains, encouraged the growth of individual city-states (answer C). The mountains also provided a great natural wealth of stone and fine-grained marbles (D). The mild weather encouraged outdoor activities, such as the religious rites held outside the temples (A). However, even though they were surrounded by water, the Greeks only used the sea to travel from city to city, thereby avoiding the mountains. They were not known for any great maritime ability (answer B is the incorrect answer).

2. **A**  An entablature is the upper part of a Greek or Roman order and consists of a cornice, frieze, and architrave (correct answer A). A capital is the topmost feature of a column (B is incorrect), a plinth is a flat slab member beneath the base of a column (C is incorrect), and a pedestal is construction upon which a column is elevated (D is incorrect).

3. **D**  The *Pantheon* is considered one of the great Roman structures: daring in design (A) and geometrically simple and perfect (C). Light was provided by an *eye* at the apex of the dome (B). However, 20-foot-thick walls were required to support and buttress the immense dome's weight and thrust. Therefore, D is incorrect and the answer to this question.

4. **C**  Greek temples used a post-and-beam style in stone, little advanced beyond the structure of *Stonehenge*, although the Greeks did have knowledge of the arch form (A and B are incorrect). Temples were

used as shrines, with rites held outside; therefore, the greatest refinements were on the exterior (D is incorrect, C is correct).

5. **A** Distinguishing features of the *Aegean* period include *cyclopean masonry* (III), *inverted tapered columns* (II), and *corbelled arches* (IV). The *elevated stylobate* (V) and the *surrounding peristyle* (I) both apply to the *Hellenic* temple (A is the correct answer).

6. **C** The Romans found concrete construction highly desirable for a number of reasons: it was easily handled by unskilled labor (A), the component raw materials were available throughout the Empire, allowing the Romans to use concrete almost everywhere (B), and with concrete construction, the Romans could span greater distances (D). Although concrete construction enabled the Romans to design buildings with arches, vaults, and domes, that was not the reason the Romans used concrete construction; it was simply an additional benefit. Therefore, C is the least important reason and the answer to this question.

7. **A** The Greek *Parthenon* is not to be confused with the Roman *Pantheon*. The Parthenon was not particularly efficient structurally (B is incorrect), it was built to house a shrine, not people (C is incorrect), and had little subsequent site planning influence, because its location on the Acropolis was so unique (D is incorrect). However, it is the most famous example of the perfected *Doric* order (A is correct).

8. **B** The Romans borrowed many Greek design features and then elaborated on them, such as creating additional orders and extending temple walls outward.

Consequently, Roman temples were significantly different from Greek temples (D is incorrect). All Roman temples were similar in plan and appearance, regardless of their location (C is incorrect). And because the Romans considered religion less important (A is incorrect), and often built temples within the *Forum*, they became an urban feature (B is the correct answer).

9. **A** The Roman *domus*, or home, combined Etruscan and Greek influences. The entrance led to an *atrium* (V), which was a central court open to the sky. In the center was an *impluvium* (I), which was a pool designed to collect rainwater. The private rooms were built at the back of the domus around a *peristyle* (II), which often contained a garden filled with fountains or sculpture. A *tepidarium* (IV), however, was one of the principal bathing rooms in a Roman bath. III is also incorrect: a *podium* added height to Roman temples, giving them the appearance of an urban monument. Therefore, the correct answer is A.

10. **B** The Romans made great use of arches, vaults, and domes. However, although the Romans had knowledge of concrete technology (A) and loved power and grandeur (C), they had a more practical reason for using an arcuated expression— they needed to shelter large crowds. The arcuated expression allowed vast, uninterrupted spaces (B is correct), since it eliminated the need for columns. The Romans readily accepted and exploited these forms (D is incorrect), which became the model for future architecture throughout Europe.

## Lesson Three

1. **C**  Although the Early Christian church wielded great influence, it did not yet own the extent of land it would have in later centuries (A is incorrect), and had not yet become a center for education and culture (B is incorrect). Though the Christian church became a ruling force after the Romans, it happened long after Constantine made Christianity the official religion of the Empire (D is incorrect). However, Christianity gained popular support and was able to unite disparate nations (C is correct).

2. **D**  *Pier buttresses*, placed at regular intervals at the external walls, served to support the vertical weight above (A is incorrect). *Flying buttresses* over the side aisles resisted, but did not reduce, the lateral thrust of the vaults (B is incorrect). *Triforium* spaces over the side aisles had no effect on lateral thrust (C is incorrect). However, the *pointed arch*, which was the great development of the *Gothic* period, exerted far less lateral thrust than the previous rounded arch (D is correct).

3. **A**  *Chartres Cathedral*, built in the 12th century, is known for its dissimilar western towers constructed hundreds of years apart (correct answer A).

4. **D**  The baptismal rite was the official initiation into the Christian church, as well as a precondition for resurrection after death. Therefore, *baptisteries* had great importance. They took the form of a centralized structure, either circular or octagonal in plan (A is correct). Since baptism symbolized the death of the old life and ways and a rebirth into the new faith, baptisteries had a theological association with thermae and tombs (B is correct). Also, since baptisms were performed only a few times each year, the buildings were usually large to accommodate the crowds (C is correct). Baptisteries evolved during the *Early Christian* period in Italy and remained a principal part of cathedral groups throughout the *Middle Ages* (D is the correct answer to this question).

5. **C**  Early Christian *basilican churches* were designed plainly and simply because of a scarcity of materials and labor (C is correct). After Constantine's conversion to Christianity, Christians no longer feared persecution (D is incorrect). And since many Christians were Roman converts, they knew of Roman construction techniques and often employed materials from Roman structures (B is incorrect). Finally, the Christian liturgy required visual and physical emphasis on the altar, which was located in a semicircular *apse* at the east end of the church (A is incorrect).

6. **D**  The structural innovations in *Gothic* structures encouraged aesthetic development and refinement. *Stone carving* (I), *wood carving* (II), *stained glass* (III), and *mosaics* (IV) filled the great churches. However, *portrait painting* (V) did not develop until the Renaissance period. Therefore, D is the correct answer.

7. **B**  *Romanesque* churches were solid and ponderous, but with developments in the *Gothic* period, churches became lightweight and skeletal (B is correct). A is incorrect, since it refers to *Early Christian* churches (horizontal) versus *Byzantine* (vertical). Traceried stained glass and rib vaulting were used in both Romanesque and Gothic design (C and D are incorrect).

8. **A**  A *pendentive* is a small triangular segment of a sphere that allows a dome to sit on an arrangement of square supports

(A is correct). Rectangular *domed basilicas* used a combination of domes and half domes (B is incorrect). Pendentives were not used to transfer a dome's thrust to pier buttresses below (C is incorrect). *Pointed arches*, not pendentives, resolved the problem of unequal vaulting arches over a rectangular bay (D is incorrect).

9. **C**   Medieval towns were generally built for easy defense (II), frequently developed around a new church (IV), and often ruled by the local bishop (V). They did not follow a strict geometric pattern (I is incorrect), which would have been difficult to defend. And there was rarely open space within city walls (III is incorrect). Therefore, C is the correct answer.

10. **B**   It was *French Gothic* cathedrals that tended to be tall and complex (A is incorrect). In addition, the French employed sophisticated vaulting and buttressing to achieve great heights (C and D are incorrect). *English Gothic* cathedrals tended to be more stately, longer, and lower than the French (B is correct).

## Lesson Four

1. **B**   The *Renaissance* originated in Italy for two main reasons. First, the Italians were constantly reminded of the past glories of the Roman Empire by the ancient Roman monuments that surrounded them (I). Second, the Gothic style had never truly taken hold in Italy as it had in other countries. Instead, the Italians clung to Roman traditions throughout the Middle Ages (IV). Although *humanism* developed in Italy, the philosophy did not emphasize pleasure-seeking; it emphasized the importance of the individual and stressed earthly fulfillment (II is incorrect). Also, religion had exerted a great influence during the previous *Age of Faith*, as

witnessed by the number of cathedrals and churches built at that time (III is incorrect). Finally, the printing press was developed in Germany by Johann Gutenburg (V is incorrect). Therefore, B is the correct answer.

2. **D**   Because of the distance, Italian artists did not venture to England (A is incorrect). Once exposed, the English quickly accepted the style, as it coincided with the end of church domination in England and the new search for a rich and free life (B is incorrect). Because of its distance from Italy, England was the last European nation to embrace *Renaissance* architecture. However, it was the classic details, not the Baroque, that were embraced (C is incorrect). However, the English were motivated by published volumes from Italy and the works of individual architects (D is correct).

3. **B**   The church described is *St. Paul's Cathedral* in London (B is correct). *St. Peter's* (A) had a *Greek cross* plan. *Santa Maria della Salute* (C) was octagonal in plan. *Church of the Invalides* (D) had a Greek cross plan within a square.

4. **C**   *Palladio* is considered to be the greatest architect of the *Late Renaissance*. However, his fame was not based on any time spent in the court of Louis XIV (A is incorrect) or on his refined structures in Vicenza (B is incorrect). His style was personal and often deviated from strict classic form (D is incorrect). His fame was mainly due to his book on the architecture of classic, ancient Rome (C is correct). Once his book was published in every country in Europe, it became essential reading for architects, ultimately having more influence than his buildings.

5. **A**   The *Renaissance* was a rebirth of the classic culture of Rome (I). With the development of *humanism* came a new awareness of the individual (IV), as well as a more worldly point of view (V). The Renaissance was not concerned with developing new building methods (II is incorrect), since it was believed that the ancients did things as well as they could be done. Consequently, Renaissance architecture did not embrace evolutionary progress (III is incorrect). A is the correct answer.

6. **D**   Started in 1540, *St. Peter's* in Rome was an enormous project, which took 110 years to complete. By the time it was finished, it was different from *Bramante's* original plan, which was a *Greek cross* plan with a Pantheon-sized dome (A is incorrect). Bramante's design stressed verticality, as opposed to the basilican horizontality of the first St. Peter's church (C is incorrect). By the time the foundation was laid, both Bramante and Pope Julius II were dead, and *Michelangelo* did not begin work on it until 1546. When he did start, Michelangelo simplified the interior and increased the dome size (B is incorrect). After 13 architects and 20 popes had finished designing and redesigning St. Peter's, the result was an immense and imposing church (D is correct).

7. **C**   The four architects came from different backgrounds: *Bruant* was French; *Bramante, Borromini*, and *Brunelleschi* were Italian (A is incorrect). Not all were originally trained as painters and sculptors (B is incorrect). And each represented a different part of the Renaissance movement: Bramante—*High Renaissance*, Borromini—*High Baroque*, Brunelleschi—*Early Renaissance*, Bruant—*Baroque/Neo-Classicism* (D is incorrect). However, each did produce important domed structures: Bramante—*Tempietto*, Borromini—*S. Carlo alle Quattro Fontane*, Brunelleschi—*Dome of the Florence Cathedral,* Bruant—*Church of the Invalides* (C is correct).

8. **B**   Curved flowing lines and complete artistic freedom were aspects of the *Baroque style* (A and C are incorrect). Unlike previous styles, the *Renaissance* did not produce any sophisticated structural concepts (D is incorrect). The architecture of the Early Renaissance was characterized, however, by symmetrical compositions with axial lines as the guide (B is correct).

9. **A**   Early Renaissance architects had no interest in the techniques of Medieval architects; they did not use ribbed vaulting or pointed arches (III and IV are incorrect). Instead, they used semicircular vaults (I), domes on pendentives (II), and classic Roman orders (V). Therefore, A is the correct answer.

10. **C**   The *Florence Cathedral* was originally a Gothic structure. However, *Brunelleschi* designed a dome that was placed on a drum with windows and crowned with a lantern, which was to become the standard for Renaissance domes (A, B, and D are correct). However, the slightly pointed shape did not become the standard for subsequent domes, as Renaissance architects preferred the classic rounded dome (C is the answer to this question).

## Lesson Five

1. **A**   Originally, the *Industrial Revolution* was meant to provide an abundance of inexpensive goods that would help improve the quality of life (D). However, factories actually contributed to a decline in the quality of life, with inhuman conditions, long hours, no job security, and no labor representation (C). Many of the workers

came from the peasantry, who moved from the country to industrialized centers (B). The Industrial Revolution traded *unregulated* craftsmanship for *regulated* manual labor, not the other way around (A is the correct answer).

2. **B**  Gaudí and Horta used flexible, free-flowing forms (I and III), Adam was a true Palladian (II is incorrect), and Nash laid out the great parks of London's West End (IV is incorrect).

3. **C**  The *Renaissance*, which preceded *Neo-Classicism,* lost its impetus when all architectural expression seemed to be further elaboration of the same styles (A), and the rules of *Palladio* no longer produced satisfying work (B). The rediscovery of ancient Greek monuments made architects realize that the prototypes of classical architecture had represented only a narrow view of classical civilizations (D). Neo-Classicism was not a natural outgrowth of the Renaissance; rather, it was predicated on ancient classical architecture, including Greek and Egyptian, and was judged on archeological accuracy (C is the correct answer).

4. **D**  *Romanticism* moved beyond *Neo-Classicism* by expressing men's dreams and fantasies. Good design was no longer sufficient, as picturesqueness (I), nostalgia (II), charm (IV), and historical association (V) all became more desirable. Formality (III), however, was not a necessary quality, since rigid compositions conflicted with the romantic nature of the period. Therefore, D is correct.

5. **B**  *Art Nouveau* was an attempt to break from the eclectic tidal wave of *Historicism* which included styles borrowed from all previous historical periods (III). The style found expression through the sensuous curves of natural forms (IV). However, the movement was merely a protest against historical allusion and was obsolete by World War I (V). Although Art Nouveau was prevalent in the decorative arts, it began in the applied arts and proliferated throughout Europe (I and II are incorrect). B is the correct answer.

6. **A**  Most 19th century architects believed that the use of iron in construction was inappropriate, since iron members had no precedent in historical architecture (A is correct). Not only did architects have an engineering knowledge of metal structures, but they believed that they could create art with any available material, not just masonry (B and D are incorrect). *John Ruskin, William Morris,* and *Viollet-le-Duc* were associated with the *Arts and Crafts* movement, which generally had a negative opinion about iron construction (C is incorrect).

7. **D**  The *Crystal Palace*, designed by *Joseph Paxton* to house the Great Exhibition of 1851 in London (V), was a masterpiece of standardization (I) with cast iron members and glass panels prefabricated in a matter of months. Because it was standardized, the Palace only took another three months to erect (II). The building was an immediate success and brought Paxton worldwide fame (III is incorrect). Paxton's design employed new technology but omitted all references to past styles (IV is incorrect). D is the correct answer.

8. **C**  The architecture of the *Historicism* movement combined details from all past styles in a haphazard and indiscriminate way, which was consequently described as *a collapse of taste* (C is correct). It was not considered *imaginative* or *creative* (B is incorrect). *Soaring and spiritual* describes

*Gothic* architecture, while *free-flowing and natural* describes *Art Nouveau* (A and D are incorrect).

9. **C**    The *Arts and Crafts* movement was based on the preachings and influence of *John Ruskin* and *William Morris* (B), who hoped for a rejuvenation of art by returning to medieval craftsmanship (A). The emphasis on basic form, sound materials, and good craftsmanship anticipated the *Modern* movement by at least 50 years (D). However, Morris did not believe that good craftsmanship could be produced with industrial tools (C is the answer to this question).

10. **A**    *Paxton, Roebling*, and *Eiffel* created a new technological aesthetic through the use of iron, during an otherwise eclectic period (A is correct). They did not follow the rules of Palladio (B is incorrect), and it took several decades for their designs to reconcile engineering and architecture (D is incorrect). The *Crystal Palace* (Paxton) and *Brooklyn Bridge* (Roebling) were accepted and celebrated almost immediately. The *Eiffel Tower* (Eiffel), however, met great resistance at first and became popular some time after its completion (C is incorrect).

## Lesson Six

1. **B**    After experiencing the New England winters, the colonists began modifying the Elizabethan design they had used for their homes. Rooms were oriented to the huge, central chimney (I), small windows were placed wherever light was needed (IV), and the house had a steep gabled roof (II). The rooms had low ceilings to keep heat in (III is incorrect), and balloon framing was not developed until the mid-1880s (V is incorrect). Therefore, B is the correct answer.

2. **D**    The Bank of Pennsylvania in Philadelphia (designed by Latrobe), the Boston State House (designed by Bulfinch), and the White House (designed by Hoban) were all neo-classic in style (A, B, and C). Only choice D, Trinity Church in New York, designed by Upjohn, was Gothic Revival in style, and it became influential in church architecture in the early years of this country.

3. **A**    The uniform style of the World's Columbian Exposition of 1893 was dictated by *Charles McKim,* who was under the influence of the Ecole des Beaux-Arts. The style became known as *Modernized Classic,* but was actually a *Neo-Baroque* expression (A is correct). Although the chief architect was *Daniel Burnham* of the *Chicago School* (B is incorrect), he was overshadowed by McKim. Although the Fair was a great success, it virtually put an end to the developments of the Chicago School, which had preceded it (C is incorrect). The one unique building was the *Transportation Building* by *Sullivan*, which was completely original and not influenced by the classics (D is incorrect).

4. **C**    The Great Fire of 1871 destroyed large areas of Chicago, which gave the talented architects in the city the opportunity to build (C is correct). Although skyscrapers do utilize expensive land economically, that would not account for their initial development in Chicago, since land in New York was more expensive (A is incorrect). The development of the steel frame made skyscrapers possible, but where the steel was manufactured had little to do with determining where skyscrapers were developed (B is incorrect). Finally, Chicago had become a key city along the east-west commercial axis of New York and San

Francisco, but it was not the commercial center of the United States (D is incorrect).

5. **D**    Knowing of Thomas Jefferson's strong affinity for Roman architecture, we can assume that he would most likely be attracted to an ancient Roman structure, such as the *Temple of Vesta* (D is correct). The *Erectheion* was a Greek temple (C is incorrect). The *Boston State House* by *Bulfinch* was an 18th-century *American* building (B is incorrect). Finally, the *Pantheon of Soufflot*, not to be confused with the *Pantheon* in Rome, was an 18th-century *French* building (A is incorrect).

6. **B**    The *Boston Public Library* was the work of *McKim, Mead, and White* and was influenced by fashionable Roman classics (A is incorrect). The *Trinity Church* in New York was built by the Gothic champion *Richard Upjohn* (C is incorrect). The *Marshall Field Warehouse* was built by *Richardson*, but it was a departure from his previous Romanesque work (D is incorrect). *Trinity Church* in Boston, by Richardson, displays his skillful handling of rugged masonry and his powerful sense of composition, giving rise to the term *Richardson Romanesque* (B is correct).

7. **D**    *Balloon framing* was an outgrowth of a technological revolution in the building industry (D is correct), which resulted in thin, easily transported studs and joists that could be fastened with machine-made nails. Although the invention of the elevator and development of the steel frame were important advancements, they applied to tall buildings and were unrelated to balloon framing (A and B are incorrect). Finally, the progressive work of *Louis Sullivan* had nothing to do with the development of balloon framing (C is incorrect).

8. **A**    The first American colonists built structures that were a precise reflection of those they had known in England (A is correct). They did not adapt anything from the Native American culture (B is incorrect), and they imported all the supplies for their homes directly from England (C is incorrect). The American Georgian style did not appear until the 18th century (D is incorrect).

9. **C**    *Burnham and Root, Holabird and Roche*, and *Adler and Sullivan* were all associated with the *Chicago School* (A, B, and D). *McKim, Mead, and White* were associated with *Academicism* (C is the correct answer to this question).

10. **B**    The plan of Washington DC is a *Baroque* plan consisting of long axial avenues that radiate from various centers, with the *White House* and the *Capitol* as the major focal points. *Pierre Charles L'Enfant* created this plan under the influence of the plan of *Versailles*, which was filled with avenues, lakes, and gardens (B is correct). Haussmann directed the rebuilding of Paris in the 1850s and 1860s, long after L'Enfant was dead (A is incorrect). *Palladio* is regarded as the greatest architect of the Late Renaissance and one of the most influential figures in Western architecture, but he did not influence L'Enfant's plan (C is incorrect). Finally, the *Royal Circus* is an example of English urban row town-houses, and in no way an influence on L'Enfant (D is incorrect).

## Lesson Seven

1. **C**    The *Tribune Tower Competition* was held in Chicago, since that was the location of the company headquarters (A is incorrect). The styles of the designs ranged from *Eclectic* to *Modern*, with everything in between (B is incorrect). The winning

design, by *Hood and Howells,* was Eclectic and in the style then called *Woolworth Gothic* (D is incorrect). Although the progressive European entries did not win, they did exert a strong influence on tall buildings thereafter (C is correct).

2. **B**   *Breton brut*—crudely fabricated concrete work, *brise soleil*—permanent sun shields, and *pilotis*—stilts, were all architectural characteristics associated with *Le Corbusier* (B is correct). *Oscar Niemeyer* was the Brazilian architect who collaborated with Le Corbusier on the *Ministry of Health Building* in Rio de Janeiro, which first used brise soleil, but he was not associated with the other two characteristics. Neither Behrens (A) nor Breuer (D) was associated with the architectural characteristics in this question.

3. **A**   *Postmodernism* was an attempt to break free from *Modernism,* which was associated with austere formality (III) and rigid consistency (IV). Postmodern structures included a diversity of expression (I), the use of historical precedents (II), and freedom from dogma (V). Therefore, A is the correct answer.

4. **B**   The *Bauhaus* at Dessau was an attempt by *Walter Gropius* to unite art and technology in order to find a sound basis for modern design (B is correct). The Bauhaus building developed new space concepts, but that was not the ultimate purpose of the movement (C is incorrect). The Bauhaus also brought together 20th-century design ideas and disseminated these through a new educational system; however, this was more a by-product than its purpose (D is incorrect). Another by-product of the Bauhaus philosophy was the production of well-designed, hand-crafted products (A is incorrect).

5. **C**   *Rudolph Schindler, Louis Kahn, and Paul Rudolph* were all influenced by *Frank Lloyd Wright* (C is correct). Schindler and Kahn worked in California, but not Rudolph (A is incorrect). Also, Schindler was the only one of the three trained in central Europe (B is incorrect). Finally, none of the three were involved in *Eclecticism* (D is incorrect).

6. **D**   At the end of the 19th century, *Neo-Classicism* prevailed (A is correct), and the World's Columbian Exposition of 1893 fostered eclectic design (B is correct). As the technology improved, photography was used to supplement historical information previously obtained through drawings (C is correct). However, early 20th century Eclecticism differed from the previous style in that it encouraged creative adaptation of style, as opposed to outright mimicry (D is the correct answer to this question).

7. **D**   *Greene and Greene* were the California pioneers responsible for developing the *California Bungalow* style (D is correct). *Irving Gill* was known for his reinforced concrete construction (A is incorrect). *Richard Neutra* designed European modernist houses (B is incorrect), and *Frank Lloyd Wright* was associated with Usonian houses, but not with the California Bungalow (C is incorrect).

8. **A**   The *Ronchamp Chapel* (*Notre Dame du Haut*) by *Le Corbusier*, the *Dodge House* by *Irving Gill*, and the *Steiner House* by *Adolf Loos* all used reinforced concrete (B, C, and D are correct). The *Werkbund Model Factory* by *Walter Gropius* used masonry and glass (A is the correct answer to this question).

9. **D**  Throughout his career, two essential principles dominated the work of Walter Gropius: design through collaboration (I) and respect for industrialization (IV). Mies van der Rohe's work is more closely associated with order and precision (II is incorrect), and Frank Lloyd Wright was better known for his sensitivity to natural forms and materials (III is incorrect). The correct answer is D.

10. **B**  The *International Style* involved austere compositions, unadorned surfaces, and a clear distinction between solid and void (A is correct). The *CIAM* conferences, which were convened to discuss the state of international architecture and related political philosophies, agreed only on the general characteristics of the style (C is correct). *Henry-Russell Hitchcock* and *Philip Johnson* not only named the International Style with their book of the same name, but they brought attention to the new European work (D is correct). The new architectural expression influenced the design of tall buildings, urban design, domestic structures, and even furniture (B is the correct answer to this question).

# EXAMINATION DIRECTIONS

The examination on the following pages should be taken when you have completed your study of all the lessons in this course. It is designed to simulate the actual exam questions on

Architectural History that may appear in any of the multiple-choice divisions of the ARE. Many questions are intentionally difficult in order to reflect the pattern of questions you may expect to encounter on the actual examination.

You will also notice that the subject matter for several questions has not been covered in the course material. This situation is inevitable and, thus, should provide you with practice in making an educated guess. A few questions may appear ambiguous, trivial, or simply unfair. This too, unfortunately, reflects the actual experience of the exam and should prepare you for the worst you may encounter.

Answers and complete explanations will be found on the pages following the examination, to permit self-grading. **Do not look at these answers until you have completed the entire exam**. Once the examination is completed and graded, your weaknesses will be revealed, and you are urged to do further study in those areas.

Please observe the following directions:

1. The examination is closed book; do not use any reference material.

2. Allow about one hour to answer all questions. Time is definitely a factor to be seriously considered.

3. Read all questions *carefully* and mark the appropriate answer on the answer sheet provided.

4. Answer all questions, even if you must guess. Do not leave any question unanswered.

5. If time allows, review your answers, but do not arbitrarily change any answer.

6. Turn to the answers only after you have completed the entire examination.

GOOD LUCK!

# EXAM ANSWER SHEET

**Directions**: Read each question and its lettered answers. When you have decided which answer is correct, blacken the corresponding space on this sheet. After completing the exam, you may grade yourself; complete answers and explanations will be found on the pages following the examination.

1. Ⓐ Ⓑ Ⓒ Ⓓ
2. Ⓐ Ⓑ Ⓒ Ⓓ
3. Ⓐ Ⓑ Ⓒ Ⓓ
4. Ⓐ Ⓑ Ⓒ Ⓓ
5. Ⓐ Ⓑ Ⓒ Ⓓ
6. Ⓐ Ⓑ Ⓒ Ⓓ
7. Ⓐ Ⓑ Ⓒ Ⓓ
8. Ⓐ Ⓑ Ⓒ Ⓓ
9. Ⓐ Ⓑ Ⓒ Ⓓ
10. Ⓐ Ⓑ Ⓒ Ⓓ
11. Ⓐ Ⓑ Ⓒ Ⓓ
12. Ⓐ Ⓑ Ⓒ Ⓓ
13. Ⓐ Ⓑ Ⓒ Ⓓ
14. Ⓐ Ⓑ Ⓒ Ⓓ
15. Ⓐ Ⓑ Ⓒ Ⓓ
16. Ⓐ Ⓑ Ⓒ Ⓓ
17. Ⓐ Ⓑ Ⓒ Ⓓ
18. Ⓐ Ⓑ Ⓒ Ⓓ
19. Ⓐ Ⓑ Ⓒ Ⓓ
20. Ⓐ Ⓑ Ⓒ Ⓓ
21. Ⓐ Ⓑ Ⓒ Ⓓ
22. Ⓐ Ⓑ Ⓒ Ⓓ
23. Ⓐ Ⓑ Ⓒ Ⓓ
24. Ⓐ Ⓑ Ⓒ Ⓓ
25. Ⓐ Ⓑ Ⓒ Ⓓ

26. Ⓐ Ⓑ Ⓒ Ⓓ
27. Ⓐ Ⓑ Ⓒ Ⓓ
28. Ⓐ Ⓑ Ⓒ Ⓓ
29. Ⓐ Ⓑ Ⓒ Ⓓ
30. Ⓐ Ⓑ Ⓒ Ⓓ
31. Ⓐ Ⓑ Ⓒ Ⓓ
32. Ⓐ Ⓑ Ⓒ Ⓓ
33. Ⓐ Ⓑ Ⓒ Ⓓ
34. Ⓐ Ⓑ Ⓒ Ⓓ
35. Ⓐ Ⓑ Ⓒ Ⓓ
36. Ⓐ Ⓑ Ⓒ Ⓓ
37. Ⓐ Ⓑ Ⓒ Ⓓ
38. Ⓐ Ⓑ Ⓒ Ⓓ
39. Ⓐ Ⓑ Ⓒ Ⓓ
40. Ⓐ Ⓑ Ⓒ Ⓓ
41. Ⓐ Ⓑ Ⓒ Ⓓ
42. Ⓐ Ⓑ Ⓒ Ⓓ
43. Ⓐ Ⓑ Ⓒ Ⓓ
44. Ⓐ Ⓑ Ⓒ Ⓓ
45. Ⓐ Ⓑ Ⓒ Ⓓ
46. Ⓐ Ⓑ Ⓒ Ⓓ
47. Ⓐ Ⓑ Ⓒ Ⓓ
48. Ⓐ Ⓑ Ⓒ Ⓓ
49. Ⓐ Ⓑ Ⓒ Ⓓ
50. Ⓐ Ⓑ Ⓒ Ⓓ
51. Ⓐ Ⓑ Ⓒ Ⓓ

1. Throughout the history of architecture, builders have attempted to reach ever increasing heights with their structures. At one time or another, each of the following distinguished buildings was known as "the tallest building in the world," EXCEPT

   **A.** Marina City Towers.

   **B.** World Trade Center.

   **C.** Sears Tower.

   **D.** Empire State Building.

2. What was the principal difference between Latin cross and Greek cross churches?

   **A.** The treatment above the crossing

   **B.** The relationship between the nave and the transepts

   **C.** The size of the church in which each was used

   **D.** The geographic location where each was used

3. Regarding the Chicago Tribune Competition of 1922, Burchard and Brown said in *The Architecture of America:* "Wright and Sullivan and Root and Jenney might as well have never lived and worked in Chicago." What did they mean?

   **A.** None of these great architects chose to enter the international competition.

   **B.** None of these men, generally considered to be the finest and most respected architects in Chicago, was invited to serve on the competition jury.

   **C.** The submissions of these architects were scarcely considered and prematurely rejected due to the regressive nature of the jury.

   **D.** The winning submission totally ignored the lessons that might have been learned from the progressive work of these modern architects.

4. Which of the following descriptions could be applied to the German Pavilion for the Barcelona Exhibition designed in 1929 by Mies van der Rohe?

   **I.** Masterly spatial composition

   **II.** Immaculate use of lavish materials

   **III.** Superb solution to functional requirements

   **IV.** One of the most influential buildings of modern architecture

   **V.** Totally original in concept, arrangement, and form

   **A.** I, II, and IV

   **B.** I, III, and V

   **C.** II, III, IV, and V

   **D.** I, II, III, IV, and V

5. Which of the following statements concerning the terms *cupola* and *tholos* is correct?

   **A.** The terms may be used interchangeably, since both refer to domed structures.

   **B.** The terms actually have the same meaning, although cupola refers to Roman architecture and tholos to Greek.

   **C.** Cupola refers to a spherical roof, while tholos refers to a circular building.

   **D.** Cupola refers to a polygonal plan, and tholos to a circular plan.

6. J. M. Richards, R. Banham, V. Scully, and H. R. Hitchcock are all well known for their

   **A.** critical essays on the historic styles.

   **B.** perceptive writings on modern architecture.

   **C.** pioneering work in the field of urban planning.

   **D.** original theories in the field of modern design.

7. Henri Labrouste was the first architect to

    **A.** make cast iron architecturally acceptable in a monumental public building.

    **B.** introduce Neo-Baroque details to the existing Beaux Arts vernacular.

    **C.** introduce the Italian-inspired Beaux Arts style to France.

    **D.** use cast iron structurally.

8. Which of the following statements about Greek Revival architecture in the U.S. during the mid-19th century is correct?

    **A.** It was a logical expression of a new nation which longed for the classic symbols of imperialism, since American developments so closely paralleled those of the Greeks.

    **B.** It was largely based on American admiration for the Greek ideals of noble simplicity, classical refinement, and democratic culture.

    **C.** The style became so popular that entire structures were built as perfect copies, in every detail, of famous Greek buildings.

    **D.** Its chances for national popularity were doomed from the start, since many viewed the Greek forms as related to an ancient pagan civilization, rather than to a modern nation.

9. By the year 1900, the characteristics and behavior of reinforced concrete had been established. After 1925, during the period of the International Style, the use of reinforced concrete became widespread. However, between 1900 and 1925, several architects and engineers experimented with pioneering designs using reinforced concrete. Which of the following were among these avant garde designers?

    **I.** Robert Maillart

    **II.** Auguste Perret

    **III.** Tony Garnier

    **IV.** Walter Gropius

    **V.** Le Corbusier

    **A.** I and II

    **B.** I, III, and IV

    **C.** II, III, IV, and V

    **D.** I, II, III, IV, and V

10. Which of the following statements concerning mastabas is INCORRECT?

    **A.** The earliest mastabas were constructed of mud bricks, but were later built of stone.

    **B.** Mastabas were rectangular in plan and built with battered walls and flat roofs.

    **C.** Mastabas were contemporary with the great Egyptian pyramids, such as Cheops.

    **D.** Mastabas were ancient tombs constructed for the burial of all Egyptians other than the pharaohs.

11. St. Peter's in Rome and St. Paul's in London are considered to have two of the five greatest domes in the world. Which of the following does NOT belong in that group?

    A. Pantheon in Rome

    B. Paris Opera House

    C. Duomo in Florence

    D. Hagia Sophia in Byzantium

12. Starting about 1950, there was a popular urban trend to create high-rise office towers that were set back from the street in order to provide open plazas for pedestrian use. All of the following projects followed this popular trend EXCEPT

    A. Lever House.

    B. Ford Foundation Building.

    C. Seagram Building.

    D. John Hancock Building.

13. The ancient Greek and Roman civilizations contrasted with one another in several important ways, including which of the following?

    I.    The Greeks were primarily great engineers, whereas the Romans were prolific builders.

    II.   The Greeks regarded architecture as art, whereas the Romans regarded architecture primarily as structure.

    III.  The Greeks were an intellectual people, whereas the Romans were pragmatic.

    IV.   Greek temples were conceived as shrines, whereas Roman temples were visualized as monuments.

    V.    The Greeks employed lavish architectural ornament, while Roman structures exhibited utilitarian simplicity.

    A. I, II, and III     C. I, III, and V

    B. II, III, and IV     D. II, IV, and V

14. The Mannerist expression used classical elements in an arbitrary and occasionally illogical way to fulfill lofty objectives. One of the finest examples of this style was the

    A. Dome of Sta. Maria del Fiore.

    B. Palazzo Strozzi.

    C. Church of S. Carlo alle Quattro Fontane.

    D. Biblioteca Laurenziana.

15. Vallingby, Stevenage, and Saynatsalo had one thing in common: they were all

    A. pioneers in the use of reinforced concrete.

    B. located in Scandinavia.

    C. examples of new town plans.

    D. influential writers on the modern movement.

16. Nikolaus Pevsner, in his *Outline of European Architecture*, made the following statement: "A bicycle shed is a building; Lincoln Cathedral is a piece of architecture." What did Pevsner mean?

    A. In addition to enclosure, architecture, which is primarily spatial, requires a space that is purposefully shaped.

    B. The term architecture should be applied only to buildings designed with a view to aesthetic appeal.

    C. In addition to enclosing space, architecture must involve a human activity, the design for which is resolved in an architectural way.

    D. Architecture is a term applied only to structures which have a particular scale, dignity, and usefulness.

**17.** The Palace of Versailles represented an enormous, grand, and raw display of power. Some 25 years after its completion, a similar palace was designed in England by Sir John Vanbrugh for the Duke of Marlborough. The palace was known as

   **A.** Castle Howard.

   **B.** Banqueting House.

   **C.** Blenheim Palace.

   **D.** Wilton House.

**18.** One of the most characteristic details of Gothic architecture throughout Western Europe was the pointed arch. Which of the reasons listed below were among the most significant in the development and use of this singular feature?

   **I.** It was easier to construct than the semicircular arch.

   **II.** It allowed a rectangular bay to be vaulted with arches of equal height.

   **III.** It reduced the overall lateral thrust of the vaults.

   **IV.** It made possible greater heights, which was symbolic of the religious aspirations of the Middle Ages.

   **V.** Through its unique form, it expressed, in the most logical way, the use of small stones laid with thick mortar joints.

   **A.** I, II, and III    **C.** II, III, and IV

   **B.** I, III, and IV    **D.** II, IV, and V

**19.** The language of architecture is as specialized, and often as obscure, as the language used by doctors or attorneys. For example, what is the correct interpretation of the following phrase? "The trabeated system required supports that were borne by the stylobate and that exhibited a subtle entasis."

   **A.** Beams were supported by columns that rested on a stepped base and that had a slight outward curve.

   **B.** The structural system was borne by a foundation that had the effect of a solid platform.

   **C.** Posts and beams were supported by a slightly curved base.

   **D.** Tapered, outward curving columns supported beams or arches and rested on a podium-like base.

**20.** When Robert Venturi wrote, "Main Street is almost all right," he offended a considerable segment of the architectural community. The probable reason that Venturi's remark provoked this reaction was that

   **A.** most architects totally misunderstood Venturi's real meaning.

   **B.** most architects were offended by Venturi's assumption that ordinary design might be acceptable.

   **C.** billboards, parking lots, and electric signs had always been viewed as urban visual chaos.

   **D.** non-designed structures had always been considered inferior to and competitive with good architecture.

21. Which of the following statements concerning the use of stone in ancient Egypt is correct?

    A. Its popularity was largely the result of its permanence and impregnability.

    B. It was commonly employed in structures because it was the only natural building material readily available.

    C. Its widespread use led to the development of the earliest arcuated construction.

    D. Regardless of the project, it was employed in a consistent fashion: small dressed stones in a thick mortar bed.

22. Architects have always been limited by the epoch in which they lived. For example, the architectural arrangement of a dome on a drum could only have been employed by

    A. Vitruvius.

    B. Anthemius.

    C. Arnolfo di Cambio.

    D. Vignola.

23. Two respected historians, Sybil Maholy-Nagy and Bernard Rudofsky, wrote books dealing with *anonymous* architecture. The point of their books was that

    A. there is a great body of non-pedigreed architecture, created by untutored builders, about which we know little, but from which we might learn a great deal.

    B. there is a vast amount of minor work in the Western architectural tradition, but historians have ignored all but the conventional monuments.

    C. architectural examples produced by non-architects are frequently indistinguishable in most ways from historically acceptable examples.

    D. most urban dwellers have an unconscious desire to escape to primitive surroundings that provide a unique source of architectural inspiration.

24. Throughout the history of modern architecture, many architects have designed excellent furniture that was later commercially produced. In this regard, which of the following statements is INCORRECT?

    A. The Wassily chair was designed by Marcel Breuer.

    B. The Tulip pedestal chair was designed by Eero Saarinen.

    C. The Cantilevered chair was designed by Le Corbusier.

    D. The Brno chair was designed by Mies van der Rohe.

25. The vast structural concrete surfaces created by the ancient Romans were invariably covered by a wide variety of facing materials, such as stucco, brick, and marble. The principal reason for this was

    A. to keep available soldiers and slaves fully employed.

    B. to improve the durability of the concrete surfaces.

    C. because the use of raw concrete was simply unpopular.

    D. because the Romans possessed an abundance of fine veneering materials.

26. *Architect* is defined as *one who designs or creates buildings or is engaged in the profession of architecture.* The word is derived from the ancient Greek *architekton*, which means

    A. constructor of buildings.

    B. master of the noblest art.

    C. arch builder.

    D. chief builder.

**27.** Which of the following statements concerning the Monadnock Building is correct?

  **A.** It was the first steel-framed tall building of the famous Chicago School.

  **B.** It was the last great skyscraper designed by the firm of Adler and Sullivan.

  **C.** It was the ultimate expression of traditional masonry construction in Chicago.

  **D.** It was a highly derivative design, based largely on Gothic proportions and details.

**28.** All of the architects listed below have names beginning with B, and all were born in Italy. However, which architect is conspicuously out of place?

  **A.** Borromini          **C.** Bernini

  **B.** Belluschi          **D.** Brunelleschi

**29.** Which of the following statements concerning the Art Nouveau movement is INCORRECT?

  **A.** It was essentially an aesthetic undertaking, born out of a fear of increasing industrialization.

  **B.** It was an attempt to integrate art with social life through renewed contact with nature.

  **C.** It was a decorative expression employing curved forms that were probably floral in origin.

  **D.** It was an anti-historical movement having little influence on design outside of Belgium, where it originated.

**30.** The Villa Savoye, Unité d'Habitation, and Pavillon Suisse all have which of the following in common?

  **I.**   France—their country of origin

  **II.**  Marcel Breuer—their architect

  **III.** Reinforced concrete—their principal structural material

  **IV.**  Modern country homes—their primary function

  **V.**   Pilotis—their system of support

  **A.** I, II, and III          **C.** I, II, and IV

  **B.** I, III, and V          **D.** III, IV, and V

**31.** Throughout the history of architecture, the greatest monuments were created

  **A.** in support of a strong common belief, which was often religious.

  **B.** when the people were unified by a single powerful ruler.

  **C.** at a time when artists were in rebellion against society.

  **D.** as the result of an authoritarian society with a large slave population.

**32.** The styles in which H. H. Richardson and McKim, Mead, and White worked were respectively

  **A.** Roman and Classical.

  **B.** Modern Industrial and Roman.

  **C.** Romanesque and Italian Renaissance.

  **D.** Gothic and Romanesque.

**33.** When the Yale Art and Architecture Building was completed by Paul Rudolph in 1963, it created a great deal of interest and excitement. The building was analyzed and reviewed by virtually every major critic in the country, and direct influence for the provocative design was ascribed to several other architects, including

**I.**   Walter Gropius.

**II.**  Louis Kahn.

**III.** Le Corbusier.

**IV.**  Frank Lloyd Wright.

**V.**   Mies van der Rohe.

**A.** I, II, and III          **C.** II, III, and IV

**B.** I, III, and IV         **D.** II, IV, and V

**34.** Concerning the Renaissance style of architecture in Italy, which of the following statements is INCORRECT?

**A.** The earliest achievements of the Renaissance were virtually a Roman Revival, and complete Roman models proliferated throughout the Tuscany landscape.

**B.** Regardless of the number of churches that were built in 15th-century Italy, Renaissance architecture was primarily an expression of the mercantile and royal establishments.

**C.** The Renaissance was born in Italy because that country had known so little of the Gothic glories, but remembered so vividly the glories of the Roman Empire.

**D.** During the Renaissance, buildings became distinct aesthetic phenomena, and architects, who during the Gothic period were primarily craftsmen, now became artists.

**35.** Much has been written about the Modulor, which was developed by Le Corbusier. It was a system

**A.** that employed a related series of proportional dimensions.

**B.** that employed a basic module of 10 centimeters (about 4 inches).

**C.** that employed standardized building components.

**D.** of proportional dimensions based on da Vinci's human figure.

**36.** The following quotation comes from Sir Bannister Fletcher: "We next see Europe rising like a strong man from the lethargy of a long sleep. He yawns, rubs his eyes, stretches his giant limbs, and stumbles to his feet to look out again upon the workaday world and the treasures scattered around. He finds himself surrounded by the achievements of a proud past, and as he becomes conscious of his own needs he realizes the possibilities of the present. Then with dazed eyes and groping hands he collects these treasures of art and applies them to his daily needs." In this colorful passage, Fletcher was referring to the

**A.** beginning of Renaissance architecture.

**B.** origins of Early Christian architecture.

**C.** creation of Etruscan architecture.

**D.** birth of Romanesque architecture.

37. Which of the following statements concerning various architectural features in specific historical periods is INCORRECT?

    A. A triglyph formed part of a Greek Doric frieze.

    B. Pendentives were spherical triangles used by Byzantine architects to adapt a circular dome to a square base.

    C. A cella was the main body of a Greek or Roman temple.

    D. Quoins were projecting blocks of stone carved with foliage and used decoratively on Gothic church spires.

38. After the first harsh winter, the early American colonists emerged from their temporary shelters to build permanent dwellings. These new structures were largely influenced by which of the following?

    A. Native American architecture

    B. Dutch Colonial architecture

    C. French Gothic architecture

    D. English Medieval architecture

39. From the decline of the Roman civilization to the beginning of Rome's rebirth in the Renaissance, the majority of new communities were planned and most often situated

    A. adjacent to rivers, streams, or large bodies of fresh water.

    B. in a secure, easily defensible, and frequently radiocentric arrangement.

    C. in a pattern that permitted religious or military processions on a grand scale.

    D. in a geometrically logical form that permitted long, interesting vistas.

40. Which of the following statements concerning Byzantine architecture is INCORRECT?

    A. The overwhelming planning and structural problems of the Byzantine architects was that of building circular domes over square or polygonal spaces; this was ultimately solved by the development and common use of pendentives.

    B. Although Byzantine decoration generally involved marble panels on the flat surfaces, glass mosaics were employed on the curved surfaces, since the small tessera could form a continuous covering running from one irregularly shaped surface to another.

    C. Columns in Byzantine structures were generally subordinate to massive piers and bearing walls; however, when they did appear, they invariably followed the conventional designs of the original Roman orders.

    D. The Byzantine domed bay was somewhat comparable to the Gothic vaulted bay in that a series of bays could be placed alongside one another, producing a more extended plan or even a crossed plan.

41. Throughout history, the design of certain architectural monuments has been enhanced by their dramatic siting near water. Among the following buildings, which had this relationship?

    I.   Chandigarh High Court Building

    II.  Chateau de Chenonceau

    III. Hagia Sophia

    IV.  Unité d'Habitation

    V.   Kaufmann House

    A. I, II, and III        C. II, IV, and V

    B. I, II, and V          D. III, IV, and V

**42.** During the Middle Ages, fortified structures were often built with distinctive architectural elements intended for defense. For example, parapets along the tops of buildings were frequently notched to provide protection for warriors, while allowing space for their weapons. Another device was the projecting parapet with floor openings through which boiling oil or molten lead could be poured on the enemy below. Which of the following terms represent these features, in the same order as described?

A. Trabeations and turrets

B. Machicolations and battlements

C. Rustications and turrets

D. Crenelations and machicolations

**43.** Consider the following statement:

*Pre-industrialized society found its artistic inspiration in the natural or spiritual world, whereas our society found its stimulus in a scientific-mechanical one. In America, mechanization has been encouraged, and with mechanization have come many forceful ideas that have changed our way of regarding and responding to things. For example, the idea that there is some virtue in exposing the elements of structure is comparatively recent. Previous historical periods were actually quite equivocal about it.*

This statement is

A. generally true.

B. generally true up to the time of the Renaissance.

C. generally true, with the exception of the Gothic period.

D. merely a personal opinion having little basis in historical fact.

**44.** In recent years an increasingly larger proportion of a building's volume, as well as its budget, has been devoted to mechanical services, which has led architects to express this phenomenon architecturally. The earliest major structure which helped establish this trend was the

A. Ford Foundation Building by Roche.

B. Air Force Academy by SOM.

C. Place Beaubourg by Piano & Rogers.

D. Richards Laboratories Building by Kahn.

**45.** It has been said that throughout history, architecture has provided a key to the habits, thoughts, and aspirations of the people for whom it was intended, and, moreover, has reflected the dominant concerns of civilization. In this regard, which of the following is INCORRECTLY matched with the dominant concern of the time?

A. Middle Ages—religion

B. Ancient Greece—beauty

C. Ancient Rome—mysticism

D. Renaissance—learning

**46.** Which of the pioneers of modern architecture said the following: "…the creative spark originates always with the individual, but by working in close collaboration with others toward a common aim, he will attain greater heights of achievement through the stimulation and challenging critiques of his teammates, than by living in an ivory tower"?

A. Mies van der Rohe

B. Walter Gropius

C. Marcel Breuer

D. Le Corbusier

**47.** At the beginning of the 20th century, several architects came to California and developed a distinct expression that had great influence in later years. Both the Southern California style and the Bay Area style were rare examples of regionalism in America. Which of the following were involved in this early California work?

**I.**    Bernard Maybeck

**II.**   Adolf Loos

**III.**  Rudolph Schindler

**IV.**  Ernest Kump

**V.**   Irving Gill

**A.** I, III, and V          **C.** II, IV, and V

**B.** I, II, and III         **D.** I, III, IV, and V

**48.** Which of the following statements concerning Early Christian architecture is INCORRECT?

**A.** The basilican plan, as adapted from ancient Rome, consisted of little more than a nave, aisles, and an apse.

**B.** The Early Christians never considered using the Roman temple form, since temples were denounced as places of idolatry.

**C.** The basilican church always employed closely spaced columns carrying entablatures, because the method of constructing arches was lost after the fall of the Roman Empire.

**D.** Early Christians rarely attempted structural innovations, since they relied on ancient Roman methods and, in many cases, actual elements from Roman buildings.

**49.** After the First World War, there was a conservative period in American architecture that was apparent in commemorative monuments. For example, in the Lincoln Memorial in Washington DC, designed by Henry Bacon in 1923, the classical inspiration was a(n)

**A.** Hellenic temple.

**B.** Aegean agora.

**C.** Corinthian monument.

**D.** Greek propylaea.

**50.** The history of modern architecture is replete with sayings that have been attributed to various famous architects. In this question, which of the following phrases is matched INCORRECTLY?

**A.** A house is a machine for living—Le Corbusier.

**B.** Art and technology—the new unity—Louis Sullivan.

**C.** Less is more—Ludwig Mies van der Rohe.

**D.** Ask the space what it wants to be—Louis Kahn.

**51.** Sustainable Design is primarily concerned with the following issues?

**I.**    Economics

**II.**   Aesthetics

**III.**  Environment

**IV.**  Mechanical systems

**A.** III

**B.** I, II, III

**C.** I, III

**D.** All of the above

The examination answers and explanations will be found on the following pages.

Do not look at the answers until you have completed the exam.

1. **A**   When the 102-story *Empire State Building* (D) was erected in 1931, it was the tallest building the world had ever seen, and remained so for over 40 years. In 1972, the twin towers of *Yamasaki's World Trade Center* (B) in New York became the world's tallest, but the honor lasted for only one year. In 1973, the *Sears Tower* (C) in Chicago, designed by *SOM*, captured the title. The *Marina City Towers* in Chicago (A is correct) by *Bertrand Goldberg* rose 60 stories, but even when it was built in 1959, it was far from the world's tallest building.

2. **B**   The difference between a *Latin cross* and a *Greek cross* church was in the shapes, that is, the relationship between the nave and transepts (B is correct). The Latin cross had a long nave with short crossing transepts (†), while the Greek cross had transepts equal in length to the nave, making all the legs of the cross equal (+). The treatment over the crossing and the church size and location had little to do with the plan shape (A, C, and D are incorrect), although most churches with a Greek cross plan were built in the Mediterranean area.

3. **D**   Although none of the four great Chicago architects in this question submitted a design or served on the jury, this is not what Burchard and Brown were referring to (A, B, and C are incorrect). They were instead referring to the fact that the progressive influence of the Chicago School was entirely ignored (D is correct), and the winning entry by Hood and Howells was totally retrogressive. It was a Gothic-inspired arrangement of derivative details that had little to do with the structure it covered. According to the authors, "the whole thing was a fraudulent stage set."

4. **A**   The *Barcelona Pavilion* had no exhibits or other functional requirements (III is incorrect). The building itself, together with the sculpture, pools, and now famous furniture, was the entire exhibit. Also, Mies was undoubtedly strongly influenced by the ideas found in Frank Lloyd Wright's early *Prairie Houses*, which were published in 1910 in Berlin (V is incorrect). Masterly spatial composition (I) and immaculate use of lavish materials (II) accurately describe the Pavilion, and it was one of the most influential buildings of modern architecture (IV). Ironically, it probably inspired Wright's later *Usonian houses*. Therefore, A is the correct answer.

5. **C**   A *cupola* is a spherical roof placed like an inverted cup over a square, polygonal, or circular plan. It also refers to an architectural element placed on a dome or a roof, such as a lantern. A *tholos,* on the other hand, is simply a circular building, which is often covered by a dome (C is correct, D is incorrect). The terms, therefore, do not have the same meaning and may not be used interchangeably (A and B are incorrect).

6. **B**   Each of the authors listed is recognized for his writings on modern architecture (A, C, and D are incorrect; B is correct). Richards wrote *An Introduction to Modern Architecture,* Banham's book was *Theory and Design in the First Machine Age,* Scully wrote *Modern Architecture,* and Hitchcock was the author of *The International Style.* Each of these books was of considerable historic interest and enjoyed wide popularity.

7. **A**   Many others may have used cast iron for structural purposes before Labrouste (D is incorrect), but it was in his *Bibliothèque Ste.-Genèvieve* in Paris that cast iron was first elevated to an important role in

architecture (A is correct). Though the library's exterior resembled a restrained Florentine palace, the interior reading rooms, framed with slender, exposed cast iron columns and vaults, appeared more delicate and elegant than any interior space previously constructed. In later years, Labrouste was viewed as a courageous pioneer for this early and rational use of exposed iron (B and C are also incorrect).

8. **B**   Admiration for the ancient Greeks, which led to the early American architecture revival, was a logical result of the values of the young democratic society (B is correct). It was only in later years that the classic symbols were construed by critics of the Revival as imperialistic, rather than democratic (A is incorrect). Critics also attacked the Greek expression for its pagan implications, although the religious issue had little effect until later years when the more "Christian" Gothic Revival began (D is incorrect). Finally, Greek Revival structures were rarely exact reproductions of classic buildings; they were most often sensitive adaptations employing the spirit, rather than the precise details, of Greek structures (C is incorrect).

9. **D**   All five designers in this question produced original designs using reinforced concrete. The Swiss engineer *Maillart* (I) created contemporary bridges, *Perret* (II) built a reinforced concrete frame for his *Rue Franklin house* in Paris, and the French architect *Garnier* (III) made use of reinforced concrete in his scheme for a *Cité Industrielle*. Both *Gropius* (IV) and *Le Corbusier* (V) began their long careers with reinforced concrete structures—Gropius with the construction of the *Bauhaus* in 1925, and Le Corbusier with his *Domino houses* in 1914. Therefore, D is the correct answer.

10. **D**   *Mastabas* were originally built with mud bricks, but later were constructed out of stone (A is correct). They were rectangular in plan (B is correct) and contemporary with the great Egyptian pyramids (C is correct). Although mastabas were ancient tombs, they were meant for the burial of noblemen, not the general public (D is incorrect and the answer to this question).

11. **B**   The building which does not belong in this group is *Garnier's Opera House* in Paris, built in 1862 (B is correct). It was a sumptuous and festive collection of *Renaissance* and *Baroque* elements, but its small, low dome over the auditorium was a relatively unimportant component of the overall composition. The domes of the *Pantheon* (A), *Florence Cathedral* (C), and *Hagia Sophia* (D), however, were all great works of design, engineering, and architectural drama.

12. **B**   It was the *Ford Foundation Building* in New York that, in 1967, departed from the open plaza trend (B is correct). The architects, *Roche and Dinkleloo*, chose instead to create a lush inner garden around which the multilevel offices were placed. Among the famous office towers that included urban plazas, *Lever House* in New York was the first, in 1952 (A). This was followed in 1958 by *Mies' Seagram Building* (C), and in 1969 by the *John Hancock Center* in Chicago (D). Both Lever and Hancock were designed by *Skidmore, Owings, and Merrill*.

13. **B**   The Greek and Roman civilizations differed from each other in a number of respects. The Greeks were an intellectual people, interested in learning, whereas the Romans were pragmatic and interested in power (III). Also, the Greeks viewed architecture as art, conceiving their

temples as shrines. The Romans, however, approached architecture as structure and visualized their temples as monuments (II and IV). The Greeks were not considered great engineers; they simply adapted a simple wood post-and-beam style to stone construction (I is incorrect). Additionally, the Greeks did not employ lavish architectural ornament, nor did the Romans exhibit utilitarian simplicity (V is incorrect). Therefore, B is the correct answer.

14. **D**   Choices A and B were two of the earliest examples of the 15th century *Renaissance* in Florence. *Brunelleschi's Dome* and *Il Cronaca's Palace* were scholarly, classic, and restrained (A and B are incorrect). *Borromini's* church in Rome, on the other hand, was a wildly ingenious example from the *Baroque* period, in which the classic details were distorted almost beyond recognition (C is incorrect). Finally, it was *Michelangelo's* library in Florence for the Medici family that was truly *Mannerist* (D is correct). In this fine example, there was no struggle against the laws of nature, only an arbitrary use and slight misinterpretation of classical elements. It was a brilliant sculptural composition carried out in tones of white and grey.

15. **C**   The three names listed were all new towns designed after World War II (C is correct; A, B, and D are incorrect). *Vallingby*, near Stockholm, was designed by *Sven Markelius, Stevenage* was planned near London, and *Saynatsalo* was a town in Finland designed by *Alvar Aalto*. For this new town, Aalto designed the *Town Hall* in 1950, which was one of his finest and most famous buildings.

16. **B**   Whether or not one agrees, Pevsner clearly distinguished between mere

building and architecture on the basis of aesthetic appeal (B is correct; A, C, and D are incorrect). Just exactly why a bicycle shed could not be made architecturally appealing was never explained by Pevsner. However, his point was that aesthetic intent is generally lacking in strictly utilitarian buildings, such as storage sheds.

17. **C**   *Vanbrugh's Blenheim Palace*, completed by *Nicholas Hawksmoor* in 1724, was the palace described (C is correct). *Castle Howard* was an earlier mansion by Vanbrugh (A is incorrect), the *Banqueting House* was designed 100 years earlier by *Inigo Jones* (B is incorrect), and the *Wilton House*, also by Jones, was built around 1640 (D is incorrect).

18. **C**   Among the reasons for the development of the *pointed arch* were that it allowed a rectangular bay to be vaulted with arches of equal height (II), while reducing the overall lateral thrust of the vaults (III). It also made possible the great heights desired in the Middle Ages (IV). However, the pointed arch was no easier to construct than the *semicircular arch* (I is incorrect), nor was its form particularly more expressive or logical than any other kind of arch (V is incorrect). Therefore, C is the correct answer.

19. **A**   *Trabeated* refers to an architectural style in which beams or lintels are used. *Stylobate* is a continuous base, often stepped, on which a colonnade is placed. *Entasis* is the outward curve of a column shaft. The phrase, as more simply stated in correct answer A, might very well describe the ancient *Parthenon*, since all these terms apply to classic Greek architecture.

20. **B**   *Venturi* opened the eyes of architects to environmental elements that were either previously ignored or regarded as purely

negative. Most could acknowledge that billboards and bad design existed, but very few could agree that they were acceptable (B is correct; A, C, and D are incorrect). Venturi's inclusive philosophy recognized the *richness and ambiguity of the modern experience.* One was encouraged to accept the environment as it was in order to appreciate the native beauty and charm of ordinary work.

21. **A** First of all, the Egyptians had other building materials, such as sun-dried bricks and even wood, which was used in houses and other utilitarian structures (B is incorrect). Secondly, the use of stone led to a trabeated (post-and-beam), not an arcuated (arched) expression, although the Egyptians may have had knowledge of the arch (C is incorrect). Finally, stone was used consistently, but in the form of large blocks that were set dry, without the use of mortar (D is incorrect). Small dressed stones in thick mortar was a construction technique developed much later by Medieval cathedral builders. The ancient Egyptians used stone because of its permanence and impregnability (A is correct).

22. **D** The *Renaissance* architect *Vignola* was the only architect of those mentioned who could have employed a dome on a drum, as he did in the *Church of Il Gesu*—a much copied *Mannerist* design from about 1570 (D is correct). The other architects predated Vignola, as well as that architectural feature, by many years. *Vitruvius* (A) was a first century Roman architect who laid down the rules of classical architecture, which, incidentally, did not include the placement of domes on drums. *Anthemius* (B) was one of the original Byzantine architects of *Hagia Sophia. Arnolfo* (C) was the Italian architect who began the *Florence Duomo* in 1296. This Gothic cathedral did end up with a dome on a drum, but it was *Brunelleschi,* not Arnolfo, who was responsible for that development well over 100 years later.

23. **A** Although there is some truth in each of the answers, the message of *Maholy-Nagy's Native Genius in Anonymous Architecture* and *Rudofsky's Architecture Without Architects* is best expressed in correct answer A. Architectural history has only been concerned with a few select cultures in a relatively small part of the world, and most historians have concentrated on personalities and projects by and for the privileged and the powerful. The two books introduced readers to work outside the conventional Western tradition, work which was performed anonymously, spontaneously, or in the indigenous vernacular of some generally obscure area.

24. **C** The *Wassily chair* was designed by *Marcel Breuer* (A), the *Tulip pedestal chair* was originated by *Eero Saarinen* (B), and the *Brno chair* was from *Mies van der Rohe* (D). The *Cantilevered chair* was designed by *Alvar Aalto*, not *Le Corbusier* (C is the incorrect answer we are looking for). Happily, these original designs are still commercially available today—for those who can afford them.

25. **B** The Romans used surface veneers primarily to protect concrete from the weather and thereby make it more durable (B is correct). They also used these veneers to decorate plain surfaces and make them appear more finished (C). Roman construction employed many soldiers and slaves, thereby minimizing unemployment (A). The Romans did have an abundance of veneering materials (D). However, the principal reason for the Roman use of

facing materials was practicality—the need to protect raw concrete surfaces.

26. **D**  *Architect* is derived from two Greek words: *archi*—meaning chief, master, or foremost and *tekton*—meaning builder or worker. Thus, the best literal meaning is found in answer D: chief builder. A trivial fact, perhaps, but one that every architect should know.

27. **C**  The *Monadnock Building*, built in Chicago in 1891, was designed by the firm of *Burnham and Root* (B is incorrect). It was a great and elegant skyscraper that expressed the ultimate limits of masonry construction (C is correct, A is incorrect). The weight of its unadorned 16 stories necessitated 12-foot-thick walls at the base (D is incorrect). With the continued development of taller buildings, masonry became impractical as a structural material, and a few years later, the steel frame completely overtook the Chicago School.

28. **B**  *Pietro Belluschi* (correct answer B) is the modern American architect who is noticeably out of place among the group of Italian Renaissance architects. In the early 1950s, Belluschi gave up his successful practice in Oregon in order to teach and collaborate with other firms on such projects as the *Bank of America Building* in San Francisco and the *Pan Am Building* in New York. *Francesco Borromini* (A) and *Giovanni Bernini* (C) were *Baroque* architects (*S. Carlo alle Quattro Fontane* and the *Piazza of S. Peter*), and *Brunelleschi* (*Pitti Palace, Florence Cathedral Dome*, etc.) was considered the first architect of the *Renaissance* (D).

29. **D**  The *Art Nouveau* movement was an aesthetic undertaking born out of a fear of increasing industrialization (A). It attempted to combine art with social life via nature (B), taking much of its influence from flowing, natural forms such as hair, the sea, and flora (C). Art Nouveau was an extensive and influential movement which affected all of Europe between 1890 and 1910 (D is the incorrect answer for which we are looking). From Scotland to Spain, the romantic forms were applied to decorative arts, graphics, textiles, furniture, and architecture.

30. **B**  All of the buildings mentioned were located in France (I). They all employed reinforced concrete construction (III), and each was raised up on *pilotis* (V), or stilts, in order to free the space beneath the buildings. They were designed by *Le Corbusier*, not *Breuer* (II is incorrect). The *Villa Savoye* was a country house, but the *Unité d'Habitation* was an apartment in Marseilles, and the *Pavillon* was a dormitory at the *Cité Universitaire* in Paris (IV is incorrect). Therefore, B is the correct answer.

31. **A**  At one time or another, great architecture was created under each of the conditions listed. However, the inspiration for the greatest monuments has always been a strong common belief, religious or otherwise, which unified the greatest architectural skills (correct answer A). In support of such a profound belief, society has lavished on these creations its talent, expertise, and wealth.

32. **C**  The new technology of the 19th century caused architects to withdraw to the familiar, to an eclectic architectural expression that borrowed freely from all past styles. With *Richardson*, the style was *Romanesque*—a romantic and robust expression in stone—and with *McKim, Mead, and White*, the stylistic expression came from the early *Italian Renaissance* (C is correct). The McKim firm carefully

reproduced whole buildings with classical details, while Richardson, rather than imitating, created an original architecture inspired by historic forms.

33. **C**   In an amazing variety of ways, *Rudolph's Art and Architecture Building* at Yale recalled diverse influences from many earlier projects. In appearance, the structure most closely resembled the *Richards Medical Research Laboratories* by *Kahn* (II), as well as *Wright's* earlier *Larkin Building* (IV). However, Rudolph's use of sculptured concrete forms and general composition also recalled *Le Corbusier's Monastery of La Tourette* completed a few years earlier (III). Although Rudolph was under the *Gropius* influence at Harvard, he abandoned the rational approach of the Internationalists soon after establishing his own practice (I is incorrect). Finally, Rudolph's Art and Architecture Building at Yale did not show any overt influence from *Mies van der Rohe* (V is incorrect). Therefore, C is the correct answer.

34. **A**   The *Italian Renaissance*, for all its churches, was primarily financed by and designed for the mercantile and royal establishments (B). It began in Italy, where the *Gothic* period had little influence, but the glories of Rome were vividly remembered (C). During the Renaissance, architects moved up in esteem from the status of mere craftsmen to that of respected artists (D). However, early Renaissance buildings were not deliberate copies of completed Roman models. That type of imitation did not occur until the *Classic Revival*, several hundred years later (A is the incorrect answer we are looking for).

35. **A**   The *Modulor* was a system of proportions (correct answer A) that had nothing whatever to do with modular,

which refers to a system of standardized units (B and C are incorrect), nor was the Modulor based on *da Vinci's* human figure (D is incorrect). The Modulor was a complex system based on the *Golden Section* and related to the human figure, which was established arbitrarily at six feet in height. The system was intended to replace actual dimensions, in meters or feet, with standardized proportions that increased geometrically, rather than in an arithmetical progression.

36. **D**   *Fletcher* was referring to the birth of the *Romanesque* style (correct answer D). The *long sleep* was the 500-year-long *Dark Ages*, and the *treasures scattered around* referred to the multitude of ancient Roman monuments that remained throughout most of Europe. Romanesque was built upon Roman foundations, using ancient Roman fragments, Roman building forms, and Roman technology (A, B, and C are incorrect).

37. **D**   A *triglyph* formed part of the Greek Doric frieze (A), *pendentives* were spherical triangles used by Byzantine architects to adapt a circular dome to a square base (B), and a *cella* was the main body of a Greek or Roman temple (C). But, crockets, not quoins, were projecting blocks of stone that were carved with foliage and used decoratively on Gothic church spires (D is the incorrect statement we are seeking).

38. **D**   The earliest American dwellings were new world versions of *English Medieval houses* (correct answer D). The 17th century colonists merely repeated in this country what they had known at home—the *Saxon cruck house*, which soon took on distinctive American characteristics. Although several lesser details from other architectural styles found their way into this

early expression, the original influence was decidedly English.

39. **B**   Most Medieval communities began with a monastery or a castle which was located, for defensive reasons, at the top of a hill (A is incorrect). The natural growth of such towns generally followed a radiocentric pattern in which easily defensible, narrow streets wound around the nucleus (B is correct). The grand scale of wide avenues and long vistas were features of Renaissance planning (C and D are incorrect), as can be seen in the city of Paris today, which was originally laid out during the 19th century by *Baron Haussmann.*

40. **C**   Byzantine architects developed and commonly used the *pendentive* to solve the problem of building circular domes over square or polygonal spaces (A). They also used marble panels for flat surfaces and glass mosaics on curved surfaces (B). The Byzantine domed bays could be placed alongside one another, thereby producing a more extended, or even a crossed, plan (D). Byzantine columns were generally subordinate to piers and bearing walls; however, when they were used, they consisted of a simple shaft and a simplified, cubiform capital, carved with incised foliage or abstract geometric patterns resembling woven baskets (C is the incorrect answer we are looking for).

41. **B**   Water has frequently been used to enhance the siting of architectural monuments, such as the 16th-century *Chateau du Chenonceau* (II), which spanned the river Cher. *Frank Lloyd Wright* achieved similar drama with his famous *Kaufmann House* (V), known as *Fallingwater*, portions of which actually projected over a waterfall by means of great cantilevers. Although a natural body of water did not exist in the hot locale of Chandigarh, *Le Corbusier* created a vast, shallow lake which reflected his monumental *Court Building* (I) and served to create an illusion of coolness. The *Hagia Sophia* (III) and *Unité d'Habitation* (IV) were not located near water. Therefore, B is correct.

42. **D**   The notched parapets of Medieval fortress structures are known as *crenelations.* Projecting parapets with floor openings are known as *machicolations.* Therefore, D is correct. The defensive functions of both features were abandoned with the coming of the Renaissance.

43. **C**   This statement, ascribed to *Paul Heyer*, is generally true, with the exception of the Gothic period (correct answer C). The great monuments erected during that period included several distinctive features that were determined principally by structural necessity, such as exposed vaults, ribs, piers, buttresses, etc. Gothic architecture, therefore, relied on the honesty of its exposed structural features, which became part of its artistic expression, as well as its drama and beauty.

44. **D**   It was in the *Richards Laboratories Building* that *Louis Kahn* introduced his logic regarding *servant spaces and served spaces* (D is correct). This building expressed exhaust towers, stair towers, and the central utility tower as *servant* spaces, while the laboratories represented the *served* spaces. In articulating the mechanical elements, Kahn attempted to create a new hierarchy of spaces, which became a philosophy influencing many later projects. The culmination of this approach was seen in *Place Beaubourg* (C is incorrect) in Paris, which comprised a dramatic amalgamation of mechanical equipment. The *Air Force Academy* by

*SOM* was known for its *Miesian* purity (B is incorrect), and the *Ford Foundation Building* by *Roche* was known for its glass-enclosed interior garden and open office design (A is incorrect).

**45. C**  Although no epoch can be completely described by a single word, the terms listed represent a dominating theme that consistently ran through the periods listed. Religion dominated the *Middle Ages* (A), beauty guided *Ancient Greece* (B), and learning led the *Renaissance* (D). However, power, not mysticism, ruled Ancient Rome (C is the incorrect match we are looking for).

**46. B**  Walter Gropius believed that the whole is greater than the sum of its parts—that a design group working collaboratively can accomplish much more than the total work of the individuals working separately (B is correct). Although Gropius also believed that final decisions must be left to the individual in charge of the job, he clearly developed the modern idea of teamwork that exploited the group consciousness of the *collective personality*.

**47. A**  *Adolf Loos* was a pioneering Viennese architect who, around the turn of the century, published an influential essay declaring that the use of ornament was a crime (II is incorrect). *Ernest Kump* was a relatively modern California architect who was known for his educational projects, such as the much-admired *Foothill Junior College*, completed in 1961 (IV is incorrect). Regarding the other architects, *Maybeck* (I) worked in the Bay Area, while *Gill* (V) and *Schindler* (III) developed a style in Southern California that was simple, restrained, and rational. Therefore, A is the correct answer.

**48. C**  Early Christians chose not to use the Roman temple form, since they believed the temples were places of idolatry (B is correct). However, they did adapt the ancient Roman *basilica* (A is correct) and, in many cases, used actual elements from Roman buildings (D is correct). They often used Roman-inspired semicircular arches for structural support (C is the incorrect answer we are looking for). In fact, the Early Christian basilican church became the key that linked the historical Western tradition of Roman architecture with that of the later Medieval period.

**49. A**  *Bacon's* famous monument was a refined *Hellenic temple* in the *Doric order* that was crowned by a flat-roofed Roman attic story, rather than a sloping pediment (A is correct; B, C, and D are incorrect). Aside from its derivative style, the structure provided a relatively modest background for the majestic statue of Lincoln by Daniel French.

**50. B**  Familiar or not, these old sayings have been used so often that the original significance has practically vanished. They are attributed to the listed architects as follows: "a house is a machine for the living"—Le Corbusier (A), "art and technology—the new unity"—Walter Gropius, not Sullivan (B), "less is more"—Mies van der Rohe (C), and "ask the space what it wants to be"—Louis Kahn (D). Therefore, B is the incorrect match we are seeking.

**51. D**  The holistic approach to sustainably designed projects encourages the design team to examine the impact of environmental, economic, mechanical, and aesthetic architectural decisions.

# INDEX